Your Attitude Is Showing

Your Attitude Is Showing

A Primer of Human Relations

Twelfth Edition

SHARON LUND O'NEIL
University of Houston

ELWOOD N. CHAPMAN

PEARSON

Prentice
Hall

Upper Saddle River, New Jersey 07458

Library of Congress Cataloging-in-Publication Data

O'Neil, Sharon Lund.
    Your attitude is showing/Sharon Lund O'Neil.—12th ed.
      p. cm.
    ISBN 0-13-242904-7
1. Psychology, Industrial. 2. Industrial sociology. 3. Interpersonal relations. I. Title.
HF5548.8.C36 2008
158.7—dc22

2006026276

Editor-in-Chief: Vernon R. Anthony
Senior Acquisitions Editor: Gary Bauer
Editorial Assistant: Dan Trudden
Development Editor: Deborah Hoffman
Marketing Manager: Leigh Ann Sims
Marketing Coordinator: Alicia Dysert
Managing Editor-Production: Mary Carnis
Manufacturing Buyer: Ilene Sanford
Production Liaison: Denise Brown
Full-Service Production and Composition: Lynn Steines/Carlisle Publishing Services
Media Production Project Manager: Lisa Rinaldi
Senior Design Coordinator: Christopher Weigand
Cover Designer: Rob Aleman
Cover Image: Getty Images
Printer/Binder: Courier Westford
Cover Printer: Phoenix Color

This book was set in GoudyWtcTReg by Carlisle Publishing Services. It was printed and bound by Courier/Westford. The cover was printed by Phoenix Color.

Pearson Education Ltd.
Pearson Education Singapore Pte. Ltd.
Pearson Education Canada, Ltd.
Pearson Education—Japan

Pearson Education Australia Pty. Limited
Pearson Education North Asia Ltd.
Pearson Educación de Mexico, S. A. de C.V.
Pearson Education Malaysia Pte. Ltd.

10 9 8 7 6 5 4
ISBN 13: 978-0-13-242904-7
ISBN 10:   0-13-242904-7

Dedication

Dear Reader,

You, as one of the million-plus readers of *Your Attitude Is Showing* around the world, have made this book extremely popular. More importantly, however, is that you have used this book to improve your human-relations skills.

Without a doubt, you deserve credit for making our world a better place; and that is why this twelfth edition of *Your Attitude Is Showing* is dedicated to **you**.

Thank you!

Brief Contents

Contents

PART I   UNDERSTANDING YOURSELF   1

1

You Can't Escape Human Relations   3

The importance of human relations should never be underestimated. Because all jobs have a human-relations responsibility and present challenges, it is important to improve your human-relations skills. There is no time like the present to start improving your human-relations skills and to continue improvement throughout life.

2 Human Relations Can Make or Break You

There are several important factors that make human relations more than just common sense. By learning and acquiring as many of the specific human-relations skills as you possibly can, you will discover very quickly that practicing good human relations can lead to greater success on the job and in life.

3 Hold on to Your Positive Attitude

Your positive attitude is a priceless personal possession. What you see in life influences your attitude and, thus, influences your relationships. Because your attitude is, for the most part, under *your* control, your positive attitude is an extremely valuable career asset.

4 When People Step on Your Attitude   41

People will step on your attitude from time to time, but it is to your advantage to explore some of the techniques you can use to quickly "bounce back" from ego-deflating encounters with others. Also, if you are sensitive and respectful of others, you show that you deserve the same consideration.

PART II RELATIONSHIPS WITH OTHERS   53

5 Vertical and Horizontal Working Relationships   55

Relationships are created by being near people as well as by working and communicating with people. Good relationships in all directions, including vertical and horizontal working relationships, need to be understood, consciously created, and carefully maintained.

6 Your Potential and Productivity— A Closer Look   67

People seldom reach their potentials because gaps exist between what they can do and what they actually do. Both supervisor and employee roles are important to closing productivity gaps of individuals and groups. Good human relations plays a significant part in increasing individual and group productivity.

7 The Winning Combination   81

There is a positive correlation between good human relations and productivity. If you give attention to horizontal relationships, personal productivity can be increased. Productivity ultimately involves quality, a service attitude, and customer satisfaction.

8 Your Most Important Working Relationship 95

The relationship with your supervisor is your most important working relationship. Because supervisors create a working climate in which you must work, it is important to practice good ethical behavior while making the relationship with your supervisor as strong as possible.

9 Understanding the Nature of Relationships   109

Human-relations competencies that are essential to creating, maintaining, and repairing good work-related relationships include characteristics such as respect and the mutual-reward theory. Using the insights gained from analyzing relationships will yield greater objectivity and longevity in relationships.

PART III MAXIMIZING YOUR RELATIONSHIPS   129

10 Your Success as a Team Player   131

The importance of teams, the team approach, and being a team member are important to an organization and to your career success. Several attitudinal factors contribute to the success of building strong team working relationships which are needed by teams and team members.

11 Emotional Intelligence: Managing Stress, Frustration, and Aggression   **147**

Frustration is the inner feeling you experience when you meet a temporary block to your immediate goals. Understanding frustration and learning several techniques to manage and harmlessly release tension caused by stress and frustration will help you to avoid aggressive behavior.

12 Restoring Injured Relationships   **163**

The power of communication is extremely strong in restoring damaged relationships. Applying the basic principles and strategies for restoring a damaged relationship is critical to avoid the possibilities and consequences of leaving an injured relationship unrepaired.

13 Attitudes among Culturally Diverse Coworkers   175

Attitude improvement toward *all* workers, including culturally diverse coworkers, can contribute to greater individual and group productivity. Your attitude (the mental set you have either for or against those from cultures other than your own) can enhance or stifle the contribution cultural diversification makes in the workplace.

PART IV BUILDING YOUR CAREER   187

14 Succeeding in a New Job or Assignment   189

Human-relations skills, especially in a new job or assignment, are critical to your job success. Following several pragmatic tips, along with your commitment to your positive attitude, will help you make a smooth and effective transition to a new work role in a new environment—and will contribute to the success of *all* your interactions.

15 Initiation Rites—Coping with Teasing and Testing   201

Employee teasing and testing may help you, as a new employee, become an accepted member of a work group. If you understand the differences, purposes, and consequences of personal and organizational testing, you will be better able to successfully address or avoid any prolonged or negative testing.

16

Absenteeism Can Damage Relationships   **215**

Most organizations have a specific policy for absenteeism and lateness—two problematic areas for management. While absenteeism and lateness pose challenges, there are several ways to avoid abusing your company's policy while helping you to improve your human-relations skills and build your career.

17

Avoiding Six Common Human-Relations Mistakes   **231**

Of the six common human-relations mistakes that both new and experienced employees make, poor communication (especially listening skills) may be the most damaging to your relationships and career. Several tips, including providing your own motivation, are offered to help you build and strengthen your human-relations skills.

18

Business Ethics, Rumors, and the Confidence Triangle   **247**

Your ethical behavior is reflected in your attitude and actions. While there are several factors that contribute to high ethical standards and building relationships, you also should be aware of the pros and cons associated with personal and organizational rumors, the grapevine, and the confidence triangle.

PART V SUCCESS AT EXPANDING YOUR ASSETS 261

19 Goal Setting and Your Attitude 263

The connection between goals and attitude points to the importance of discovering and adopting goals that motivate you to succeed. Designing a "goal pattern" with a time management system that meets your individual needs will help you move toward career and lifestyle success.

20 Strategies for Advancing Your Career 277

There are both advantages and disadvantages to staying with one organization versus moving from one organization to another as you build your career. Also, seven human-relations factors and the development of a Plan B and a "personal" business plan can contribute to both your positive attitude and your career success.

21

Keeping a Positive Attitude through Plateau Periods and Reorganizations   293

Plateau or waiting periods and reorganizations are normal in all organizations; however, there are ways to shorten plateaus and convert them into learning and preparation periods. A negative attitude can result in a productivity drop as well as lengthen, rather than shorten, plateau periods.

22

When You Are Tempted to Scramble   305

A job resignation should be seriously considered if you have been unhappy and unproductive at work for a considerable period of time. Personality conflicts and human-relations problems are the basis for most resignations. Here are ten basic tips for resigning gracefully and four ways to protect your positive attitude.

23 Attitude Renewal   319

Stress contributes to the fact that everyone needs some type of attitude renewal or restoration from time to time. Attitude renewal starts with self-appraisal; and it is a daily, weekly, and sometimes even a "major overhaul" process. Five basic attitude adjustment techniques can help you avoid attitudinal "ruts" and keep your attitude positive.

24 Leadership/Management: Your Career on the Move 333

Several career advancement factors should be considered, especially if you plan to move up to leadership/management. A positive attitude and good human-relations skills developed as an employee are especially valuable skills for leadership/management roles. The more you put your human-relations skills into practice, the more self-confident you will become to manage your career.

Preface

A PROVEN TRACK RECORD

For more than three decades, the first eleven editions of *Your Attitude Is Showing* have been used in the classroom and workplace to train both new and experienced employees. Over one million copies of the book have been distributed. *Your Attitude Is Showing* remains one of the most highly regarded primers in the field of business human relations.

Your Attitude Is Showing has helped individuals of all ages and backgrounds play their human-relations roles with greater understanding and sensitivity. Everyone who seeks self-improvement will welcome this twelfth edition.

The flexibility and modularity of this text-workbook allows it to be used in a variety of ways: as a core text in human-relations courses, as a supplemental text-workbook in other management courses like organizational behavior, or as a training manual in corporate training programs.

NEW AND RETAINED FEATURES IN EACH CHAPTER

- **"Thought for the Day"** chapter openers provide food for thought for the reader.
- **Performance Competencies** help the reader identify, as well as focus on, the four-to-six main concepts discussed in the chapter and set the stage for forthcoming material.
- **Attitude-Related Margin Statements** provide the reader with salient points and added emphasis of the chapter material.
- **Interactive Activities** throughout the text augment the chapter discussion and allow readers to stop and analyze how they feel about concepts presented in the chapter.
- **End-of-Chapter Summaries** help readers review and tie together important chapter concepts.
- **Attitude Boxes** at the end of each chapter provide short, thought-provoking statements for readers to consider—statements for readers' self-evaluation toward attitude improvement.

- **"Test Your Understanding"** end-of-chapter assessments, consisting of three types of items (true and false, multiple choice, and short answer), are designed to reinforce the reader's understanding of the chapter. Answers to the Test Your Understanding assessments are provided at the end of the book.
- **NEW "Think and Respond"** assignments provide five short-answer questions that cover the main concepts of the chapter and reinforce writing skills.
- **NEW "Summary Activity"** end-of-chapter interactive exercises allow readers to apply chapter concepts. Each Summary Activity is similar to and extends the interactive activities found within the chapter discussion. All of the interactive activities give you practical experience to better understand and apply the chapter concepts. You are encouraged to complete the activities in a conscientious way to reinforce your understanding of the chapter. In so doing, you will be in a better position to apply what you have learned to your own life.
- **NEW "Case Study" Enhancements** allow readers to analyze and research a situation that represents an all-too-common reality in the workplace. The end-of-chapter Cases have two parts. In the first part, "A. Discuss", readers are encouraged to carefully evaluate each Case to find the best solutions and recommendations for each Case. The second part of each Case, "B: Expand Your Understanding", involves a research-related assignment. By completing the second part of each Case, readers will get an extended understanding of the chapter and will improve both their research and writing skills. One or both parts of the Cases can be completed individually or in teams.

WHAT IS THE SIGNIFICANCE OF THE AMOEBA?

As you read and study *Your Attitude Is Showing*, keep in mind that people who balance their technical skills and knowledge base with human-relations competencies find greater on-the-job happiness; contribute more to the productivity of organizations; and, in general, have more successful careers and satisfying lives. This book could be appropriately subtitled *Gaining Personal Success in Business*, for nothing has more impact on career success than your attitude.

Illustrations like the amoeba that follows will help you become more aware of the strong impact your attitude has on every aspect of your life. Why an amoeba—a microscopic one-celled creature who is constantly changing in size and shape and who is often referred to as the lowest form of animal life? We hope the little amoeba will act as a reminder that, no matter who you are, where you are, or what you are doing, *Your Attitude Is Showing!*

"After all, I'm just an amoeba."

SUPPLEMENTS
RESOURCES FOR STUDENTS
COMPANION WEBSITE

Go to www.prenhall.com/o'neil to access links to online resources for each chapter and to prepare for tests. Here you will find links to helpful online resources for self-grading quizzes for each chapter including multiple choice and true/false questions with immediate feedback and assessment.

PRENTICE-HALL SELF-ASSESSMENT LIBRARY (S.A.L.)

S.A.L. is a CD-ROM product developed by Steve Robbins that contains 51 research-based self assessments that provide students with insights into their skills, abilities, and interests. It is easy to use, self-scoring, and can be packaged with this text at a discounted price. Please contact your Prentice-Hall representative to obtain a review copy.

RESOURCES FOR INSTRUCTORS

All instructor resources are available on the **Instructor's Resources CD** or you can download them from the **Instructor Resource Center** at www.prenhall.com. Register once and gain access to instructor materials for all of your Prentice-Hall textbooks.

INSTRUCTOR'S MANUAL WITH TEST ITEM FILE

The instructor's manual for this text contains a large number of multiple-choice and true/false test questions, chapter outlines and lecture notes, and comments about the assessments, cases, and activities.

PRENTICE-HALL TEST GENERATOR

This computerized text generation system gives you maximum flexibility in preparing tests. It can create custom tests and print scrambled versions of a test at one time, as well as build tests randomly by chapter, level of difficulty, or question type. The software also allows online testing and record-keeping and the ability to add problems to the database.

POWERPOINT LECTURE PRESENTATION PACKAGE

Lecture Presentation screens for each chapter are available online and on the Instructor Resources CD.

JWA HUMAN RELATIONS VIDEOS

JWA Videos on human relations and interpersonal communication topics are available to qualified adopters. Contact your local representative for details.

ACKNOWLEDGMENTS

Many people have reviewed and contributed to this work over the years. I would like to specially thank the reviewers of the current edition whose insights help keep this book a top-notch teaching tool: Sandy Boyd, Ed.D, College of Marin; Eugene E. Pettis, Ph.D, Wayne County Community College; Susan R. Gustin, West Virginia University; and Debbie Collins, Black Hawk College.

About the Author

Sharon Lund O'Neil, author of *Your Attitude Is Showing*, is a widely published author. In addition to her friendly writing style and practical advice, she has a common sense approach to problem solving. Her human-relations cases, based on the corporate work environment, are popular with both trainers and educators.

As a frequent national speaker and facilitator on leadership and engaging teams, Sharon advocates the importance of "soft skills"—the human-relations skills that are so critical for building strong relationships. Sharon has been actively involved in many professional groups and has provided leadership for several prominent national professional and educational organizations. She has been the recipient of numerous awards including several distinguished national teaching, research, and service awards.

Sharon's most recent books published by Prentice Hall include *Leadership: Essential Skills Every Manager Needs to Know*, third edition, and *Motivation: An ATM Card for Success*. Some of her books, including *Your Attitude Is Showing*, have been published in several languages. Translations include Chinese, Croatian, and Polish.

Sharon holds a Ph.D. degree from the University of Illinois and is currently a professor at the University of Houston.

PART I
Understanding Yourself

CHAPTER 1

You Can't Escape Human Relations

"I've heard all that old stuff before."

Thought for the Day: Relationships are only as good as your commitment to what you want them to be.

PERFORMANCE COMPETENCIES

- Understand that the importance of human relations should never be underestimated—a good reason to continue to improve your human relations throughout life.

- Appreciate the value of a positive attitude for yourself and others around you.

- Recognize that, in addition to productivity expectations, all jobs have a human-relations responsibility and present challenges.

- Understand that management views your work contribution as part of a team's productivity.

Most employees, even those with considerable experience, greatly underestimate the importance of human relations in building their careers. They pass it off as nothing more than common sense—something one handles intuitively. They are blind to the significance of the subject because they wrongly assume they are good at it. So what is human relations?

IMPORTANCE OF HUMAN RELATIONS

On the simplest level, human relations is being sociable, courteous, and adaptable. It is avoiding trouble with fellow workers. It is following the rules of simple etiquette. But as important as these qualities are to personal success, they only scratch the surface. Human relations is much more than behaving courteously so that people will like you. There is a second, more complex level.

Human Relations: A Basic Foundation for Your Career. Human relations is also understanding and practicing emotional intelligence (understanding yourself and others) and knowing how to handle difficult problems when they arise. It is learning to work well under demanding and sometimes unfair superiors. It is managing conflict effectively. It is understanding yourself and how you communicate with others. It is building and maintaining long-term relationships with family, friends, and coworkers. It is knowing how to restore a working relationship that has deteriorated. It is learning to live with your frustrations without hurting others or jeopardizing your own career. It is communicating the right kind of attitude during an employment interview. It is the foundation upon which good management careers are built. It is also the foundation—a "skill set," so to speak—for you to be successful in life.

Good human-relations skills are multifaceted

In short, human relations is building and maintaining relationships in many directions, with many kinds of people, in both good and bad working environments.

Because this book is devoted to helping you increase the effectiveness of your relationships, the following activity is provided to give you a starting point to assess your human-relations skills. In addition to this activity, the activities that augment the concepts in the chapters ahead will give you many opportunities to learn about and practice the skills needed to be good at human relations. If you take the activities seriously, you will find that the concepts presented in this book will be more meaningful as you acquire the human-relations skill set needed for developing and building good relationships on a daily basis.

ACTIVITY

My Human-Relations Foundation

Rate yourself as honestly as possible on how you, as well as others, view your effectiveness on the thirteen basic human relations elements that follow. Read each statement; then place a check mark (✓) in the column that best describes (a) how you view yourself and (b) how you believe others view you. Respond "Yes," "Not Sure," or "No" to each statement.

Level 1 human relations	My view of myself			Others' view of me		
	Yes	Not Sure	No	Yes	Not Sure	No
1. I am sociable.						
2. I am courteous.						
3. I am adaptable.						
4. I practice generally acceptable etiquette.						
Level 2 human relations	My view of myself			Others' view of me		
	Yes	Not Sure	No	Yes	Not Sure	No
5. I handle difficult problems successfully.						
6. I work well with demanding and sometimes unfair superiors.						
7. I am good at managing conflict.						
8. I understand myself (e.g., my strengths, weaknesses, etc.).						
9. I communicate well with others.						
10. I build and maintain long-term relationships.						
11. I am able to restore damaged relationships quickly and effectively.						
12. I am good at managing frustrations.						
13. I communicate a positive attitude.						

Review your responses. Your responses should give you a good perspective of yourself, as well as a perspective of how others see you. If you are unsure about what others think of you, ask a family member or close coworker to rate you on the thirteen items. Keep in mind that, no matter what skill levels you have, human relations needs constant attention and it is important to continue to work on improving your human relations throughout your life. There's no time like the present to get started!

The rest of this book will give you some suggestions about how to get good results from your human-relations efforts. Periodically, repeat this activity to measure your progress toward improving your personal and career success.

POSITIVE ATTITUDES APPRECIATED

Attitudes of Popular, Productive People. The most popular and productive people in any work environment are usually those with the best attitudes. Their positive attitudes

- inject humor into what otherwise would be just work. Everyone misses these individuals when they are on vacation.

- add to the team spirit by "bonding" everyone together in a more positive and productive mood. Many are unofficial leaders greatly appreciated by supervisors.

- make it easier for coworkers to maintain their upbeat attitudes. A positive attitude, in turn, helps coworkers maintain productivity and enhance their own careers.

Negativism Adds Tension. Employees who are consistently negative put an added strain on their coworkers. Their negative attitudes

- make it more difficult for others (especially the supervisor) to stay positive. Because negative attitudes thwart creativity, everyone operates under a needless handicap.

- act like a spoiled apple in a barrel, causing fellow employees to lose their enthusiasm and motivation to contribute. (Why produce more when Jack or Claire gets by with being so negative?)

- repress the fun and harmless horseplay that would normally surface and make everyone feel better about what they are doing. It often takes many highly positive attitudes to offset one that is negative.

Attitudes travel

When most people make a considerable effort to remain positive in their work environment, a single negative attitude can act as a cloud over the entire atmosphere. Productivity can drop. Customers can be treated poorly. Positive employees may seek opportunities elsewhere. While not everyone can be an attitude "star," negative attitudes damage human relationships in the workplace. Those who find it difficult to remain positive are invited to concentrate on the chapters that follow.

Another Dimension of Human Relations. In the business world, human relations (reflected in your attitude) is viewed best in terms of productivity because productivity is the goal of all group activity. Human relations, of course, is not a substitute for work; it cannot replace or camouflage poor performance. Employees are valued primarily for the amount and quality of work they turn out. Your employer will expect you to do your share of the work; and, if you are interested in moving ahead, you will want to do more than your share. An employer will not be interested for long in an employee who has a great attitude but produces very little.

Go the extra mile for career success

YOUR HUMAN-RELATIONS RESPONSIBILITY

Sensitivity to Coworkers. Getting the work out is only one side of the coin. You should accomplish your work and still be sensitive to the needs of those who work with you. You should perform your work without trying to show up your fellow workers or antagonize them. You should carry your full load in such a way that others will be encouraged to follow rather than reject you.

There's No Human Relations Escape. No matter how ambitious or capable you are, you cannot become the kind of employee you want to be (or the kind of employee management wants you to be) without learning how to work effectively with people. It would be career suicide to join an organization and ignore the people who work around you. You simply cannot escape human relations.

Does this mean that you should deliberately set out to play a game of human relations on your new job? The answer depends upon what you mean by "playing a game."

If you mean that you should play up to those who can do you the most good and pay little attention to others, the answer is, of course, "no."

If you mean that you should devise a master strategy that will give you the breaks at the expense of other people, the answer is, again, "no."

If, however, you mean that you should sincerely do everything you can to build strong, friendly, and honest working relationships with all of your coworkers—including those from diverse cultures—the answer is an unqualified "yes."

Build the best relationships you can

If this comes as a shock, think about it. Working hard is not enough in our modern society. It may have been thirty years ago, but it is not today. You, as a new or experienced employee, have a definite human-relations role to play. You can't ignore it. You can't postpone it.

A Balance of Responsibilities. From the moment you join an organization, you assume two responsibilities: (1) to do a job—the best job you can do with the work assigned to you—and (2) to get along with all of your coworkers to the best of your ability. It is the right combination of these two factors that spells success.

Perhaps you are a highly qualified, experienced employee happy in your present work environment. Or perhaps, after working a number of years for a particular company, you are making a career change. Perhaps your firm eliminated your position and you are seeking a similar one elsewhere. Or you may be graduating from an educational institution soon and you are preparing to launch your career. The possibilities are endless, but no matter what your personal condition is now or what it may be in the future, human relations will play a dominant role.

It would be wrong, of course, to say that the skills or abilities you possess are unimportant. If you are employed as an office manager, your computer competencies are vital. If you are employed as an apprentice machinist, your mechanical ability is important. If you are a registered nurse hoping to get into management, your professional training and background are vital. These skills helped you get where you are, and they will help you make progress.

Human-relations skills enhance technical expertise

But they are not enough. To make your education and experience work for you as effectively as possible, you must become competent in human relations. You must learn the technique of working with others.

Why? Because your behavior has a direct bearing on the efficiency of others. Your contribution will not always be an individual contribution; it will often be a component of a team effort, and you will only be a part of the group. What you accomplish will be in direct proportion to how well you get along with the people who work with you, above you, or for you.

Your Actions Affect Others. Almost everything you do will have an effect on other people. If the effect is good, people may do a better job. If the effect is bad, they will be less productive. Your personal work effort will not be enough. You should conduct yourself in such a manner that those who work with you and near you will also become effective. As you move into supervisory roles, you will be judged less on your personal productivity and more on the team you manage.

HOW MANAGEMENT VIEWS THE TEAM

Productivity Is a Standard. *Productivity* has become a significant word in business, industry, and government. Every organization operates either to make a profit or to reach a certain level of excellence.

Management has its own ways of measuring work quality and productivity. Some jobs are more easily measured than others. If you are employed as a factory worker, for example, your productivity is measured by the amount of work you perform over a certain time.

Some organizations employ time-study experts to measure the time required to perform a given task and to establish standards of performance.

As an employee of such a company, you are expected to exceed this standard. If you are employed in a sales organization, for instance, you may be given a sales quota that you will be expected to reach or exceed.

The point is that everyone's productivity is measured. We must all live up to the standards that prevail in our particular business. There is some form of measurement or evaluation for every job.

Never underestimate your contribution to the bottom line

Everyone Is Part of a Team. Our value is measured not only by the actual work we do but also by the contribution we make to the department or organization as a whole. The contribution to a work unit includes getting along with your team; and everyone, as management sees it, is part of a team. Workers are expected to get along with each other because exhibiting good human relations is important to a team's productivity. Productivity is not only an individual matter but also a divisional or departmental matter. Management has discovered that the way people get along together has a considerable impact on the total productivity of a department.

Consider the example of Janna and Harrison who are checkers at a local supermarket. The productivity of a checker is usually measured in three ways: speed, accuracy, and relations with customers. But it doesn't stop there. Why? Because the way customers as well as coworkers react to Janna and Harrison is important to both individual and combined productivity. That is, the way Janna and Harrison interact with each other has a bearing on their own and each other's productivity as well as on the productivity of other workers in the market. Each worker has an influence on other workers.

If Janna is an excellent checker and measures above others in all three categories, one would think Janna would be the best checker of all. But this is not necessarily true.

Let us assume that it is a peak period in the supermarket and all checkers are extremely busy. Shoppers are lined up in front of each checkout stand. Harrison suddenly runs out of paper sacks and calls for Janna, the "superior" checker, to toss him a few bags. What if Janna says, "Come and get 'em if you want 'em"? What would happen? No doubt, a psychological barrier would immediately arise between the two checkers. Harrison, who requested the bags, would be embarrassed in front of the customers. As a result, Harrison's speed, accuracy, and relations with customers would deteriorate.

Good human relations has value in any setting

Additionally, Janna's customers also may be embarrassed by her remarks. Her quick comment may stop any conversation at her station or, at the very least, may affect the way customers view her in the future. While her rather snide response may not affect her immediate efficiency, it could have an influence (even a momentary drop in efficiency) on any other checker who may have heard her. Certainly, Janna's response would have some effect on the thoughts of anyone within hearing distance of her comments.

Janna's human-relations error of just a few words could yield quite damaging results. Why? Because some of the customers who heard and saw the interaction between Janna and Harrison now may have a different relationship with them or other checkers the next time they come into the supermarket. Even worse, some customers may decide to take their business elsewhere. The checkers themselves, especially Harrison, also may make a mental note to be careful about asking for Janna's assistance in the future.

So even though Janna, the superior checker, is exceptional in all three categories, she has hurt the total productivity of the market. She may have hurt her relationships with other checkers. She may have even hurt the bottom line (profit) of the supermarket if some of the customers do not return to the store. Nobody can beat Janna as far as doing her assigned job is concerned. However, she has failed to live up to good human-relations standards.

Your Work Contribution and Productivity Influence. Productivity is not only what you do yourself. It is also the influence—good or bad—you have on others. You not only have a job to perform but also have a contribution to make to your fellow employees. It is not a contribution that always comes easily. On occasion, you may find it necessary to work effectively with someone you do not like. If you succeed, you have made a worthwhile contribution. If you fail, try to learn something from the experience. Then wait for another chance, for it is a challenge you should eventually meet successfully.

Human relations has significant power

The worker who keeps his (or her) personal productivity high and at the same time is sensitive enough to have a beneficial influence on others is the worker management will probably reward.

Summary

Human relations and a positive attitude know no age or experience level. You may be a recent high-school or college graduate starting your first job, a middle-aged person entering the labor market for the first time, a senior citizen taking up a new career, a housewife returning to a job left years ago, or a longtime career employee just promoted to a management position. Whatever your situation is, human relations and a positive attitude are greatly valued and will play a vital role in the years that lie ahead.

You have a responsibility to your employer to do the best job you can on your job as your personal productivity is extremely important to your department and organization. Your work performance also includes how well you get along with other people. Thus, your overall contribution to your department or unit involves a dual responsibility: (1) completing the work you are assigned to do and (2) exhibiting good human-relations skills for your whole work team to be productive. Management values workers who bring a balanced combination of both elements to the work team—a team that works together and a team that management expects to be productive.

Your contribution toward promoting a positive and productive work environment for everyone around you can be maximized if you harness the power of practicing good human relations. Because there is no escape from human relations, it is vitally important for you to capitalize on improving your human-relations skills every single day throughout your life. As you do, you will reward yourself and be in a position to receive the greatest compliment of all: to be recognized, perhaps by a supervisor or a fellow employee, as having the ability to work harmoniously with others. Your knowledge about human relations will have earned you that distinction.

Test Your Understanding

Respond to the following items to test your understanding of the chapter.

Part A: Circle the correct answer (T = True; F = False) for each of the following statements.

T　F　1. Human relations plays a far more important role in career success than most people will admit.

T　F　2. To achieve career success, an individual should place human relations first and productivity second.

T　F　3. Human relations, among other things, is devising a strategy that will give you the breaks at the expense of others.

T　F　4. A positive employee adds to a team spirit by bonding everyone together in a more enthusiastic mood.

T　F　5. Human-relations competencies can be learned.

Part B: Circle the letter of the correct answer for each of the following items.

6. The most popular and productive people in any work environment are usually those with the (a) best technical expertise, (b) most friends, (c) best attitudes, (d) highest IQs.

7. When management considers the value of a worker's contribution to a work unit or department as a part of the actual work performed, management is measuring the worker's (a) psychological productivity, (b) human relations, (c) supervisory competence, (d) leadership potential.

Part C: Write a short response to demonstrate your understanding related to the following item.

8. Explain why human relations is important for all ages and at all levels.

Turn to the back of the book to check your answers.

> What you accomplish
> can be magnified
> by the relationships you build
> in getting it accomplished.

Think and Respond

Respond to the following items with two or three complete sentences.

1. Define human relations and discuss why human relations is important to every person.
2. Why are positive people appreciated as well as usually being the most popular and productive?
3. Describe two essential human-relations responsibilities that you have as an employee.
4. How is your work contribution measured?
5. Why is it important to improve your human relations throughout your life?

SUMMARY ACTIVITY

Careers and Human Relations

Some careers require more human-relations skills than do others. For example, a customer service associate must be more competent in interacting with people than a mechanic needs to be.

This exercise will help you evaluate the importance of human relations in diversified careers. *List three of your career goals in the spaces provided at the bottom of the exercise before you begin.* Then rate, by placing a check mark (✓) under the appropriate column, the relative importance of human relations in each career, *including your own.*

Computer technician	_____	_____	_____	_____
Office manager	_____	_____	_____	_____
Flight attendant	_____	_____	_____	_____
Waitperson	_____	_____	_____	_____
Bank manager	_____	_____	_____	_____
Police/security	_____	_____	_____	_____
Salesperson	_____	_____	_____	_____
Laboratory technician	_____	_____	_____	_____
Research scientist	_____	_____	_____	_____
Electrician	_____	_____	_____	_____
Nurse	_____	_____	_____	_____
Librarian	_____	_____	_____	_____
Travel agent	_____	_____	_____	_____
Customer-support representative	_____	_____	_____	_____
Administrative assistant	_____	_____	_____	_____
Accountant	_____	_____	_____	_____
Teacher	_____	_____	_____	_____
Politician	_____	_____	_____	_____
Manufacturing supervisor	_____	_____	_____	_____
_____	_____	_____	_____	_____
_____	_____	_____	_____	_____
_____	_____	_____	_____	_____

Review your responses to evaluate the importance of human relations in your career choices as compared to other careers.

A positive attitude costs nothing but gives much. It enriches those who receive, without making poorer those who give. It takes but a moment, but the memory of it sometimes lasts forever. No one is so rich or mighty that you can get along without it and no one is so poor that you can be made rich by it. It can be your most priceless possession.

CASE 1

Reality

"It's *whom* you know that counts."

When Rod and two equally qualified people were hired at a fast-paced, innovative, high-tech firm, they knew there would be good promotion opportunities. Rod was pleased to be assigned to a department that was known for its high productivity and teamwork. Rod's team leader told him how fortunate he was to get the assignment, and she quietly suggested that Rod make a special effort to get along with everyone.

Rod worked hard and efficiently in his new job, yet he made several human-relations errors. For example, he was rather rude to a coworker who returned some borrowed files in three batches rather than all together. Another time, he complained that he had to take a late lunch because a fellow employee had failed to return on time. On still another occasion, he openly expressed his displeasure when his workload was temporarily increased because a coworker had to go home sick.

Only a few weeks had passed when the team leader called Rod into her office for a serious talk. The team leader focused her remarks on the importance of getting along with coworkers instead of unintentionally rubbing them the wrong way. At the end of the discussion, Rod asked if his work was satisfactory. The team leader told him that it was substantially above average, but was quick to add that Rod's human-relations skills were below par and needed improvement.

Some months later, promotions were given to the two people who were hired at the same time Rod was hired. What was Rod's response? He passed it off by saying, "In this outfit, it isn't what you know but who you know that counts."

A. Discuss: Was Rod justified in feeling this way? What might Rod's team leader have done to help Rod with his human-relations problems?

B. Expand Your Understanding: Make a list of human-relations actions that Rod should consider. Also, suggest some ways he and his team leader can be more "in sync" to improve the productivity (work contribution) of all members of his unit (including himself, his coworkers, and his team leader). Find at least two Internet sources to back up your recommendations. Draw some conclusions about human relations that can be useful to anyone.

CHAPTER 2

Human Relations Can Make or Break You

"Me? A split personality?"

Thought for the Day: To question how you are being perceived is a healthy way to assess the effectiveness of your human-relations skills.

PERFORMANCE COMPETENCIES

- Understand that self-confidence and other important factors make human relations more than just common sense.

- Appreciate the power of human relations as a dimension of your experience and competence.

- Consider how developing and practicing good human relations can contribute to your career opportunities.

- Recognize that high academic performance does not guarantee good human relations but a good attitude will enhance learning (and vice versa).

- Appreciate the symbiotic relationship between personality and attitude—factors that personify your human relations in achieving success.

As with most people, you may have several questions about human relations in your mind. In this chapter, you will find answers to some of the most frequently asked questions that have human-relations implications.

PROJECTING SELF-CONFIDENCE IN YOUR ATTITUDE

How Significant Is Attitude during the Job-Interview Process? Critical. Everything on your application form is vital, but your attitude, the way you view work, is equally significant. Assessing your attitude, of course, is the purpose of the personal interview. Prospective employers hope to pick up a few signals on how you will work with others and handle problems. During an interview, you communicate via your attitude as well as with your words. Many employers will hire the positive versus negative interviewee even if the knowledge and skills of the positive person are less impressive.

Will Learning More about Human Relations Give Me More Self-Confidence When Meeting People for the First Time? Yes. Without a doubt, the number one reward from a study of human relations is greater confidence. More self-confidence will help you take the first step in meeting others, instead of standing on the sidelines and thinking about it. You will greet your fellow workers pleasantly, even though they may not return the courtesy. You will feel more at ease about communicating with others. And your increased confidence, of course, will greatly help you during the interview process.

Is a Quiet Person Handicapped When It Comes to Human Relations? Sometimes. People who tend to be quiet need to make a special effort, especially at the beginning of a new venture. It is difficult to build good relationships with strangers if you back away and refuse to give them a chance to know you.

Good communications enhance human-relations skills

People who are very quiet or self-sufficient sometimes forget that their silence may be interpreted as aloofness, indifference, or even hostility. To avoid misinterpretation, you should learn to communicate frequently and openly with the people with whom you work.

However, it should be encouraging for you to know that many quiet people become highly skilled at human relations later on. The same sensitivity that makes them reserved and reticent also makes them more aware of others' needs.

Are Extroverted People Automatically Good at Human Relations? Not necessarily. Human relations is sensitivity to others. Extroverted people are often too concerned with themselves to be good at building relationships with others. The skills and principles outlined in this book can be learned and applied by both extroverts and introverts.

HUMAN RELATIONS: A DIMENSION OF EXPERIENCE

Can Good Human Relations Help One Overcome the Handicap of Inexperience?
If you can learn to create and maintain good relationships with all people, young and old and including those with much more experience than yourself, inexperience need not be much of a handicap. One way to gain experience is to respect other people's experience and to learn as much as possible from them. Keep in mind, too, that you may have frequent contact with all types of people who have invaluable experience. Always have an open mind toward expanding your knowledge base and developing good relationships. The building of such relationships will test your human-relations skills.

Why Is It That Some Sophisticated, Capable Employees—Even Managers—Seem to Ignore Good Human Relations?
It is difficult to understand. Perhaps some assume that they already practice good human relations, that the subject is too elementary, or that hard work and the work product are all that count. Perhaps they permit the pressures of their jobs to push human relations to the bottom of their priority list. They do not realize that when they let this happen, they stall their career progress.

Can One Become Competent in Human Relations the Same Way One Can Become Competent as a Computer Operator, Mechanic, or Technician?
In a way, yes. It is far more difficult, however, to measure human-relations skills. Nevertheless, people will react in a positive way when you practice good human relations and in a negative way when you don't.

Practicing good human relations contributes to positive interactions

Your human-relations skills will be observed, even if they can't be measured precisely. (A list of human-relations competencies is presented on the inside of this book's front and back covers.)

OPPORTUNITIES HUMAN RELATIONS PROVIDE

Does Paying More Attention to Human Relations Give One a Brighter Future?
In general, management experts agree that those who concentrate on good human relations get the best jobs and eventually rise to the top in most organizations. Those who pay little attention to human relations seem to get lost and are pushed into the least desirable jobs. All

organizations are built around people. And when you build healthy relationships with your fellow workers and supervisors, you open doors that would otherwise be closed.

Look at it this way. You have energy; you have high potential; you have the desire to succeed. All of this is great, but you can't put it to work unless you work well with people—because people, if they want to, can put up roadblocks at every corner. Whether you accept it or

ACTIVITY

Human Relations: Past, Present, and Future

For each statement that follows, answer the question, "Is human relations more important today than it was a few decades ago?" Check (✓) the appropriate box, "Yes" or "No," that corresponds to what you believe about each item.

Importance of human relations	Yes	No
1. In previous years, more employees worked alone and did not have to concern themselves with the interpersonal relationships necessary to achieve high standards of excellence in a modern business enterprise.		
2. Today, more workers are employed in service occupations in which the future of the organization depends on how well the customer is served. Thus, human relations is more important throughout the company.		
3. Higher productivity among employees is the key to improved profit and an increase in the standard of living for everyone. To build superior work teams, employees need greater competence in human-relations skills.		
4. More and more supervisors are being trained in human relations. Training can cause a supervisor to set higher human-relations standards and to expect greater human-relations efforts from all employees.		
5. Today, the workforce is composed of a mix of personalities and cultures. Thus, the necessity—and challenge—of building strong human relations with all kinds of people is becoming increasingly important.		

If you answered "Yes" to all five items, you are correct! Over the decades, human relations has been the number one reason why most people are hired and fired; yet, the practice of good human relations continues to become even more critical for most businesses. In fact, human relations is cited as a main reason that one business is more successful than another when the competitive playing field is evaluated. Good human relations and a positive attitude are a good combination for success—for your career success and for the success of your employer.

not, people will control your job future; and the better the relationships you build with them, the better things will be for you.

Is Human Relations as Important in Small Organizations as It Is in Large Ones? Yes. There are some important differences, though, between functioning in large organizations and functioning in small organizations. Your progress over the long run may depend more on good human relations in a large company than in a small company. Why? Because there is more supervision and more human-relations responsibility in a large company. Some higher positions in these organizations are almost exclusively leadership positions, where human relations is 60 or 70 percent of the total job.

Also, the big companies were the first to introduce human-relations training for supervisors. They are likely to place more importance on it. It follows that because smaller companies may not provide as much training and assistance, you may have to develop human-relations skills on your own.

Will Becoming Competent in Human Relations Help One Become a Better Supervisor or Team Leader? Emphatically, yes. Not only will you become a better supervisor or team leader, but you will become one sooner. The degree to which you develop your human-relations skills now will strongly influence your progress later. Of course, other factors, such as your willingness to work, also play an important role. But the daily application of the techniques you learn through this book will unquestionably have something to do with the pace of your progress.

LEARNING AND ATTITUDE

Does High Academic Performance Guarantee High Performance on the Job? No. An individual can be outstanding academically but very weak in human-relations skills. The work environment is different, people are different, and the objectives in business are different from those in the classroom. It is frequently true that a student who is average in the classroom is outstanding on the job, and vice versa. Thus, some students who are high achievers academically may have more of an adjustment to make to the world of work than those who get more practical experience along the way.

Is There a Relationship between Attitude and Learning? Yes. The expression "openness to learning" is used to communicate that when a mind is open (free of blocks, fears, prejudices, hang-ups), it will more readily accept and retain new data and ideas. For example, if a student dreads taking a required course (calculus, chemistry, English, etc.), the chances of success are diminished because the fear constitutes a block to learning. However, through an "attitude adjustment" counseling session with the instructor, the block may be partially eliminated. Learning is easier because the student's attitude is more positive toward learning.

Do Some People Needlessly Carry around a Poor Image? Unfortunately, yes. Carrying around a poor image can be very damaging because it places a person at a real disadvantage for building relationships. A poor image also leads to a negative attitude. However, a good image of yourself promotes a positive attitude and brings your best traits to the surface. Learning to be positive outweighs all the alternatives because your positive attitude is your most priceless possession.

YOUR PERSONALITY AND HUMAN RELATIONS

Why Are Some People So Obviously Awkward at Human Relations? That's a tough question because each personality is different. Here are a few possibilities. Some individuals are so self-centered that they think only of themselves and therefore give little consideration to the feelings of others. Some are blinded by ambition to the point where they seriously jeopardize their relationships with others. Still others let their emotions spill over at the wrong time, destroying relationships they have carefully built. It may be hard to admit, but we all make mistakes in building and maintaining relationships with people. None of us will ever be perfect, but we should never stop trying to improve.

Continuously strive to improve your Human Relations Skills

Must One Change One's Personality to Become Better at Human Relations? You are what you are, and you cannot become someone else. However, you can change many of your habits, attitudes, and behaviors in working with people. You can develop the personality you already have by becoming more effective in human relationships.

What Is the Connection between Attitude and Personality? There is a symbiotic relationship between the two. Personality is generally considered to be the sum total of special physical and mental characteristics that allow you to transmit a unique image to others. The special blend that comes through constitutes your personality. When your positive attitude is in charge, the image communicated is at its best.

You may be proud of one or more of your physical characteristics (eyes, posture, smile, etc.). The same may be true of mental traits (ability to learn, patience, determination, etc.). Attitude, however, is the only characteristic that transcends other traits and pulls them together into a more attractive image. The magic of a positive attitude is that it has a way of making your eyes sparkle more brightly, causing your smile to be more engaging and generally improving your total countenance.

A positive attitude improves all your attributes

Your positive attitude can best be viewed as a background "light" that enhances your other characteristics. When you are positive, the traits you desire to feature come to life. They are highlighted. Even your less-favorable traits appear more attractive. Your total personality is appreciated and enjoyed more by others.

What Is Charisma? Charisma is a special blend of a few physical and mental characteristics that seem to communicate a touch of magic. To most people, presidents John F. Kennedy and Bill Clinton had charisma. Many movie stars have it. Most of us do not have recognizable charisma; but when we have a positive attitude, we come close. And even those individuals who have charisma usually lose it if they don't keep positive attitudes.

Summary

Some of the human-relations questions and responses presented in this chapter should demonstrate to you how important human relations is in your personal life and career. While you may have some concern about the many facets, elements, and factors of human relations (e.g., the human-relations skill set), you will find that the chapters throughout this book discuss the important human-relations competencies and provide a wealth of ideas how to maximize your human-relations skills.

The really good news about human relations is this:

1. Human relations can be learned and, with practice, can be enhanced.
2. Human relations will give you self-confidence in your attitude.
3. Human relations will expand your knowledge base and provide a dimension of experience that will lead to greater competency in all that you do.
4. Human relations will open doors to many opportunities on and off the job.
5. Human relations will boost your attitude; and, in turn, you'll be more receptive toward learning.
6. Human relations will be reflected in your personality.

No doubt, human relations is a powerful asset to you and everyone around you!

So, to sum up our discussion in this chapter, an important question is, *Will this book really help me become human-relations competent?* If you give it a try, yes. Your biggest job, of course, will be to apply what you learn in this book to your present job and in your personal life. If you practice a technique long enough, it becomes a habit and you do it automatically. It won't be easy, though, because no one is ever human-relations perfect. Your goal is not to become perfect but to become substantially more effective, which, in turn, will improve your self-confidence.

As you become more aware of and gain experience in the specific human-relations skills you may practice and acquire for more effective interactions, place a high value on your positive attitude. With a positive attitude as your most priceless possession, you have a distinct advantage of improving your human relationships. Practice good human relations to make the difference you need to become successful in your personal life as well as in your career. And, because there is a symbiotic relationship between personality and attitude, frequently ask yourself how you are being perceived by others. Knowing that human relations can make you or break you, opt for a win-win outcome!

Test Your Understanding

Respond to the following items to test your understanding of the chapter.

Part A: Circle the correct answer (T = True; F = False) for each of the following statements.

T F   1. Employers often hire applicants based as much on their attitudes as on their job skills.

T F   2. It is important to build strong relationships because people can put up roadblocks.

T F   3. There is an extremely high correlation between high mental ability and human-relations competency.

T F   4. A major personality change is necessary if one is to become skillful at human relations.

T F   5. A positive attitude will give you both more confidence and a better self-image.

Part B: Circle the letter of the correct answer for each of the following items.

6. The number one reward from the study of human relations is (a) greater confidence, (b) less competition, (c) more challenges, (d) fewer challenges.

7. Freeing your mind of blocks, fears, and prejudices makes you (a) less susceptible to criticism, (b) less awkward in explaining your viewpoint, (c) more vulnerable to sensitivity, (d) more positive toward learning.

Part C: Write a short response to demonstrate your understanding related to the following item.

8. Contrast some of the human-relations challenges that may face people with quiet versus extroverted personalities.

Turn to the back of the book to check your answers.

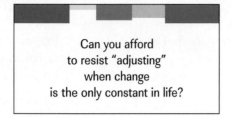

Can you afford
to resist "adjusting"
when change
is the only constant in life?

Think and Respond

Respond to the following items with two or three complete sentences.

1. Suggest two ways self-confidence will contribute to good human relations.

2. Why should good human relations augment and expand your experience?

3. Identify work opportunities that can be a direct result of practicing good human relations.

4. How do academics and learning factor into human-relations development?

5. Discuss two ways a positive attitude contributes to your personality and human relations.

My Self-Confidence Inventory

This self-evaluation exercise is designed to help you measure your personal confidence in initiating communications with others, which, in turn, can lead to the building of better human relationships. Read both statements associated with each item that follows. Then, circle the number that indicates where you fall in the scale from 10 to 1 on each of the factors.

1. I am completely at ease when it comes to speaking up in class or in other groups.

    10 9 8 7 6 5 4 3 2 1

    I never take the initiative to speak up in groups of any kind.

2. When I have all the facts, I do not hesitate to present my opinion.

    10 9 8 7 6 5 4 3 2 1

    I never present my opinion even though I know I am right.

3. I enjoy initiating a conversation with a stranger if there is no danger involved.

    10 9 8 7 6 5 4 3 2 1

    Even under ideal (safe) conditions, I would never talk to a stranger.

4. It does not bother me at all to join informal groups already involved in communication.

    10 9 8 7 6 5 4 3 2 1

    I would feel so awkward, I would never join an informal group of any kind without an invitation.

5. If a coworker and I had a personality conflict, I would initiate a meeting to reconcile our differences.

    10 9 8 7 6 5 4 3 2 1

    If a coworker and I had a personality conflict, I would let time solve it.

6. I would have complete confidence to approach my supervisor on any matter important to me.

    10 9 8 7 6 5 4 3 2 1

    I would never approach my supervisor under any circumstances.

7. I would quickly volunteer to speak over a microphone at a dinner meeting.

    10 9 8 7 6 5 4 3 2 1

    Under no condition would I volunteer to speak in front of any group.

8. I enjoy walking into strange social environments when I do not know anyone.

    10 9 8 7 6 5 4 3 2 1

    I refuse to walk into strange social environments even if I know I will meet a friend.

9. In conversations, I always look people in the eye.

    10 9 8 7 6 5 4 3 2 1

    I never look anybody in the eye.

10. I have more than enough self-assurance to initiate a relationship with anyone.

    10 9 8 7 6 5 4 3 2 1

    My self-assurance is zero when it comes to initiating relationships with others.

    Total Score _____

Total your scores for the ten items. If your point total is 50 or above, you are doing your part or more in building relationships. If your score is under 50 points, more initiative on your part probably would be desirable. Building self-confidence can enhance many aspects of your life. In fact, *most* people should strive for more self-confidence in building relationships with others.

CASE 2

Adjustment

"Don't ask me . . . I just work here."

Aria and George were both young, aggressive, and competent information systems specialists. They met during a training program in preparation for identical jobs involving considerable contact with fellow employees.

Although it was not easy, Aria made a good adjustment to her work environment. Adjusting was easy for her because of her warm, flexible personality. She also applied the human-relations skills she had learned and developed in college. George, however, had some difficulty with his assignment. He appeared to be rigid and distant to those who worked around him. To a few older and experienced employees, he even seemed aloof and hostile. George's supervisor watched him from a distance. The supervisor felt George waited or expected others to approach him and be friendly. George seemed to stand on the sidelines, unable or unwilling to initiate interaction or communication, let alone to meet people halfway.

A few weeks after joining the company, George told Aria during lunch that he was going to look for another job. When asked why, he said some coworkers were unfriendly. He also resented some of his fellow employees who were excessively critical of him. Furthermore, his supervisor was trying to push him into a mold of conformity that was simply not his style. Why should he go all out to adjust? After all, building working relationships should be a two-way street. He felt confident he could find another company that would appreciate him more and give him all the freedom he needed to be himself.

A. Discuss: What chance do you think George has of finding a job environment that would make him completely happy? How could Aria help George? Assume that you are George's supervisor and are willing to spend thirty minutes in a two-way communication session trying to help him and keep him with the firm. What points would you attempt to cover?

B. Expand Your Understanding: Interview two managers, asking them how they help employees like George. Identify some Internet sources for desirable personality traits George needs to acquire over time. Also suggest some recommended strategies he can use to adjust his outlook.

CHAPTER 3

Hold on to Your Positive Attitude

"It's hard to stay positive under pressure."

Thought for the Day: If your attitude has thorns, you cannot expect others to want to get close to you.

PERFORMANCE COMPETENCIES

■ Understand the importance of communicating a positive attitude and how your perspective (either positive or negative) influences how you are perceived.

■ Identify several ways you can build and protect your positive attitude for it to become a valuable career asset.

■ Recognize the significance of making frequent self-assessments for initiating attitude improvement.

■ Appreciate the value of a serendipitous attitude—an attitude you control—and how it can be contagious.

Attitude is a common word. You hear it almost every day. Managers discuss it at work. Professors use it on campus. Employment counselors look for it among applicants. You hear people say, "He's got an attitude" (indicating a possible problem), while others say, "I wish I had her consistently positive attitude." No other attribute will have more influence upon your future. A positive attitude can be your most priceless possession.

If you can create and keep a positive attitude toward your job, your company, and life in general, you should not only move up the ladder of success quickly and gracefully but also be a happier person. If you are unable to be positive, you may find many career mobility doors closed to you and your personal life less than exciting.

COMMUNICATING YOUR ATTITUDE

There are three basic forms of communication between people. One is the written form—letters, memos, faxes, e-mails, and so forth. The second is the verbal form—face-to-face conversations, telephone conversations, voice mail, intercom discussions, video conferencing, and so forth. The third involves the transmission of attitudes.

The first two forms of communication are so important to the profitable operation of an organization that we tend to think they are the only ones. We forget that we also communicate our attitudes through facial expressions, hand gestures, and other more subtle forms of body language. Sometimes people will greet others with a positive voice, but their body language (negative facial expression) sends a contrasting signal.

As the expression claims, sometimes your attitude speaks so loudly that others cannot hear what you say.

Your attitude speaks loudly

Your Attitude Is Showing. Every time you report for work, every time you attend a staff meeting, every time you go through a formal appraisal, every time you take a coffee break, and every time you go out socially, be aware that your attitude is showing.

Because attitude can play such an important role in your future, let's take a closer look at the meaning of the word itself. *Attitude* is defined by most psychologists as a mental set that causes a person to respond in a characteristic manner to a given stimulus. You have many attitudes, or mental sets. You have attitudes toward certain makes of automobiles; toward certain social institutions (schools, churches, and the like); and toward certain careers, lifestyles, and people.

You also have a wide variety of job attitudes. You build attitudes toward your supervisor and the people with whom you work, toward the job you do, toward company policies, and toward the amount of money you are being paid. In addition to these specific attitudes, you have a basic, or total, attitude toward your job and toward life itself. Strictly speaking, then, attitude is the way you look at your whole environment.

Your Perspective Influences Your Attitude. What you see in life truly is up to you, but remember that your perspective also is reflected in your attitude. For example, you can look at your job in any way you wish. On the one hand, you can focus your attention on all its negative aspects (odd hours, close supervision, poor location). On the other hand, you can focus your attention on the more positive factors of the job (harmonious work environment, good learning opportunities, good benefits). All jobs have both positive and negative factors. How you choose to perceive yours is an important decision.

Attitude is the way you view and interpret your environment. Some people can push unpleasant things out of sight and dwell largely on positive factors. Others seem to enjoy the unpleasant and dwell on these negative factors.

Your attitude is the way you look at things

If you go around looking for what is wrong with things, wondering why things are not better, and complaining about them, then you will be a negative person in the minds of most people. If you do the opposite—look for what is good and focus on pleasant things—you will be a positive person in the minds of most people.

Some people (through imaging) keep their positive attitudes by viewing life with both positive and negative factors competing to gain as much "mind time" as possible. Negative factors constantly try to command attention, pushing positive factors to the side.

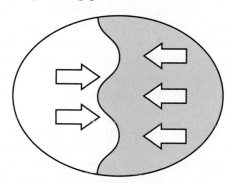

To offset a negative drift, positive people discipline their minds to concentrate primarily upon positive factors, thus pushing the negative to the outer perimeter of their thinking.

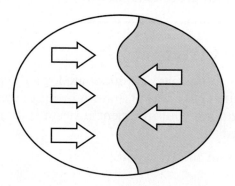

There is no perfect job or position. One job may have more favorable aspects than another, but all jobs have some unpleasant ones. The employee who dwells on the unfavorable factors has a negative attitude. The employee who is determined to look for factors that are favorable will slowly become a more positive person.

Therefore, even if you start a new job or assignment with a positive attitude, you must make sure that it remains positive. It is possible that you will meet a few people with negative attitudes who will attempt to persuade you to think as they do. These factors could influence you and destroy what otherwise would have been an excellent start.

To be a positive person, you need not think your world or company is perfect. That would be foolish. You would eventually become disillusioned. However, unless you feel that the majority of factors are favorable, you will eventually become negative and you will show it.

Negative Attitudes Diminish Success. This really means that the moment you can no longer be positive about your career with your company, your chances for success are reduced. No one can be positive all the time. You will naturally have periods of doubt. These temporary periods will not hurt you seriously. But a consistently negative attitude that persists for weeks or months will destroy your future with the organization. If you find your negative attitude cannot be improved in your present setting and you honestly feel such an attitude is justified, you should resign.

It is important to realize that a positive attitude involves far more than a smile. A smile, of course, is helpful in transmitting a positive attitude. However, some people transmit a positive attitude even when they seldom smile. They convey positiveness by the way they treat others, the way they look at their responsibilities, and the perspective they take when faced with a problem.

Attitude is a highly personal thing. It is closely tied to your self-concept, or the way you look at yourself. Because attitude is so personal, talking about it is not easy. People often freeze when the word is mentioned. As a result, management may never talk to you about your attitude. You may never hear, for example, "Let's be honest. Your attitude is negative. What are you going to do about it?" But everyone will know when your attitude is showing.

ACTIVITY

A Positive Attitude Is Essential to Career Success

1. When you are positive you are usually more energetic, motivated, productive, and alert. Thinking about negative things too much has a way of draining your energy. Put another way, a positive attitude opens a gate and lets your inner enthusiasm spill out. A negative attitude, however, keeps the gate closed.

   Name two things that seem to energize or motivate you.

2. First impressions are important on the job because they often have a lasting effect. Coworkers you meet for the first time appear to have little radar sets tuned in to your attitude. If your attitude is positive, they receive a friendly, warm signal and they are attracted to you. If your attitude is negative, they receive an unfriendly signal and they try to avoid you.

   Name one positive signal you can give to others.

3. A positive employee contributes to the productivity of others. A negative employee does not. Attitudes are caught more than they are taught. Both negative and positive attitudes are transmitted on the job. They are picked up by others. A persistently negative attitude, like the rotten apple in the barrel, can spoil the positive attitudes of others. It is very difficult to maintain a high level of productivity while working next to a person with a negative attitude.

   Name one attitude you admire in another person.

4. Coworkers like you when you are positive. They like to be around you because you are fun. Your job is more interesting and exciting because you are in the middle of things and not on the outside complaining. When you are negative, people prefer to stay clear of you. A negative person may build good relationships with a few other people (who are perhaps negative themselves), but such a person cannot build good relationships with the majority of employees.

   Name one positive element you have that attracts others.

5. The kind of attitude you transmit to management will have a considerable influence on your future success. Management constantly reads your mental attitude, even though you may feel you are successful in covering it up. Supervisors can determine your attitude by how you approach your job, react to directives, handle problems, and work with others. If you are positive, you will be given greater consideration when special assignments and promotion opportunities arise.

   Name one way a positive attitude influences an employer.

If your job involves customer, client, or patient contacts, you should place additional emphasis on everything stated in the preceding list. Your attitude is significant in all relationships, but it is crucial when you are in a service position.

Now, review all of your responses and write a general summary statement that encompasses all your responses.

You are definitely on the right track if your summary statement reflects that "a positive attitude contributes to my success" or that "everyone knows when my attitude is showing."

BUILDING AND PROTECTING YOUR POSITIVE ATTITUDE

How, then, do you make sure you keep your positive attitude when things get tough? How do you keep a good grip on it when you are discouraged? How do you keep it in good repair on a day-to-day basis over the years? Here are a few simple suggestions.

Build a More Positive Attitude in One Environment and You Will Be More Successful in Another. Your positive or negative attitude is not something that you can hang on a hook. It follows you wherever you go. It is reasonable to assume, then, that if you make a greater effort to be a more positive person in your social and personal life, your effort will automatically spill over and help you on the job. By the same token, if you make a greater effort to develop a more positive attitude at work, your effort will make a contribution to your social and personal life. One effort will complement the other.

Talk about Positive Things. Negative comments are seldom welcomed by fellow workers on the job; nor are they welcomed by those you meet in the social scene. The best way to be positive is to be complimentary. Constant gripers and complainers seldom build healthy and exciting relationships with others.

Positive people see positive things in others

Look for the Good Things in the People with Whom You Work, Especially Your Supervisors. Nobody is perfect, but almost everybody has a few worthwhile qualities. If you dwell on people's good features, it will be easier for you to like them and easier for them to like you. Make no mistake about one thing: People usually know how you react to them even if you don't communicate verbally.

Look for the Good Things in Your Organization. What are the factors that make it a good place to work? Do you like the hours, the physical environment, the people, the actual work you are doing? What about opportunities for promotion? Do you have chances for self-improvement? What about your wage and benefit package? Do you have the freedom you seek? No job is perfect, but if you concentrate on the good things, the negative factors may seem less important. Seeing the positive side of things does not mean that you should ignore negative elements that should be changed. Far from it! A positive person is not a weak person. A positive person is usually confident, assertive (within limits), and an agent of change within an organization. Management is not seeking passive people who meekly conform. They want spirited, positive people who will make constructive and thoughtful improvements.

If you decide to stay with an organization for a long time, you would be wise to concentrate on its good features. Staying positive may take a considerable amount of personal fortitude, but it is the best way to keep your career on an upward track. If you think positively, you will act positively and you will succeed.

Shun Potential Negative Traps That Will Drag Your Attitude and Career Down.
It is unfortunate, but all too common, that students frequently fail academically and drop out because of financial problems. It also appears that employees troubled with financial worries often become negative and lose the promotions that would provide the extra money that could help them pay off their bills. If financial problems are not addressed quickly through planning and discipline, many people do not understand how the resulting damage can go far beyond financial losses. Unfortunately, few of these individuals realize that their positive attitudes are being sacrificed along with their credit ratings. Instead of seeking and accepting family or professional financial counseling, they permit their insolvency to lead them into attitudinal bankruptcy. When attitudinal bankruptcy happens, they pay a double penalty.

Avoid attitudinal bankruptcy at all costs

Don't Permit a Fellow Worker—Even a Supervisor—Who Has a Negative Attitude Trap You into His (or Her) Way of Thinking.
You may not be able to change a negative person's attitude, but at least you can protect your own positive attitude from becoming negative. The story of Chandi will emphasize this point.

Chandi. Chandi was a little uneasy about her new job. It was a fine opportunity, and she knew the standards were very high. Would she have the needed skills? Could she learn fast enough to please her supervisor? Would the older employees like her? Although Chandi's concern was understandable, it was not justified. In addition to being highly qualified for the job, she had a happy, positive attitude that wouldn't stop. She was seldom depressed.

Everything went very well for Chandi for a while. Her positive attitude was appreciated by all. Slowly, however, her fellow workers and supervisor noticed a change. Chandi became more critical of her colleagues, her job, and the company. Her usual friendly greetings and helpful ideas were gradually replaced by complaints. What had happened? Without realizing it, Chandi was showing the effects of the friendships she had made on the job. Needing acceptance in a strange environment, she had welcomed the attention of a clique of employees who had negative attitudes—a group that management already viewed critically.

Chandi was not able to confine her negative attitude to her job. Soon, again without realizing it, she let her negative attitude spill over into her social life. In fact, it troubled her boyfriend so much that he had it out with her one night. His words were a little rough. "Look, Chandi. When you are happy, you are very attractive and fun to be around. But frankly, when you are negative you are a real bore, and I never have a good time with you. I think those so-called friends you hang around with on the job are killing what was once a beautiful personality."

It wasn't a happy evening, but Chandi got the message. She made a vow to recapture and hang on to the positive attitude she had previously enjoyed. Not only was she successful in recapturing her positive attitude, but she also converted a few of her previously negative friends to her way of thinking. Her action saved her career.

MAKE FREQUENT SELF-ASSESSMENTS

When friends casually ask me, "How are you doing?" I often jokingly reply, "I'm not sure, but I intend to sit under a tree tomorrow and ask myself some questions to find out." Most employees make the mistake of waiting around for their organizations to complete an annual formal appraisal instead of frequently sitting under a shady tree somewhere and asking themselves questions similar to these.

Am I currently transmitting a positive or negative attitude?

Is my attitude influencing the quality and quantity of my personal productivity in a positive way?

Am I sufficiently positive to be considered a fun and comfortable coworker?

Am I communicating to superiors through my attitude that I seek career advancements?

Are my customers, clients, or coworkers responding to my attitude in an upbeat manner?

John. John's boss is a believer in formal appraisal programs. Instead of annual evaluations, he would prefer going through the process twice each year. In discussing the good showing John made on his current appraisal, his boss said, "John, I have noticed that your attitude and productivity always improve shortly before appraisal time and then settle back a few weeks afterward. I think it would be smart for you to appraise yourself every few weeks during the year. By periodic appraisal checks, you would keep a more positive attitude and deserve a higher rating than I can give you now. Consistency is a big factor, and I recommend frequent self-appraisals."

┌ ACTIVITY

My Positive Attitude Self-Assessment

In the space that follows, formulate some questions to help you in the self-assessment of your attitude. While you may be able to only come up with one or two questions now, come back to this activity frequently to review your questions, to assess your progress, and to add, delete, or modify your questions. Be sure to honestly answer the questions, evaluate your answers, and chart your progress toward self-improvement.

Questions for Self-Assessment	Progress I Have Made
1.	
2.	
3.	
4.	
5.	

Whatever form your self-assessment takes (attitude is a most personal matter), use it frequently. Check your attitude as you would the amount of gasoline in your car. Talk to yourself about the progress you are making. Don't sit around expecting someone else to do it for you. Fill up your tank—and top it off—with positive-attitude fuel.

A SERENDIPITOUS ATTITUDE

There are many techniques that can help you hold on to your positive attitude. Some are discussed later in this book. One that will help you get started, especially when an irritating problem surfaces, is saying the word *serendipity*.

The word *serendipity* was coined by Horace Walpole in 1754 when he put the fairy tale *The Three Princes of Serendip* to paper. A more modern version by Elizabeth Jamison Hodges was published in 1964. It is a delightful story of three princes who travel from kingdom to kingdom in a lighthearted, compassionate manner. In helping others solve their problems, they are led to the solution of a problem in their own kingdom.

Serendipity lends itself to many interpretations. To some, it is a gift to help them find agreeable things not sought. To most everyone, it is a "happiness" word. The magic comes into play when we realize that a "lighter approach" can often not only solve a problem, but cause something good to happen in our lives.

In short, serendipity is an attitude—an apparently frivolous mental set that can help us view our work environment in a more humorous and forgiving manner. It is an attitude that temporarily moves responsibility aside and encourages one to rise above any negative situation. A serendipitous attitude is within the reach of everyone; and, when achieved, fortuitous things may happen. For example, when you have a lighthearted, mischievous, festive way of looking at things, others are intrigued and may invite you to share beautiful experiences

Be in control of your attitude

with them that, in turn, can enhance your life. Serendipity is a state of mind. It is a wonderful attitude to take to a party. There are also times when it can be a lifesaver in the workplace.

Summary

Because your attitude speaks so loudly to those around you, it is critical that you aspire to develop the most positive attitude you can. Display your positive attitude in everything you do. Strive to keep your perspective of things positive. If you do, you will be in a better position to ward off the negative elements that inevitably seem to be abundantly present.

Holding on to your positive attitude will never be easy; however, your success in doing so depends on how much you work at it. Continually working on your positive attitude will achieve positive results—you'll find greater success on your job and you'll enjoy better relationships with the people in your life. So it makes sense to frequently assess your attitude to see where you can be more positive. As a result of your assessments and the positive actions you take, you will probably be successful in helping others to be more positive, too. Remember, a serendipitous attitude can travel far and wide—it can be delightfully contagious—and it can come back to you in a way that will increase your positiveness. What great rewards come with showing off your positive attitude!

Test Your Understanding

Respond to the following items to test your understanding of the chapter.

Part A: Circle the correct answer (T = True; F = False) for each of the following statements.

T F   1. Attitude can be defined as the way you look at things mentally.

T F   2. People who are totally negative about their jobs and remain so for an extended period of time should find a new job.

T F   3. Attitudes are always caught and cannot be taught.

T F   4. There is no relationship between attitude and the number of friendships one enjoys.

T F   5. The more an individual concentrates on the positive factors in life, the more positive she (or he) will be.

Part B: Circle the letter of the correct answer for each of the following items.

6. When you keep a positive attitude, you are usually (a) more energetic and motivated, (b) focused on negative factors, (c) closed minded, (d) more critical of others.

7. Good advice for assessing your attitude is to (a) wait for your organization's assessment before you act, (b) frequently conduct your own self-assessment for improvement, (c) ignore feedback from your

supervisor unless it is to your liking, (d) do an assessment only when you get a drift from others that your attitude is negative.

Part C: Write a short response to demonstrate your understanding related to the following item.

8. Describe several ways to keep your attitude positive (especially when the going gets tough or when there are negative elements all around you).

Turn to the back of the book to check your answers.

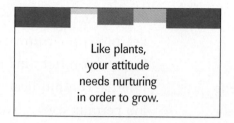

Like plants,
your attitude
needs nurturing
in order to grow.

Think and Respond

Respond to the following items with two or three complete sentences.

1. Name two ways you can communicate your attitude effectively.
2. Explain how your perspective positively or negatively affects your attitude.
3. Suggest two things that will help you build and protect your attitude.
4. What is the purpose of making frequent self-assessments?
5. Describe the meaning and potential effect of a serendipitous attitude.

Keeping a Positive Attitude on the Job

All jobs or careers have both plus and minus factors. The more an employee concentrates on the positive factors, the more positive the attitude of the individual is apt to be.

To help you separate the positive from the negative in your present job or one you have had in the past, rate the following factors that employees respond to in either a positive or negative manner. Place a "P" in front of each factor about which you are positive and an "N" in front of each factor about which you are negative. Add other important factors about your job in the blanks provided, and rate those as well.

_____ Job permits you to go to school   _____ Working hours

_____ Salary   _____ Compatible coworkers

_____ Company benefits   _____ Parking facilities

_____ Physical working environment   _____ Learning opportunities

_____ Promotional possibilities   _____ Recognition from management

_____ Quality of leadership in management   _____ Internal communications

_____ Quality of your immediate supervisor   _____ Job permits you to live where you please

_____ Amount of personal freedom   _____ You are doing what you want to do

_____ Opportunity to dress as you please   _____ Equipment is up-to-date

_____ Transportation and commuting distance   _____ Advancement opportunities

_____ Diverse company culture   _____ Regular breaks

_____   _____

_____   _____

_____   _____

_____ Total Positive Factors   _____ Total Negative Factors

If you counted more positive than negative factors (and they are equally or more important to you than those you rated as negative), you should become even more positive about your job if you concentrate on them. Try to be less concerned with negative factors and talk about them less. This change will have a good influence on your attitude.

If, however, you counted more negative than positive factors, you have three choices: (1) Convert some negative factors to positive. (Perhaps you made a mistake in these ratings.) (2) Uncover some positive factors you previously ignored. (3) Seek a new work environment where more positive factors exist.

A person not considered beautiful by physical standards can still be regarded as "beautiful" with a cheerful, positive outlook. A positive attitude can provide higher energy levels, greater creativity, and an improved personality.

CASE 3

Credit Blues

"Financial solvency helps keep my attitude positive."

Manuel, a graphic artist with multimedia skills, was constantly praised by his college professors for his creative works. He was also rewarded by winning a number of prizes in campus art shows. Upon graduating, Manuel made many attempts to find a job in commercial art. No luck. After many disappointments, he reluctantly accepted a position with a large retail chain that would have only limited use for his talent in the area of merchandising display.

Manuel decided to make the most of his situation and began his career with a positive attitude. He quickly demonstrated that he had both talent and managerial ability. His future looked bright. He was happy. Some time later, however, his supervisor noticed that Manuel's enthusiasm had started to dwindle. He began giving excuses for not getting things done on time. Manuel's merchandise displays were not up to previous standards. His relationships with other workers started to deteriorate.

In a heart-to-heart talk with his sensitive and supportive manager, Manuel revealed that he was having serious financial problems. Manuel's quest for finding satisfying challenges had led him to obsessive and impulsive Internet shopping and stock trading. As it took more and more stimuli to satisfy his "needs," Manuel's acquisitions and debts grew, too. Due to the purchase of a new sports car and other consumer items, Manuel was behind on his credit payments, and the high interest rates were keeping him in a financial hole. Manuel's manager told him he was suffering from a severe case of "plastic blues" and sent him to a company counselor with expertise in financial planning.

A. Discuss: Would you agree that financial problems can damage a positive attitude and derail one's career? What suggestions would you give to Manuel to help him stay positive while he digs himself out of his financial hole?

B. Expand Your Understanding: Conduct a survey of several people as to the best financial advice they would give to another person to avoid attitudinal bankruptcy (e.g., how does one stay positive through financially tight times?). Find some magazine and Internet sources for suggestions about holding on to your positive attitude. Draw some conclusions from which both you and Manuel can benefit.

CHAPTER 4

When People Step on Your Attitude

"Another day on the job!"

Thought for the Day: Adjusting your attitude in a positive direction—and often—will only improve it.

PERFORMANCE COMPETENCIES

- Anticipate the fact that people will step on your attitude.

- Understand and explore some of the techniques for "bouncing back" quickly from ego-deflating encounters with others.

- Learn to be sensitive and respectful of others if you expect to deserve the same consideration.

- Appreciate the true value of your attitude and treat it as your most prized possession.

Holding on to your positive attitude does not just happen without any effort on your part. It takes work, and it takes commitment. If you become passionate about the value of your attitude, you will quickly see the many rewards of your efforts. You will protect your attitude as an important personal and career asset. In fact, you will quickly realize that your attitude is your most prized possession. Protecting your attitude, then, must become a continuous, daily activity. Why? Because others can take it away from you in an instant—or at least try to do so—if you aren't prepared to guard your attitude with a strong conviction.

OUCH! I'VE BEEN STEPPED ON

On any given day, three or four different people might step on your positive attitude and render you negative for a short period of time. For example, an insensitive coworker or teacher might press you to deliver an answer to a difficult question in such a way as to embarrass you; or a friend or someone in your family might back away from keeping an important promise you were depending upon; or a person you've known for a long time or a coworker you thought was your friend might "snub" you in an off-the-job social environment.

Your effectiveness is strongly linked to your attitude

Even in simple situations, stepping on your attitude is like stepping on your ego. It deflates your personal confidence and destroys your effectiveness.

Although the damage to your attitude may be slight, it takes effort on your part to bounce back. In more serious situations, bouncing back can be a major challenge.

Gregg. About a month ago, Gregg missed what appeared to be a "sure" tackle in a key college football game. Furious, his coach pulled him out of the game and chewed him out in front of others. The verbal lacing hit Gregg's attitude so hard that he was tempted to turn in his equipment. "After all," Gregg told his teammates, "the turf was wet and I slipped. It could have happened to anyone." With encouragement from others, however, he discussed the incident with his coach, pumped up his depressed attitude, and finished the season at such a high level that he kept his athletic scholarship.

Jennifer. Last week, due to a misunderstanding, Jennifer got into a conflict with her boss and emotionally unloaded some stored-up grievances. Her boss, Ms. Bailey, came down on her hard. Rather than attempting to resolve the problem so she could keep and enjoy her part-time job again, Jennifer nursed her grievance, which kept her positive attitude from bouncing back. Result? She was given notice and quickly discovered that she had lost a job that was better than any she could find.

Jill and Roberto. Having been married almost a year, it became obvious that things were not going to work out for Jill and Roberto. After the separation process was underway, it was also obvious that Jill was allowing the whole matter to get under her skin. Roberto's outward acceptance of the separation, the legal conferences with the lawyers, and the breaking up of their apartment all combined to step on Jill's attitude in a devastating manner. She finally went to her older sister for guidance. Her sister made this statement: "Face it, Jill, your attitude has taken a beating and bouncing back is a do-it-yourself project. Don't you think it is time to get started? I will do everything I can to help."

Human conflicts both on the job and in our personal lives can turn our attitudes negative. The damage can sometimes be severe. But if such conflicts are permitted to destroy our positive attitudes on a permanent basis, we are paying a price that is much too high. What can we do to "bounce back"? What can we do to restore our positive attitudes? The following section of this chapter provides some suggestions for protecting your attitude from permanent damage when others have contributed to turning it in a negative direction.

BOUNCE-BACK STRATEGIES

Take Immediate Action. It is a mistake to wait around and "nurse" your deflated attitude. Quickly do something to restore your positive attitude so that additional damage will not occur. In some cases, this may mean an apology that you don't want to make.

Erlan. Yesterday, Erlan made a foolish mistake that could have been minimized if he had reported it to his boss immediately. However, before Erlan could offer his boss an explanation, an insensitive coworker stepped on Erlan's attitude. Erlan became so upset with getting his attitude stepped on, he forgot to report the mistake to his boss. Not reporting the mistake caused Erlan to have a poor night's sleep. To restore his attitude, Erlan got to work early the next morning and apologized to his boss. Erlan was in full possession of his positive attitude by noon.

Generally speaking, the longer you allow your attitude to be depressed, the longer it takes to bounce back. Quick action, even if it is embarrassing, is advisable.

Place a High Value on Your Positive Attitude. The more you respect and covet your positive attitude, the more you will want to take quick action to preserve it. Normally, we only protect those possessions that we deem priceless.

Protect your attitude as if your life depends on it!

When you come to the conclusion that your positive attitude is the golden key to your future, you will want to restore it as soon as possible once it has been stepped on.

Genelle. Some coworkers pile extra, uninteresting work on Genelle because she has the reputation of being so easygoing. When she belatedly discovered that being such a "pushover" around the office was turning her negative, she did an about-face and, as a result, she is respected more and fewer coworkers step on her attitude these days.

Learn to See Both Sides of Situations. Sometimes a friend or coworker may step on your attitude because she (or he) is under pressure and is rendered insensitive to your needs. When this happens, you have two choices. You can allow your attitude to remain depressed and become the victim. Or you can give the other party the benefit of the doubt and restore your attitude to its normal positive stance without making a major issue out of what happened.

Sylvia. Immediately, Sylvia knew her attitude had been stepped on when her coworker didn't show up at the appointed location and was seen later with another person. What Sylvia didn't know was that there had been a family emergency and the coworker was headed for the hospital with her sister. When she arrived at work the next morning, her friend was waiting to explain what had happened. Sylvia could feel her positive attitude returning before the discussion had ended.

Protect Yourself So Attitude Damage Won't Happen Twice. Some people will step on your attitude once and, if they get away with it, will step on it again. The behavior of some people is such that they are either insensitive to your needs or they do not give you the respect you deserve. Some supervisors are this way. Some family members or coworkers are also this way. In these situations, you need to protect your attitude by standing up for yourself, isolating yourself from the individual, or using other techniques to open up a two-way discussion with this person so that you and your attitude will be treated with respect and sensitivity.

Hank. Hank's boss kept stepping on his attitude by making unkind snide remarks, giving him undesirable assignments, and generally treating him like a second-class employee. Finally, Hank asked for a private appointment and confronted his boss with the question: "Am I not entitled to the same kind of treatment as my coworkers?" Hank's boss replied: "I was only testing you. You have now made the grade, so we will have a different kind of relationship from now on."

Of course, you'll want to do everything you can to avoid letting others diminish your positive attitude. And there are no guarantees that, even after taking deliberate action, your attitude will not get stepped on a second time by a person who has stepped on it before, especially if you are overly sensitive. But if a threat to your attitude comes over and over again by the same person, you need to be particularly alert to stopping the repeat threats while avoiding any negative fallout.

Keep Your Sensitivity in Check. It's up to you how you address the challenges facing you. And, as most people with positive attitudes must do, you probably will need to work hard at keeping your attitude positive and upbeat in trying situations. Try to keep your sensitivity in "check." Use the power of positive thinking and positive actions to combat negativism. Call on the "bounce-back" strategies that work for you—and call on them as often as they are needed to capitalize on getting your attitude back on track as quickly as possible.

Building relationships is not an easy feat and must be continually reinforced throughout life. With a concerted resolve, however, you're bound to appreciate your positive attitude more and more. You're bound to get better at protecting yourself from others trying to turn your positive downward. As you do, you will be rewarded for the progress you've made by enjoying a more positive attitude.

AVOID PUTTING OTHER PEOPLE DOWN

If you expect people to respect you and be sensitive to your needs, don't step on other people's attitudes. One of the best ways you can keep your attitude from being stepped on is making sure you give other people the same consideration you expect. Value and respect the views, perspectives, and feelings of others. There is always more than one side to an issue and more than one way to solve a problem.

Respect for others will earn you respect

It may take more effort on your part to avoid stepping on another person's attitude, but it will be worth it in the long run. You will increase your sensitivity to plausible alternatives, and you will get to know people better. As a result, you will be able to get your ideas across more effectively. It is vital to watch and listen to others for a better understanding of their perspectives. Be sure you seek this type of feedback to ensure you truly are communicating.

Steve. Frequently Steve played the "one upmanship" game by building himself up in front of groups of people. One on one, he would be very careful not to give out too much information. But in a meeting it was a different story. When an issue was discussed in a group setting, Steve was very quiet until near the end of the discussion, when he would give his opinion. His opinion always seemed to be the way the "wind was blowing" by his supervisor. He was so good at rephrasing others' views, the key point he made frequently could solve the problem. His coworkers, however, felt his comments were offered at their expense. He took great pride in his ability to make people understand "he was the only one who had complete information" or that "he should always be consulted."

ACTIVITY

Bounce-Back Checklist

Assume an authority figure of some kind (supervisor, teacher, parent, etc.) or a family member, friend, or colleague has stepped on your attitude so hard that you are emotionally upset. Which of the following action steps would you consider taking to restore your positive attitude in the shortest period of time? Place a check mark (✓) in the square of the three suggestions you like best.

1. ❑ Play it "cool" and allow time, but not too much time, to restore your positive attitude.
2. ❑ Have a serious talk with yourself in which you convincingly explain why your positive attitude is too valuable to allow any authority figure to "steal" it from you.
3. ❑ Make an appointment to openly discuss the matter with the authority figure or person who stepped on your positive attitude.
4. ❑ Sulk.
5. ❑ Figure out a way to retaliate so you can, in effect, step on the authority figure's or the other person's attitude.
6. ❑ Forgive and forget; and, above all, refuse to take being stepped on personally.
7. ❑ Position yourself where it won't happen again.
8. ❑ Tell yourself you are too "big" a person to allow such a little thing to get under your skin.
9. ❑ Realize that your attitude will be stepped on from time to time and quickly employ bounce-back strategies.
10. ❑ Seek counseling and guidance from a professional, especially if you have tried other strategies and they don't seem to work for you.

Review your responses. Have you selected all "positive" actions (all but numbers 4 and 5). If not, consider why selections 4 and 5 are not appropriate. Remember, the way to make the most of other physical and mental characteristics is to communicate them through a positive attitude.

YOUR ATTITUDE: A PRICELESS POSSESSION

If you consider your attitude to be your most priceless possession, as many people do, you cannot—under any circumstances—permit others to turn it negative. When others knowingly or unknowingly step on your positive attitude, you must resort to whatever technique is comfortable and appropriate to restore it. If you do not quickly restore your attitude, you are, in effect, allowing a person to "take" or "steal" your positive attitude from you.

Your attitude belongs to you

Should someone try to damage your positive attitude, keep in mind that your attitude belongs to you alone. It cannot be given or transferred to another person. It is not negotiable. You have the right to protect your positive attitude from anyone who might damage it over an extended period of time. It is one thing to have another person step on your attitude unknowingly and then apologize or make amends in other ways. In these situations, you can bounce back quickly and no harm is done. It is another thing altogether when someone steps on your attitude over and over again. Should this happen, action on your part to build a more mutually rewarding relationship is suggested.

Summary

Without question, you must bounce back and be the most positive person possible! Here are some important things to remember for building a strong positive attitude:

1. In one way or another, we all get our attitudes stepped on from time to time. When we bounce back quickly, no harm is done.

2. Bouncing back quickly is not always easy. Sometimes the utilization of certain techniques is necessary to speed up the process.

3. Respect the ideas of other people. If you learn this important rule, you will frequently find your good ideas will become even better and your attitude won't get in the way of solving problems.

4. Your positive attitude is a priceless possession and belongs only to you. Keeping it positive may be your greatest challenge in life.

Test Your Understanding

Respond to the following items to test your understanding of the chapter.

Part A: Circle the correct answer (T = True; F = False) for each of the following statements.

T F 1. When someone steps on your positive attitude, it is like stepping on your ego.

T F 2. The longer you allow your attitude to be depressed, the more difficult it is to bounce back.

T F 3. It is a good idea to apologize when you advertently step on another person's attitude.

T F 4. Sometimes a boss can come down on your attitude so hard that it is impossible to bounce back.

T F 5. If someone steps hard on your positive attitude and you allow yourself to turn negative for a long time, you have, in effect, permitted this person to "steal" your positive attitude.

Part B: Circle the letter of the correct answer for each of the following items.

6. The golden key to your future is placing a high value on (a) keeping your attitude positive, (b) making lots of money, (c) becoming a creative person, (d) putting up a barrier so people cannot step on your attitude.

7. Expecting people to respect you and be sensitive to your needs can be enhanced if you (a) make others see that your ideas are best, (b) leave most of the communication up to others, (c) find quick solutions to complex problems, (d) value and respect the views and feelings of others.

Part C: Write a short response to demonstrate your understanding related to the following item.

8. Suggest some strategies for "bouncing back" when someone has stepped on your positive attitude.

Turn to the back of the book to check your answers.

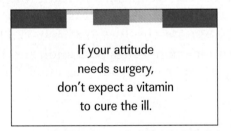

If your attitude
needs surgery,
don't expect a vitamin
to cure the ill.

Think and Respond

Respond to the following items with two or three complete sentences.

1. Explain the statement: "Anticipate that people will step on your attitude."

2. Discuss two "bounce-back" strategies to use when your attitude is stepped on.

3. How can you avoid getting your attitude stepped on by the same person again and again?

4. What is one of the best ways to earn respect of others?

5. Explain the statement: "Your attitude belongs to you alone."

My "Bounce-Back" Strategic Plan

In the space provided, list at least five ways you can use to bounce back when people step on your attitude. Keep in mind that there may be minor as well as very serious situations that can contribute to deflating your ego and confidence. Once you have listed some techniques you can practice in your life, add a summary statement about the value of your attitude.

1. _____

_____

_____

2. _____

_____

_____

3. _____

_____

_____

4. _____

_____

_____

5. _____

_____

_____

Summary:

_____

_____

Revisit your list and summary frequently. Practice your techniques to improve your ability to protect and strengthen your positive attitude.

CASE 4

Bounce Back

"I recover quickly."

Sue Ellen is a physical therapist for a sports medicine clinic in a prestigious hospital. She is highly disciplined, has outstanding work skills, and is quietly effective. Sue Ellen's only problem is that she is supersensitive to comments and actions from others. She lets her attitude get stepped on and is too easily hurt by people. Sue Ellen is particularly vulnerable to any strong demands from doctors, supervisors, and even patients. When anyone comes down hard or steps on Sue Ellen's attitude, she has a difficult time bouncing back. It is now quite noticeable that Sue Ellen's personal productivity and interaction with people are lowered whenever she gets "down" on herself.

From time to time, Frank, a male nurse in the clinic, is Sue Ellen's immediate supervisor. Frank is well aware of Sue Ellen's sensitivity to demands of others. In fact, on more than one occasion and with increasing frequency, Frank has unavoidably stepped on Sue Ellen's attitude to the point that she has had to step away for a few moments to gain her composure. Frank has never had a heart-to-heart talk with Sue Ellen about why she is so sensitive and why it appears so easy for people to step on her attitude. In recent weeks, Frank feels that Sue Ellen is retreating and, as a result, becoming even more sensitive. Frank has decided there is no time like the present to try to help Sue Ellen become a stronger person so that, regardless of what people say, they do not psychologically step on her attitude.

A. Discuss: Even though Frank supervises Sue Ellen only "from time to time," why should he try to help her? How should Frank go about trying to address Sue Ellen's sensitivity problem? What should he say and do to help her?

B. Expand Your Understanding: Make a list of actions that Sue Ellen should consider for developing her human-relations skills. Categorize your list into three parts: (1) sensitive issues and suggestions, (2) interaction issues and suggestions, and (3) productivity issues and suggestions. Support your lists with Internet and other sources. Write a short summary of your conclusions.

To the Reader

You have now completed Part I of this book. Part I was designed to help you understand yourself and especially the potential of your positive attitude. Part II introduces you to ways you can use your positive attitude to build and maintain better human relations.

Before going on to Part II of this book, you may want to go back to the beginning of each chapter and think about each of the opening "thought for the day" statements. Also, go to the end of each chapter and read the thoughts provided in each "attitude box." The ideas presented at the start of each chapter and in the attitude boxes were designed for you. Ponder and contemplate these important concepts about attitude as you assess your attitude—and as you make changes toward becoming a more positive person.

PART II

Relationships with Others

CHAPTER 5

Vertical and Horizontal Working Relationships

"Relationships are *that* important?"

Thought for the Day: Become the kind of person *you* value as a friend or colleague.

PERFORMANCE COMPETENCIES

- Recognize the differences in relationships that are created by being near people as well as by working and communicating with people.

- Understand the importance of building vertical working relationships.

- Understand the importance of building horizontal working relationships.

- Appreciate why good communication is needed for consciously creating, building, and maintaining relationships in all directions in the workplace.

Understanding yourself and the power of your positive attitude makes it much easier to meet new people and establish meaningful relationships with them. For example, when you meet a supervisor or coworker for the first time, a psychological reaction takes place: Each person instantaneously interprets the other. It is a feeling that is hard to define. You know something is happening, but you can't put your finger on it. Slowly, as you and the other individual see each other more frequently and get to know each other better, these initial feelings mature into what is called a relationship.

THE NATURE OF RELATIONSHIPS

A Relationship Is a "Feeling Thing" That Exists between Two People Who Associate with Each Other. You can't see, taste, smell, or touch a relationship; you can only feel it in a psychological sense. Job relationships are usually different from social relationships. Job relationships exist only because you selected a certain company and were assigned to work with certain people in a specific department. In other words, in your social life you have a choice; on the job you do not. Nevertheless, working relationships are extremely important to you and your future because they will have a strong influence on your personality and personal productivity.

Working relationships of this nature are fascinating to study. For example, one interesting characteristic is that two persons cannot meet regularly on the job or work in the same general areas without having a relationship. So the first thing to learn about working relationships is that, *whether you like it or not, a relationship exists between you and every employee or supervisor with whom you have regular contact.* While you need not work next to this person, speak to this person, nor even have a desire to know this person, a relationship still exists.

Relationships are felt even without contact

There appears to be no way to neutralize a relationship under these conditions. The very fact that you may decide to ignore a person does not destroy the relationship; in fact, the opposite may happen. The relationship may become more tense and psychologically powerful. Let us take a specific example.

You notice Francine, an employee working in a department next to you. In an attempt to be friendly, you say hello in a very pleasant way to this person the first day on the job and you receive no reply.

Does this mean that the relationship is cut off at this point?

Far from it! You may feel that Francine's failure to reply is slighting you, and this may naturally disturb you. You may decide not to take the initiative again. Nevertheless, you will remember this person clearly and wonder what will happen in the future.

The person to whom you said hello, however, has had some kind of reaction to your friendly gesture. She may feel that she treated you in an unfriendly manner (perhaps she was not feeling well that day) and may welcome another opportunity to be more friendly. Or, she might have interpreted your hello as being a little too forward on your part as a new employee and decided to be cool toward you.

You could ignore her. You could avoid verbal contact. You and she could see each other only a few times a week.

Would a relationship exist?

Yes, indeed. Two persons have made contact with each other. They see each other occasionally. They work for the same company. As long as these factors exist, a relationship must exist. Under these conditions, you cannot erase a relationship. The attempt on the part of one person to withdraw serves only to make the relationship more emotionally charged; it does not in any manner eliminate it.

You Cannot Consistently Work with or Near People or Communicate with Them Frequently without Having Working Relationships with Them. There is another interesting characteristic about working relationships when viewed objectively. They are either strong or weak, warm or cool, healthy or unhealthy, friendly or distant. There appears to be no absolute neutral ground. Every relationship has a very small positive or negative content.

Don't count on having "neutral" relationships

Have you ever heard someone say, "I can take her or leave her"? The phrase usually means that it doesn't make any difference whether the person referred to is around or not. But the very fact that one makes such a comment indicates that it would be better if the person were not around. The relationship still exists, and in this case it is a little cool.

Each Relationship You Have Has Its Own Characteristics. Another characteristic of relationships is that each is different. You must build relationships with all kinds of people, regardless of race, religion, age, sex, or personality characteristics. Each relationship is unique. Each is built on a different basis. Each has its own integrity.

As you look around and study your coworkers and your supervisor, you will see that they are all separate personalities. At the same time, your supervisor and coworkers are studying you. Do they all see the same person?

Strange as it may seem, they do not. You do not look the same to different people. You make a different impression on each of them because they interpret you differently.

There is another way of saying this: You do not have a single personality in the eyes of others. Each person interprets you differently, based on his (or her) own unique background, prejudices, likes, dislikes, and so on. Your personality, to that person, is different. The way he interprets your personality is your personality to that person.

Why all this emphasis on the way people view your personality? How will this help you become more sensitive to human relationships? Because everybody sees you differently, you will have to build good relationships with different people differently. And make no mistake here. Good relationships must be built. They seldom come about automatically.

┌─ **ACTIVITY** ───

Relationship Differences Focused on Similar Outcomes

In the following spaces, describe the relationship you have with two of your coworkers (or with two friends, family members, or associates). Then describe how and why the relationships are different and how you can strengthen each of them.

1. My relationship with (name_____) is:

2. My relationship with (name_____) is:

   A. The difference(s) between these two relationships is (are):

   B. The reason(s) for the difference(s) in these relationships is (are):

To strengthen my relationship with (#1 name_____), I plan to:

To strengthen my relationship with (#2 name_____), I plan to:

Write a summary statement about how your proposed action can improve the relationships. Include whether or not your action will be similar for both people. As soon as possible, put your action plan into practice.

Summary of proposed action:

Once your plan is implemented, describe here how your action plan is working (if you need to modify your proposed action to achieve success at building stronger relationships, do it as quickly as possible).

My action is working because:

If, in your summary, you included being more positive in your interactions, you are on your way to enhancing your positive attitude. Also, if you said you will give more consideration to the feelings and needs of the other people, you probably will build even stronger relationships than without such consideration. Practice your plan at every possible opportunity. (Hint: Your continued study of this book will give you more ideas for successfully building human-relations skills.) As you actively work at building better relationships, enjoy your successes and positive outcomes!

You Will Rarely Build a Strong, Warm, or Healthy Relationship with Two Persons in the Same Way. Because good relationships don't happen by accident and must be consciously built, you will always have to take into consideration the person at the other end of the relationship. To start with, some people are not going to interpret your personality favorably. You are going to have to be sensitive enough to determine who these people are, and then you must build a good relationship with them on an individual basis. It is not easy to change a cool relationship to a warm one, yet you cannot afford to allow it to remain in an unhealthy state. You should make some effort to build it into a stronger relationship.

Be considerate of others as you build relationships with them

To build a stronger relationship, you should consider the person at the other end of the relationship and remember that she (or he) sees you differently than anyone else.

BUILDING VERTICAL RELATIONSHIPS

Building a Vertical Working Relationship Is a Critical Element of Your Job. A vertical working relationship is the relationship between you and your immediate supervisor. If, as a regular employee, you have two or more supervisors, you will have two or more vertical relationships to maintain. Normally, you will have one immediate supervisor, as illustrated here.

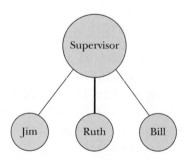

In a small department consisting of one supervisor and three employees, each employee has a different vertical relationship with the same supervisor. This relationship is indicated by the line between each employee and the supervisor, often called the job-relations line. If the relationship is strong, we indicate this by a heavy line. If it is weak, we indicate the weak relationship by a light line. Naturally, it is almost impossible for supervisors to create and maintain an equally strong line between themselves and all the employees in the department. It is their job to try to maintain strong relationships with all workers; and, the closer they come to this ideal, the better it is for the department. But supervisors are human beings and are not perfect. Consequently, the job-relations lines are seldom equally strong. The person

working next to you may have either a stronger or a weaker relationship with the supervisor than you have.

Notice the arrows in the following illustration.

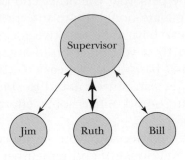

The arrows at the ends of the vertical job-relations lines have real
significance. They signify that there should be a free flow of information between the workers and the supervisor. It is extremely difficult
for a strong relationship to exist between two persons without two-way
communication. The supervisor must feel free to discuss, openly and
frankly, certain problems with Ruth, Jim, and Bill. If the supervisor hes-
itates to talk with Jim about a certain weakness in his job performance,
the relationship between the two of them is not what it could be. By
the same token, if Jim is hesitant about taking a suggestion or a gripe
to the supervisor, the relationship is less than ideal.

BUILDING HORIZONTAL RELATIONSHIPS

**Building a Strong Horizontal Working Relationship Is Another Critical
Element of Your Job.** Horizontal working relationships are those that exist between you and fellow workers in the same department—the people you work next to on an hour-to-hour, day-to-day basis. The
following diagram illustrates the horizontal relationships among three
people in a very small department.

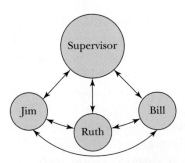

You will note that Jim has a horizontal working relationship with
both Ruth and Bill. In this very small department of three employees
and one supervisor, Jim has one vertical relationship and two

horizontal relationships to keep strong. It is easy to see that in larger departments there would be many more. In fact, the average number of employees in a department is nine.

You (not the supervisor) have the primary responsibility for creating and keeping healthy horizontal relationships. The supervisor—working at a distance in regard to these relationships—has the secondary responsibility. Once in a while, he (or she) may find it necessary to step in to help restore a good relationship between two employees. But by and large the supervisor must leave this up to the employees themselves.

The critical need for building good horizontal working relationships is often ignored by some workers. When they reject the need for building good relationships, their doors of opportunity are locked and the keys are thrown away.

Give attention to balance in building your work relationships

It is extremely important to the new employee to build and maintain good horizontal working relationships. In fact, building good relationships should be a major part of your total human-relations effort as you start your career. Much of this book is devoted to the principles and techniques that will assist you in this respect. For example, here are two mistakes you should refrain from making:

1. Avoid concentrating on building a good relationship with your supervisor and neglecting good relationships with your fellow workers.
2. Avoid concentrating on building one or two very strong horizontal working relationships and neglecting those with the remaining fellow workers in your department.

Making either mistake will cause immediate disharmony in your department and will put you in human-relations hot water. The supervisor cannot afford to have an extremely strong relationship with you and weak relationships with your fellow workers if she (or he) wants high productivity from all. It makes for dissension and immediate cries of favoritism.

From your point of view, then, an overly strong vertical relationship can cause a general weakening of your horizontal working relationships. When you make the mistake of concentrating on one or two horizontal working relationships, the remaining horizontal relationships deteriorate and your vertical relationship with the supervisor is also weakened.

COMMUNICATION AND RELATIONSHIP BUILDING

The Lifeblood of a Good Relationship Is Free and Open Communication. Good
relationships are built and maintained by free and frequent verbal

communication. People need to talk with each other, exchange ideas, voice complaints, and offer suggestions if they intend to keep a good relationship. The moment that one party refuses to talk things over, the relationship line becomes thin and weak.

The primary responsibility for creating and maintaining a strong vertical relationship rests with the supervisor. Building a vertical relationship line is a responsibility that goes with the position. If the relationship line is in need of repair, it is primarily the supervisor's responsibility to initiate a discussion that can mend the break.

Productivity is linked to good working relationships

Although the supervisor has the primary responsibility, you as the employee have the secondary responsibility to keep the relationship line strong and healthy. Some employees make the serious mistake of thinking that the supervisor is wholly responsible for making them happy and productive.

While other chapters show you how to create and maintain a good relationship with your supervisor, it suffices now to say that you can't expect the supervisor to do all the relationship building. You will have to work hard to keep a good job-relations line between you and your supervisor. Even if you have an exceptionally poor supervisor, you will have to meet him (or her) halfway. Vertical relationships need to be in healthy repair if departmental productivity is to be high. Often the supervisor finds that it requires considerable tact and delicacy to maintain vertical relationships. Small wonder that management has seen fit to give this person some special training.

All horizontal working relationships in the same department should be given equal attention and consideration. One should not be strengthened at the expense of others, even though it may be more fun and more satisfying. Balance is important.

When you concentrate on creating good horizontal working relationships with all fellow workers, you almost automatically create a good vertical relationship with your supervisor. It should be recognized, of course, that the success of this principle is assured only if the supervisor is sufficiently sensitive to the working environment. In the majority of cases, work environment sensitivity is a fair assumption. A perceptive supervisor will greatly appreciate any employee who builds a better team spirit in the department by creating and maintaining strong horizontal working relationships.

Building Good, Broad-Based Relationships with as Many People as Possible Should Be a General Goal for You. There are, of course, important relationships other than those indicated in the diagrams presented earlier in this chapter. Your relationship-building activity should not be confined to a single department. It is a good idea for you to expand your sphere of influence as quickly as possible on your new job. The more good relationships you build, the better.

As important as peripheral relationships are, they are not your primary working relationships. You cannot afford to concentrate on building relationships outside your department by neglecting those on the inside.

Summary

Two people who associate with each other, no matter how infrequent their contact may be, have feelings toward each other—that is, they have a relationship. That's the basic nature of relationships. Work relationships exist between coworkers and supervisors without communication; however, good communication contributes to building good relationships. Both building a strong vertical relationship with your immediate supervisor and developing strong horizontal working relationships with your fellow workers are absolutely essential to your personal success.

Because communication is the lifeblood of all relationships, it is critically important that you become the best communicator that you can. And that means you must ensure that your positive attitude is projected in *all* your communications in *all* directions. Creating, building, and maintaining work relationships will take your conscious effort. No other human-relations activity should have a higher priority.

Test Your Understanding

Respond to the following items to test your understanding of the chapter.

Part A. Circle the correct answer (T = True; F = False) for each of the following statements.

T F   1. Two people cannot meet regularly on the job or work in the same general area without having a relationship.

T F   2. Most good relationships usually come about automatically.

T F   3. Supervisors are in charge of creating and maintaining good horizontal working relationships.

T F   4. Building balanced work relationships is a key element for your personal success.

T F   5. The lifeblood of a good relationship is two-way communication.

Part B: Circle the letter of the correct answer for each of the following items.

6. Relationships that exist between people at work can be defined in a psychological sense as something you can (a) neutralize, (b) see, (c) feel, (d) turn off.

7. Your highest priority human-relations work activity should be to (a) concentrate on building peripheral relationships at work, (b) help others keep their work relationships positive, (c) create a strong horizontal relationship with your supervisor, (d) build strong relationships with both your supervisor and coworkers.

Part C: Write a short response to demonstrate your understanding related to the following item.

8. Discuss some of the ways or best practices for developing good work relationships.

Turn to the back of the book to check your answers.

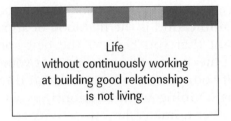

Life
without continuously working
at building good relationships
is not living.

Think and Respond

Respond to the following items with two or three complete sentences.

1. Describe what is meant by a relationship.
2. How are all relationships different yet focused on similar results?
3. What is a vertical relationship and why is it critical to build it?
4. What are horizontal relationships and why is it critical to build them?
5. Give two reasons that communication is critical to building relationships.

SUMMARY ACTIVITY

Prioritizing My Working Relationships

Although all of your job (as well as personal) relationships are important, some may be more critical to your career success than others. This exercise will help you decide whether you have been underestimating and neglecting some relationships in favor of others. As noted by a telephone company employee, "This turned out to be a profitable exercise for me because I discovered I had been neglecting a few key relationships that were influencing my personal progress."

If you are not currently employed, complete this exercise on the basis of your personal relationships (friends, family members, or other people with whom you associate or have contact). List in the spaces provided from five to ten important relationships you have in your present job, noting what you feel to be your most important relationship first and so on down the line. After analyzing the list, underline the names of those whom you feel you have neglected in recent weeks.

1.	6.
2.	7.
3.	8.
4.	9.
5.	10.

All working and personal relationships are important. The individual who concentrates on building relationships, especially job relationships, with a few people at the expense of others is demonstrating insensitivity and damaging her (or his) career.

CASE 5

Decision

"My supervisor ignores me."

Bernie, a budding engineer apprentice, was getting used to working with all types of people on project-management teams. He seemed to "fit in" wherever he was assigned and built good relationships. Recently, however, because of a realignment of personnel, Bernie was transferred (against his wishes) to the traffic department. In his new assignment, he would have to build seven horizontal relationships and one vertical relationship. Bernie was the junior member of the department. All the other employees, including the supervisor, were much older than he.

After one week in the new department, Bernie discovered that it was difficult to approach his supervisor Gloria, let alone talk to her. Bernie also found that Gloria stayed aloof from the workers in the department and that she often seemed critical of most people. Bernie could feel a psychological barrier between his boss and the rest of the department employees. Once a week, Gloria held a short staff meeting. In Bernie's first departmental meeting with Gloria and coworkers, he observed that most of the employees were silent and even seemed somewhat hostile.

How could Bernie build a strong, worthwhile vertical relationship with his boss, whose nature was so distant, within an environment that was so structured? Wouldn't he be wiser to concentrate exclusively on horizontal relationships until an opportunity presented itself to establish a better relationship with Gloria? After giving the matter some serious thought, Bernie decided to concentrate on horizontal relationships and weather it out.

A. Discuss: Was this a smart decision on Bernie's part? Would you have gone about it differently? Support your point of view.

B. Expand Your Understanding: Research the topic of building work (career) relationships. Contrast similarities and differences between the importance of building relationships vertically versus horizontally. Discuss the significance of communication and how much a conscious effort plays into building strong relationships. Support your research by citing sources from books, magazines, and the Internet. Draw some conclusions about your findings to share with Bernie.

CHAPTER 6

Your Potential and Productivity—A Closer Look

"Being productive requires more than technical skills."

Thought for the Day: Giving your best effort to an endeavor can never be faulted.

PERFORMANCE COMPETENCIES

- Realize that productivity measurement, whether by scientific measures or by management judgment, is important to an organization.

- Understand that people seldom reach their individual productivity potentials; that is, a gap exists between what you can do and what you actually do.

- Appreciate the importance of group productivity and why it is an extension of individual productivity.

- Recognize that both supervisors and workers have responsibility to help close individual and group productivity gaps.

A manufacturing plant, in order to be competitive with other operations turning out a similar product, must produce at the lowest possible cost per single item or unit. A retail store, in order to pay overhead expenses and show a profit, must produce sales at a certain level. An airline must produce a reliable service that will attract enough customers to keep the seats filled. Even a municipal organization like a fire department must produce at a level that will satisfy taxpayers. Every kind of organization must produce; when production is not sufficient to make a profit or satisfy people, changes are made. These are economic facts of life.

MEASURING PRODUCTIVITY

Productivity is key to the survival of most organizations

Because productivity[1] is so important, management has devised ways of measuring it. Productivity is easily measured on an assembly line where the worker must perform a specific function, such as connecting a wire or screwing on a nut. Assembly or production-line jobs can be time studied and a standard rate established. If the standard rate is eighty-five completions in sixty minutes, it means that the average worker can reach and sustain this number over a certain period of time.

Measurable jobs or tasks of this nature are found primarily in the manufacturing and fabricating industries. Other jobs, such as customer service and office work, are more difficult to measure. That is, factors such as how much initiative is demonstrated, how people are treated, and how the telephone is answered are difficult to measure.

Productivity, then, can be measured scientifically in some situations, but in countless others it can only be measured by management judgment. Regardless of the kind of job you now hold or the way in which your productivity is measured, understanding what is meant by productivity (from the management point of view) is important to your future.

Productivity Types There are two kinds of productivity.

- *Individual productivity.* Individual productivity is the contribution a single person makes to getting the departmental job done. It is the amount of work one person does in comparison with that of others in the group or section. It may or may not be measurable.

- *Group productivity.* Group productivity is the sum total of all individual contributions, including that of the supervisor. It can be—and often is—measured objectively; that is, it is reduced to figures and statistics.

---

[1]The reader is reminded that when using the word *productivity*, the author means *quality* performance. Management is only interested in producing more products or services when it reaches standards of excellence.

INDIVIDUAL PRODUCTIVITY POTENTIAL

Each worker has a current (day-to-day, week-to-week) level of productivity that generally remains constant, although it may fluctuate from time to time. Let us illustrate this through the use of a glass or beaker. Assume that the liquid in the glass is the current level of productivity for a person we will call Jane. Like all employees, Jane also has a potential level of productivity that is greater than her current level.

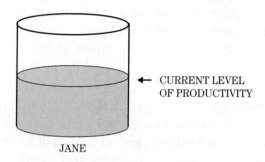

← CURRENT LEVEL OF PRODUCTIVITY

JANE

Seldom, if ever, does a person reach his (or her) full potential. Jane would be the first to agree with this.

So let us draw a dotted line across the glass to indicate Jane's potential level of productivity. We don't know exactly where Jane's potential might be. It is impossible to measure her capacity or potential scientifically because more than her mental ability is involved—and even her mental ability cannot be measured accurately. But for our hypothetical situation, we can say that Jane's potential is somewhat above her current level of productivity.

Most people don't reach their productivity potential

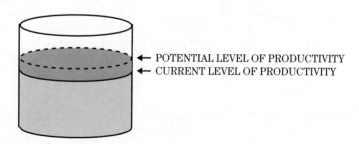

← POTENTIAL LEVEL OF PRODUCTIVITY
← CURRENT LEVEL OF PRODUCTIVITY

In the preceding diagram, then, Jane's current level of productivity is indicated by the solid line, and her potential or possible level of productivity is indicated by the dotted line. The difference between the two is what we will call her *productivity gap*.

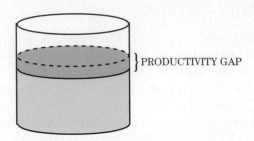

There is always a gap between what one could do and what one actually does. Of course, management would like to see Jane close the gap between her current and potential productivity levels as much as possible, but it would be asking too much to expect her to close it completely.

Why Focus on Minimizing Productivity Gaps? We are concerned, then, not so much with the gap itself as with the size of the gap. If it is small, Jane's supervisor knows she is working close to her capacity. If it is large, the supervisor knows that something is wrong and should be looked into.

Jane's supervisor should, of course, do all she (or he) can to keep the distance between Jane's potential and her current performance as small as possible. If the gap becomes too great, she may decide that Jane needs additional training, a special incentive, a change in assignment rotation, or perhaps some form of counseling. The supervisor cannot permit Jane's level of productivity to remain substandard over an extended period of time.

Jane, of course, is not the only worker in the department. In our hypothetical situation, let us assume that there are two other employees occupying positions identical to Jane's. These people are Arturo and Fred.

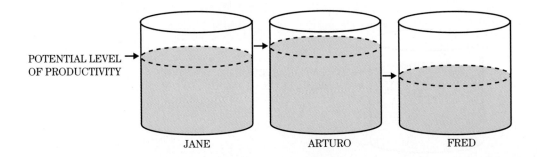

You will note that the potentials of Arturo and Fred are different from Jane's. It is somewhat disturbing at first to recognize that everyone has a different potential and that some people have higher potentials than others. However, potential variability is in fact true because everyone differs in mental ability (IQ), ability to endure physical strain (stamina and endurance), ability to perform certain manipulative skills (dexterity), creative level, inner drive, emotional intelligence (EQ), and attitude, as well as in other personality characteristics. All these features together make up an individual's potential.

Every person's potential is uniquely different

It is important not to get hung up over the word *potential*. As we are using it, potential simply means the level of productivity a worker might achieve under ideal circumstances if he (or she) pushed himself to his limit. It is seldom, if ever, reached. In using the word *potential*, however, we should remember that some employees are outstanding in some areas and average or below in others. Few, if any, are outstanding in all areas. Yet, almost everyone has at least one exceptional characteristic.

Individual Potential Differences. We need not be concerned about the measurement of potential. (In fact, there is no truly scientific way to measure it.) All that we need to be concerned about here is that individual differences exist and that, except under extremely rare conditions, there is always a gap between one's potential and present level of productivity.

In the following diagram, Arturo has been arbitrarily given a potential (shown by the dark liquid noted by brackets) above Jane's and Fred's. Fred, however, has been given a potential below Jane's and Arturo's.

Now, to complete our diagram, let us assign a current productivity level to each of the three workers.

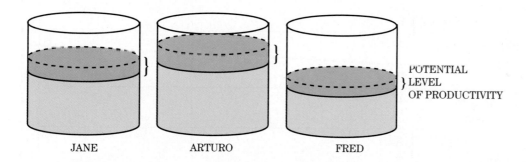

JANE ARTURO FRED POTENTIAL }LEVEL OF PRODUCTIVITY

You will note that even though Arturo has a higher potential than Jane, there is not a substantial difference between their current levels of performance (shown by the lighter liquid). This is a compliment to Jane and perhaps indicates that she is more highly motivated to succeed and consequently performs closer to her potential.

Fred also deserves a compliment because the gap between his current level of productivity and his potential is smaller than that of either Jane or Arturo. Fred is doing an excellent job in living up to his potential. Perhaps with more education and training, Fred will be able to raise his potential gradually and, in turn, increase his productivity.

Assessing My Potential for Improving Productivity

While scientific measurement of potential may not be possible, you have a responsibility to yourself and to your employer to assess your potential as it relates to your productivity. To help you assess your potential, complete the following exercise. Read all directions before starting, noting that a sample item is provided to give you guidance in maximizing the exercise.

For each of the factors listed, suggest one or two actions you can take to raise your productivity levels. Add time lines to your actions and immediately begin implementing your identified actions. As soon as you have made significant progress toward implementing your action plan (so the actions become part of your life), use the last column to describe your progress. Your progress should reflect how well you are meeting your goal to help you narrow the gap between your potential and your current level of productivity.

To assist you with getting started, a sample item, 1.A., is provided. Add one of your own suggestions for item 1 (relating to mental ability) by completing 1.B. Also note there is room for you to add at least one other factor or characteristic that you believe is important for working up to your potential. Use a separate piece of paper to add to your list.

An important factor for increasing my personal potential	Action needed and suggested timeline to improve this factor	My success in reaching my action goal
1. My mental ability (IQ)	A. Read more (specifically, job-related as well as leisure magazines); weekly. B.	Good; my interaction skills are better, too.
2. My stamina and endurance (my ability to endure physical strain)	A. B.	
3. My manual dexterity (or my ability to improve my manipulative skills)	A. B.	
4. My creativity (or my ability to increase my innovativeness)	A. B.	
5. My motivation (or my "inner drive" that spurs me to action)	A. B.	
6. My attitude	A. B.	
7.	A. B.	

In addition to completing this activity, you may want to start a file labeled, "My Potential: Ways to Improve My Productivity." Review your file frequently. Add, modify, and reevaluate your ideas related to your potential and productivity action plan as often as needed to push yourself to higher levels of success in your life. Good luck!

GROUP-PRODUCTIVITY POTENTIAL

Just as each individual has a current and potential level of productivity, so does each branch, division, or department of an organization. This we call group productivity.

The next diagram illustrates this important concept. The beaker represents the productivity level and potential of the department as a whole.

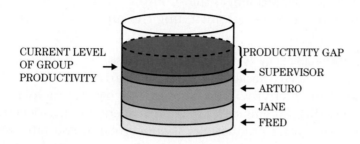

CURRENT LEVEL
OF GROUP
PRODUCTIVITY → }PRODUCTIVITY GAP
← SUPERVISOR
← ARTURO
← JANE
← FRED

You will observe that the productivity levels of Fred, Jane, and Arturo have been added to that of their supervisor. As you can see, the supervisor does not contribute as much in productivity (actually getting the work out) as do the individual employees. Why not?

The answer is simple. The primary responsibility of the supervisor is to help each worker achieve her (or his) maximum productivity. The supervisor's secondary responsibility (as a working supervisor) is to do a certain amount of the work personally. The supervisor cannot be expected to take care of the many supervisory responsibilities and also do as much work as each one of the employees in the department. The supervisor's concern is the total department productivity, for this is how the supervisor is measured by management.

Good supervisors strive to raise both group and individual productivity

Departmental Gaps Need Attention, Too. You will also notice in the preceding diagram that there is a gap in the department beaker, just as there was in the others. This is a departmental gap. Just as an individual has a certain potential for productivity, so does a department.

A crew working for a telephone company may have the potential for installing 120 telephones in a certain period of time and yet actually install only 80. A retail store may have the potential for selling $5,000 worth of merchandise on a day when everything is ideal and yet on most days, sell only $2,000 worth. A claims department for an insurance company may have the potential for processing fifty claims per day and yet may never reach this goal. Just as there is a gap with individuals, there is one with departments and organizations.

CLOSING PRODUCTIVITY POTENTIAL GAPS

It is the responsibility of the supervisor to close the gap between what the department is currently doing and what it may do in the future. There are two ways a supervisor can help to close the gap. One is by working harder, putting in more hours, and making better use of personal time. Because the supervisor is only one person, there is a limit to what he (or she) can do alone to reduce the size of the gap.

The second—and by far the more effective way to reduce the gap—is to reduce the gaps between the levels of each employee. The productivity of the department is the sum total of the productivity of all members of the department, including the supervisor.

Worker Interdependency Is Valued. A supervisor is interested in each worker's productivity because of what each can contribute to the total work team's productivity. What should this basic principle mean to you? Simply this: All employees in a department are interdependent as far as the work unit's productivity is concerned. If you raise your personal productivity but at the same time take away some of the productivity of others in the department (because of poor human relations), you have not necessarily added to the total.

Sound strange?

To demonstrate this vital fundamental, let us take Arturo as an example. The following diagram tells us that Arturo has a high potential and a good level of productivity. In fact, he is currently producing more than either Jane or Fred.

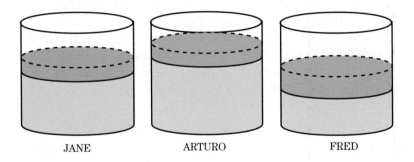

JANE   ARTURO   FRED

But let us assume for a moment that Arturo begins to ignore Jane and Fred. He is no longer interested in helping them. He refuses to pitch in and do some of their work when they are absent. He starts to rub them the wrong way. His superior attitude causes resentment. Instead of natural, healthy competition, the situation becomes personal and vindictive.

What could happen then?

The productivity of Jane and Fred could drop because of the lack of harmony in the department.

Now let us see what might happen if Arturo does just the opposite. Let us assume that he becomes more sensitive about human relations. Instead of antagonizing Jane and Fred, he starts working with them. He takes up some of the slack when they are absent. He compliments them on certain skills. He earns their respect instead of their animosity. What happens? Harmony replaces disharmony.

Good human relations in a work group can narrow productivity gaps

Instead of a wider gap between the current and potential productivity levels of Jane and Fred, there is a smaller gap as shown in the following diagram. Both Jane and Fred produce more because Arturo has strengthened his horizontal relationships with them.

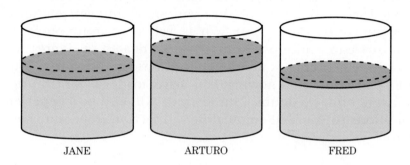

JANE   ARTURO   FRED

This interdependence between workers in a department cannot be ignored. Group productivity is the key more than individual performance. More will be said about group and team performance in other chapters of this book.

It should be pointed out, however, that sometimes a single individual can raise her (or his) productivity above that of coworkers; and even though relationships are not ideal, the coworkers will strive to increase their personal productivity so that the other worker will not show them up. The reaction of employees in each situation is different.

Summary

So, to review what we have discussed in this chapter, the following points are important for understanding productivity as you consider both your individual productivity and that of your work group.

1. Supervisors as well as workers need to understand management's perspective about the need to measure productivity, because productivity is extremely important to the well-being and effectiveness of an organization.

2. There is always a gap between an individual's current level of productivity and his (or her) potential. If the employee consistently

has a small gap, he is trying hard to contribute and should be complimented by the supervisor for working so close to his true potential.

3. A departmental gap represents the difference between what a department can do and what it is actually doing. If the departmental gap is small, the supervisor is doing a good job and should be complimented by her (or his) superiors.

4. The human-relations behavior of one worker affects the productivity gap of coworkers as well as that of the department.

The positive correlation between good human relations and work productivity is of considerable significance to you and your employer. That is, the more skillful you are at human relations, the more you contribute to your own as well as to group productivity. If you strive to work up to your potential related to all areas of productivity—including your human-relations productivity—you will find satisfaction in knowing you have made a contribution to your work unit. No doubt, your attitude will also be a benefactor of your efforts so you will enjoy more satisfaction from your personal life too.

Test Your Understanding

Respond to the following items to test your understanding of the chapter.

Part A: Circle the correct answer (T = True; F = False) for each of the following statements.

T F   1. The difference between what a worker is doing and what she (or he) could do under ideal conditions is called a "productivity gap."

T F   2. Potential and mental ability are one and the same.

T F   3. A primary responsibility of a supervisor is to help a worker achieve his (or her) maximum productivity.

T F   4. There appears to be little or no correlation between high productivity and good human relations in a department.

T F   5. The interdependence between workers in a department is extremely important to group productivity.

Part B: Circle the letter of the correct answer for each of the following items.

6. The contribution a single person makes to help get the departmental job done is called (a) group productivity, (b) individual productivity, (c) group potential, (d) individual potential.

7. The productivity of a department is the sum total of the productivity of (a) key workers, (b) all workers, (c) key workers and the supervisor, (d) all members of the department and the supervisor.

Part C: Write a short response to demonstrate your understanding related to the following item.

8. Discuss the importance of individual productivity as it relates to group productivity.

Turn to the back of the book to check your answers.

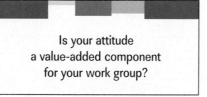

Is your attitude
a value-added component
for your work group?

Think and Respond

Respond to the following items with two or three complete sentences.

1. Describe two types of employee productivity that management measures.
2. What is meant by the terms *potential productivity level* and *current productivity level*?
3. What is a productivity gap and how is it determined?
4. Describe the contributions that individual and group productivity provide to an organization.
5. Suggest two ways productivity gaps can be reduced.

My Productivity Motivators

Some job improvements contribute to an employee's productivity more than others. Other improvements seem to provide little or no incentive to do a better job. Assume you have a job that is not highly motivating to you and management makes the improvements noted below. Place a check mark (✔) in the appropriate column opposite each improvement that you believe would contribute to your level of motivation: (A) This improvement has sustaining or long-term motivation for me; (B) This improvement has temporary or short-term motivation for me; or (C) This improvement is not motivating at all for me.

IMPROVEMENT	(A) SUSTAINING MOTIVATION	(B) TEMPORARY MOTIVATION	(C) NOT MOTIVATING
1. Higher pay	_____	_____	_____
2. Better relationships with coworkers	_____	_____	_____
3. Better retirement plan	_____	_____	_____
4. Better relationship with my supervisor	_____	_____	_____
5. More job security	_____	_____	_____
6. Receiving more recognition	_____	_____	_____
7. Less distance to travel to work	_____	_____	_____
8. Being accepted more by others, including those in my department	_____	_____	_____
9. Improved lighting, better restrooms and physical surroundings	_____	_____	_____
10. Being told more often how I am doing by my supervisor or others	_____	_____	_____
11. Improved health program paid for by employer	_____	_____	_____
12. Feeling more relaxed to have some fun on the job	_____	_____	_____
13. Having a better cafeteria with lower prices or better company recreational facilities	_____	_____	_____

14. Opportunity to communicate
    more with management   _____   _____   _____

15. Better equipment to use   _____   _____   _____

16. Being involved more in
    management decisions   _____   _____   _____

17. Better or flexible working
    hours   _____   _____   _____

18. Being treated with more
    dignity   _____   _____   _____

19. Moving to a better building
    in a better location   _____   _____   _____

20. Being trusted more; less
    supervision   _____   _____   _____

You were not told in advance that the odd-numbered statements relate to physical changes, while the even-numbered ones relate to psychological or human, relations changes. To find out which classification motivates you the most, add the check marks found in columns 1 and 2 opposite the odd-numbered improvements and place the total on the line for physical changes. Then go through the identical process for the even-numbered improvements and write the total on the other line.

TOTAL SCORE FOR ODD-NUMBERED (PHYSICAL) IMPROVEMENTS ☐

TOTAL SCORE FOR EVEN-NUMBERED (PSYCHOLOGICAL) IMPROVEMENTS ☐

If you have a larger score in the physical box than in the psychological box, it would appear that physical improvements motivate you the most. If the opposite is true, it would appear that psychological improvements are more motivating to you. Psychological versus physical improvements usually are more important for motivating the majority of people. This is often a signal that maintaining good relationships with people is extremely important to these individuals.

This interesting comparison could be valuable if you are or should you become a supervisor. As a supervisor, the more you can influence people to be motivated, the more successful you will be. Yet you may have little control over physical matters. (Your superiors may not approve the increase in salary you recommend for one of your employees.) But you *do* have control over psychological matters. If you can't give a high-producing employee an immediate raise, at least you can provide recognition or psychological support.

Most of us must learn to live in a comfortable way with our many inherited traits and characteristics. We can make improvements through better grooming, health programs, and even cosmetic surgery. But even doing our best in these areas, we must recognize that further improvement must come through better human relations and communication of what we already possess. The vehicle that will accomplish this is a positive attitude.

CASE 6

Message

"Now you tell me . . ."

Jeff, a hard-working specialty upholsterer, was one of several employees in a small manufacturing unit in which productivity depended upon the close cooperation of everyone. Jeff had high potential and lived up to it, producing more than anyone in the unit. But Jeff liked to work alone, and he seldom volunteered to help his fellow workers. Many of the people who worked with him felt he portrayed a superior attitude, and they resented it.

Jeff's supervisor gave a lot of thought to the problem. Although Jeff was producing at the highest level in the unit, the total productivity of the unit had actually gone down slightly since Jeff joined the group. Could it be that Jeff had done more damage (through poor human relations) than good (by his high personal productivity)? The supervisor came to the conclusion that Jeff was an outstanding employee when viewed alone, but a very poor one when viewed as a member of a group.

When Jeff's supervisor was promoted to a more responsible position, management selected someone from outside the unit to become the new supervisor. Jeff felt he should have been the one to be promoted and immediately demanded an explanation. He was told that he was the highest producer in the unit, but his human-relations skills were not up to standard. Management felt that the other workers in the unit would not respect him as their supervisor.

A. Discuss: Do you agree with management's decision to pass over Jeff, even though Jeff was the best producer? Give reasons why you agree or disagree. How responsible do you feel the supervisor was for Jeff's being passed over?

B. Expand Your Understanding: From the Internet and other sources such as the *Harvard Business Review*, identify several productivity measurement surveys (checklists, guides, etc.) relating to improving an organization's productivity (bottom line) and effectiveness. Review the instruments to determine the similarities (essential components) among them. Based on your findings, develop some recommendations and suggestions for improving individual and group productivity—suggestions you can also give to both Jeff and his supervisor.

CHAPTER 7

The Winning Combination

"High productivity and good relationships, too?"

Thought for the Day: A happy heart, resourceful mind, and helping hands are a good combination of skills for a successful life.

PERFORMANCE COMPETENCIES

- Understand why a positive correlation exists between good human relations, worker satisfaction, and productivity.

- Identify ways personal productivity can be increased by giving attention to a good balance of work skills.

- Recognize the characteristics, actions, and expertise of the four "plus" factors that management seeks in employees.

- Appreciate how productivity ultimately involves quality, a service attitude, and customer satisfaction.

- Understand the four quality issues valued by organizations that strive to improve services and products.

There is a danger of misinterpretation in discussing human relations and productivity. You might have deduced from the other chapters in this book that building strong, healthy vertical and horizontal working relationships automatically results in greater departmental productivity. This is not necessarily so.

An employee can be happy, satisfied, and content with his (or her) job and yet not carry his fair share of the workload. A group of employees in a department can get along beautifully with each other, and yet the productivity of the department may be far below average.

HUMAN RELATIONS, SATISFACTION, AND PRODUCTIVITY

Happy Employees Usually Are High Producers. The goal of good human relations is not just happy employees, but happy employees who produce more. The goal is greater productivity and, ultimately, greater profit. It is theoretically possible that a business organization could devote so much time and money to making employees happy and comfortable that the company could go broke and out of business. Management is, therefore, not interested in making people happy just because happy people are nice to have around or because happy people stick with their jobs longer. Management is interested in making their employees happy because happy employees, under the right leadership, can be motivated to achieve greater productivity.

Competitiveness and improvement go hand-in-hand.

Management's focus on productivity should not be interpreted as meaning that employers are sensitive to their employees' needs only because they are interested in increasing productivity. Not true. Nevertheless, management (and their employees) must fully accept the economic truth that survival under free competition requires a continual improvement in personal and group productivity.

Employees who are fun to be around, but never get down to doing their share of the work, are a burden on fellow workers. They are parasites on the productivity of others. They may be pleasant to have around, but they are far too expensive for management to keep. Why?

- The work itself must be done.

- Labor costs must be controlled.

- Customers must be well served.

Competitive Organizations Depend on Human Productivity. Greater productivity must be the goal of American business organizations if they are to survive and compete with other world markets where labor costs are much lower. The development and use of more and more highly technical equipment will take us a long way, but human productivity must do the rest.

It is only natural, then, that management should seek outstanding people for jobs that are increasingly sophisticated. It is only natural that they should try to find, hire, and train people who have already developed their human-relations skills to a high level.

A BALANCE OF ESSENTIAL WORK SKILLS

The "Right" Combination. What are the human factors management seeks? The most important one is the right combination of personal productivity and human relations.

Human productivity is multi-faceted

The best way to explain this fundamental is to present the situation of a small department composed of three employees who have identical assignments and similar workloads. For example, Alexia and Richard have been employed in their positions for over a year. Hazel, however, recently joined the organization as a replacement for an employee who resigned. She has a very high potential, substantially above that of the other two people.

Alexia and Richard have been taking it very easy, and there is a sizable gap between their current level of productivity and their potential. In other words, they have not been motivated to do the kind of job they can do. Hazel, however, is very ambitious. She wants to build a reputation for herself and, if possible, move on quickly to a supervisory position in which she will have more responsibility and remuneration. In order to gain the attention of management, Hazel decides to increase her personal level of productivity to the point at which it will surpass both Alexia's and Richard's. She has decided she can further her career in either of two ways:

1. Hazel can go all out and pass Alexia and Richard in a hurry. But, in using this approach, she would risk building poor horizontal working relationships with her fellow workers.
2. Hazel can pass Alexia and Richard in personal productivity on a somewhat slower and less obvious schedule. That is, she can concentrate on building good horizontal relationships with her fellow workers and create a harmonious environment that will increase their productivity along with her own.

What might happen if Hazel decided to follow the first approach and ignore building good horizontal relationships?

It is possible, of course, for Alexia and Richard to become motivated. Perhaps in order to make their positions more secure, they may compete with Hazel; and, as a result, the productivity of the entire department may increase.

It is just as likely that the outcome will not be positive. Alexia and Richard may resent Hazel; and, rather than work with her, may in subtle ways work against her. For example, because they are more experienced, they may let her make some mistakes that, if they wanted to, they could prevent. They could do many little things that would make her uncomfortable and her work more difficult. As a result, Hazel may become critical of Alexia and Richard and the relationships among the three could deteriorate to the point where the productivity of all three would drop. A drop in group productivity would be especially serious if customers were involved.

Lowered productivity for the group may not happen, of course—but it could. And if it did, Hazel would certainly not have helped her future with the company. It is not a safe approach for her to take. She could be asking for trouble.

Now what might happen if Hazel took the opposite approach—if she passed Alexia and Richard in personal productivity, but at the same time worked hard to build good, strong working relationships with them?

Link personal productivity with relationship building

It is likely that Hazel would make her job easier. She would be valued more by the supervisor. She would earn the support of both Alexia and Richard. She would contribute more to productivity. Instead of falling into a human-relations trap, she would demonstrate to management that she had insight and sensitivity.

Mapping the Best Route to Take. Of course, it would be easy to tell Hazel that building good working relationships with Alexia and Richard is the best route to take. But how should she go about doing it? Here are four suggestions:

1. Hazel could build better horizontal relationships with Alexia and Richard by sacrificing a little of her personal productivity to help increase theirs. She could accomplish her objective of building better relationships by looking for opportunities to help Alexia and Richard when their workloads are heavy or when they do not feel well. She could also pitch in when one of them is absent.

2. As Hazel brings her personal productivity above that of Alexia and Richard, she should be careful not to become critical of them because their performance levels are now lower than hers. She should not expect constant praise from her supervisor just because she, at this point in her career, is carrying a larger share of the workload.

3. Hazel should be careful not to isolate herself too much from Alexia and Richard. Even if she is occasionally rejected by them, she must continue to be pleasant until good relationships are built. She must be sincerely interested in both Alexia and Richard as individuals in order to win their respect. A superior attitude on her part will defeat any effort she makes to build sound relationships.

4. Above all, Hazel should stand on her own two feet and work out her own problems without complaining or running to the supervisor for help. She can achieve the support of Alexia and Richard only by demonstrating to them that she knows what she is doing and can fight her own battles.

Hazel will go a long way in communicating to management that she has one of the human-relations factors they seek if she keeps the following principle in mind: An increase in personal productivity should be accompanied by increased attention to horizontal relationships.

So what strategy did Hazel use?

Last week, Hazel was invited to have a long talk with the human-resource director of her company. During the conversation, she asked the director what kind of a person management was really seeking. The director said that management usually sought four "plus" factors in the employees they hoped to promote into management. Hazel made a real effort to remember all four. The section that follows outlines the four "plus" factors in the way Hazel would probably put it if you asked her about them now.

FOUR "PLUS" FACTORS MANAGEMENT DESIRES

The person management is looking for is . . .

1. **. . . someone who strives to work close to her (or his) personal potential regardless of the level at which fellow workers are performing.** She is always trying to close her personal productivity gap, even if others are content to do only what they have to in order to keep their jobs. She is self-motivating. She takes a professional approach to her job and gains real satisfaction when she does it well.

2. **. . . someone who is never completely satisfied with her personal potential.** She believes that she can always improve it a little. She truly believes in lifelong learning. She takes advantage of any training that the company will provide. She continues to read and study on her own. She is always learning more and more about the job ahead of her. She may even continue her formal education by attending classes at a nearby adult education center, junior college, or university. Although she is realistic about her potential, she does not go along with the idea that a person is born with a certain potential that cannot be changed. She will continue to learn and to prepare for new opportunities.

3. **. . . someone who believes human relations is important.** She puts people and the development of good human-relations skills ahead of machines, statistics, procedures, and credentials.

She accepts responsibility for building strong relationships as an interesting and inevitable challenge. She is highly productive, and at the same time, she protects her relationships with people. She does this with a sense of humor and personal understanding. She is proud of the fact that she is a good person with whom most people like to work. She endeavors to keep all relations on a sincere level. She does all of this because she knows that she contributes to the productivity of her department in two ways: through her personal work effort and through the relationships she builds with her fellow employees. She refuses to sacrifice one for the other, and she constantly tries to keep them in proper balance.

4. **. . . someone who makes a point of being loyal to her company or organization.** Being loyal does not mean that she automatically accepts all of the policies and practices that filter down from the top. Far from it. She accepts the responsibility for making changes, but she remains loyal to her company while fighting for changes. She feels that her company deserves her best effort. She refuses to let human-relations problems, the negative attitudes of others, or personal disappointments slow her down.

Hazel asked the director a second question: "How many employees have all of the four 'plus' factors?"

He replied: "It is impossible to say. There are many who are good at one or two, some who are good at three, but only a few who are good at all four. At any rate, those who demonstrate all four do not remain line employees for long, unless by choice, because they are desperately needed for supervisory positions."

Hazel then asked: "How does management single out those who have the 'plus' factors they seek?"

Stand just a little taller to be recognized

"It's easy," replied the director. "You only have to be slightly taller than others to stand out in the crowd. It's the same with the 'plus' factors. You don't have to be miles ahead of others for management to recognize you; a little is all it takes."

ACTIVITY

How I Stack Up on the "Plus" Factors

Think about how your supervisor would rate you on the four "plus" factors (refer back to the detailed description in this chapter). Then, in the following space, describe the characteristics, actions, and expertise that make up each of the four factors. Give yourself an overall rating on each of the factors, and put them in rank order to determine your strongest and weakest attributes. Consider several ways you can improve your weaker attributes and add your suggestions to the respective items.

1. I try hard to work close to my personal potential:_____
   _____

2. I am never satisfied with my personal potential:_____
   _____

3. I believe human relations is important:_____
   _____

4. I am loyal to my organization:_____
   _____

Now, begin working on improving each of the four factors toward strengthening your employability and career skills.

LINKING CUSTOMER SERVICE AND PRODUCTIVITY

Productivity Ultimately Involves the Quality of Service Provided to Customers. When new employees enter the workforce, their main interest is usually career advancement. Advancement is encouraged because a strong focus on personal goals is motivating and has many other beneficial aspects to both employee and employer. But if self-interest goes too far, it can detract from the responsibility to fulfill job duties. A primary responsibility, often neglected by otherwise excellent employees, is developing an effective service attitude.

A service attitude is a desire to satisfy customers to the point at which they will continue to use the firm's services and bring in new clients as well. All employees should take time to identify who their customers are and then serve them in every way possible with a positive attitude. Implementing a customer service strategy will create a win-win situation for the client and the company, and career advancement will be facilitated for the employee.

Everyone benefits from a good customer service strategy

It is easy to identify clients when you are on the front line providing direct customer service. A waitperson, bank teller, doctor, or salesperson receives daily reminders. But what about a machinist, software engineer, or hospital dietitian? Although these individuals may not serve clients directly, they all have service-attitude responsibilities.

The machinist's client may be a manufacturer who assembles parts he (or she) builds into kitchen appliances. Thus, the service attitude of the machinist involves building durable parts, meeting production schedules, and conforming to specifications. The machinist may never see the client, but he is building a quality product that serves the client indirectly. The hospital dietitian serves those who will eat the food prepared by others. The software engineer's clients are those who will eventually utilize the computer programs. All can benefit from a positive service attitude.

To illustrate how productivity and customer service must be linked, a good example follows.

Sid and Lisette. Both Sid and Lisette design computer software for financial institutions. Both are highly professional and career minded. The primary difference between them is their service attitudes.

Sid works closely with his own boss and the manager of the financial organization being served to get the specifics of each job before designing his software package. He does not take time to consult with the ultimate users—tellers and other front-line employees. Even so, Sid receives many compliments from his boss because he is always on or ahead of schedule.

Lisette, however, takes the time to get specifics directly from users (branch managers, new account officers, tellers), who are the ultimate clients. This takes more time, so Lisette does not always receive immediate reinforcement from her boss. Most of the time, her compliments show up later, but they are more meaningful because they demonstrate a superior service attitude.

Each individual must identify her (or his) clients and design a strategy that will best serve them, whether compliments are received or not.

Find the balance that works for you

Your job success will depend to a large degree on finding a proper balance of personal productivity and human relations that works for you. It should not be difficult to determine how you can help your coworkers if you are seriously concerned about building good working relationships. Learning about their needs as well as those of your customers will also help you to learn more about yourself and how you can improve your own productivity and work quality.

A FOCUS ON QUALITY

In recent years, employees have been exposed to a wide range of quality-related factors and issues including standards, measures, procedures, controls, assurances, and so forth. What has caused organizations to place so much emphasis on quality issues? Employers, in an effort to keep customers happy, have focused on getting workers to find ways of reducing inefficiencies while providing value-added elements to products and services.

Various models relating to quality improvement have been implemented by organizations in which change, especially in the way people think and interact, promotes a good balance between productivity and human relations. While many quality terms have become dated (such as total quality management, TQM; continuous quality improvement, CQI; total quality, TQ; and others), the quality focus continues to evolve for organizations with the emphasis being placed on quality control, process improvement, customer service, and operations improvement.

Measuring Four Areas for Quality Improvement. Quality consciousness has come a long way since some of the popular management philosophies were introduced in the early 1990s. The quality-related offshoots stemming from early quality efforts, however, have helped organizations implement needed change toward becoming more competitive and profitable. As an all-encompassing process that involves the attitudes of everyone in an organization, a quality focus today is aimed at a very critical goal: to improve every aspect of customer service and product quality. The quality focus involves the following:

- *Accountability.* A basic quality concept is that everyone is responsible for improving their performance; and their performance is to be measured over and over again based upon facts. Quality-focused organizations embrace the idea that "what gets measured gets improved."

- *Focus on customer.* The quality consciousness of most organizations starts with the customer and filters back to the production process. To achieve quality means to exceed customer expectations.

- *Group decisions.* Whenever all members of the team are involved in the decision-making process, everyone assumes more responsibility to make it work. For quality measures and processes to be implemented successfully, an organization must rely on the entire workforce.

- *Commitment to improvement.* A commitment to quality never ends; it is a continuous process. A firm that takes its quality commitment seriously will devote itself to improving products and services. It will put quality processes in place long before the customer becomes dissatisfied or the competition gains an advantage.

As you may have already guessed, the focus on quality is an attitude of management to promote a learning organization by generating action plans to improve product and service at every turn.

A quality focus promotes a good balance between productivity and human relations

Summary

In this chapter, you have learned that good human-relations skills exhibited by workers frequently translate into high satisfaction among workers. Satisfied workers with good human-relations skills give value to their employers for their contribution to the organization's overall productivity.

Workers who can successfully combine productivity with an effective service attitude also strive to develop the factors management values. These four "plus" factors include workers who work close to their potentials, who strive to reach higher potential levels, who value the importance of human relations, and who are loyal to their organization. Thus, employees who want to achieve career success are wise to develop and maintain a good balance of personal productivity and human relations—a balance that cannot be overemphasized.

With just a little creativity, the significance of this balance translates into a winning combination that can be expressed as a mathematical equation to guide you every day. That is, the "winning equation" related to productivity and relationship building can be demonstrated by a somewhat "theatrical" redefinition of Einstein's theory for mass energy equivalence, $E = mc^2$. The impact of the "theory" offers excellent advice to anyone who wants to achieve work and life success. Note here that the terms of Einstein's equation are redefined as follows:

E = energy and enthusiasm to work hard,

m = motivation to build strong relationships, and

c^2 = commitment to continuously strive for quality and self-improvement.

The "winning equation" is a good model to follow to improve your relationships, increase your productivity, focus on quality, and develop a service attitude. Why not adopt the equation as your own and put it into practice every single day?

Test Your Understanding

Respond to the following items to test your understanding of the chapter.

Part A: Circle the correct answer (T = True; F = False) for each of the following statements.

T F   1. The kind of employee management seeks is one who is willing to produce at the level of other workers.

T F   2. An increase in personal productivity should be accompanied by increased attention to horizontal relationships.

T F   3. Most employees know the work characteristics their supervisors value.

T F   4. Productivity ultimately includes the quality of service provided to the customer.

T F   5. Two of the basics of a quality organization are accountability and a commitment to improvement.

Part B: Circle the letter of the correct answer for each of the following items.

6. The human factors that management seeks include the right combination of personal productivity and (a) risk taking, (b) human relations, (c) creativity, (d) product expertise.

7. Someone who believes human relations is important capitalizes on the development of (a) statistical processes, (b) work procedures, (c) technical skills, (d) people.

Part C: Write a short response to demonstrate your understanding related to the following item.

8. Discuss what is meant by not being completely satisfied with your personal potential.

Turn to the back of the book to check your answers.

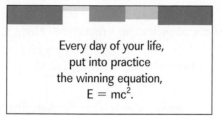

Every day of your life,
put into practice
the winning equation,
$E = mc^2$.

Note: Refer to the definition of $E = mc^2$ noted in the chapter summary.

Think and Respond

Respond to the following items with two or three complete sentences.

1. Describe why happy employees usually are high producers.
2. Discuss the importance of balancing personal productivity and human relations in your job.
3. What are two of the "plus" factors desired by management?
4. Explain why customer service and productivity must be linked.
5. Describe two important elements that contribute to quality standards of an organization.

SUMMARY ACTIVITY

Desirable Work Characteristics

This activity will enable you to discover those work characteristics that both you and your immediate supervisor appreciate the most. Identifying desirable work characteristics and striving to improve your competence of each of them will help you work better with your supervisor and improve your career progress. If you are not currently employed, have a fellow student, friend, or family member act as your supervisor.

There are two steps involved in completing this exercise: (1) You are to complete the left side of the grid below. (2) Independently, ask your supervisor (or a designee you select) to complete the right side of the grid.

Most supervisors consider the following ten factors to be vital to job success. In fact, many claim that these are the factors most managers seek in the employees they wish to promote. After studying them carefully, place them in the pyramid that follows in the order of importance to you. The factor you feel to be most important should be placed on the top, the least important at the bottom. List all ten factors.

Attitude	Creativity (submitting	Job accuracy
Human-relations skills	new ideas)	Personal productivity
Assertiveness	Willingness to assume	Attention to details
Reliability	responsibility	Follow-through

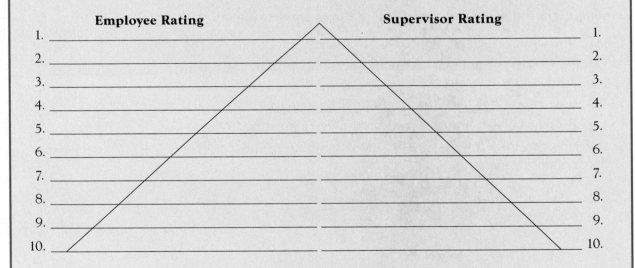

Employee Rating   **Supervisor Rating**

1. _____   1.
2. _____   2.
3. _____   3.
4. _____   4.
5. _____   5.
6. _____   6.
7. _____   7.
8. _____   8.
9. _____   9.
10. _____   10.

Once both you and your supervisor have rated the ten job factors, compare your priorities with those of your supervisor. Where your priorities are different from those of your supervisor, it may be a good idea to discuss why differences exist. As you gain a better understanding of the work characteristics desired by your supervisor and work unit, you probably will become even more valuable to the total productivity of your organization.

CASE 7

Insight

"Okay, next time I'll cool it."

Ted, an air-conditioning journeyman, had been with a large appliance repair company for more than nine months. From his first day, he had been determined to set a pace that would earn him a promotion. It took Ted a little while to catch on to the job, but within four months he was up to the average of others in productivity. After a few more months, he was the top producer in the department. In the meantime, his coworkers maintained a steady, but slower pace.

Ted felt good about his ability to pass others in the department, but he was disturbed because he had received so little recognition for his achievement. In fact, the harder he worked, the more difficult it was to get along with the others. Even his supervisor had failed to give Ted as much encouragement as he felt he deserved.

After a few weeks as top producer, Ted became more critical of his coworkers. He started to give out a few tips on how they might improve their efficiency, and he began to sound off more in staff meetings.

One day the whole situation reached a boiling point. Ted was called into the supervisor's office and was strongly counseled to be more patient and understanding with his fellow workers. "Look, Ted," said his supervisor, "you have everything going for you, but you will never get a promotion if you blow your cool with your fellow employees. You have very high potential and your productivity is great, but you can't expect others to always equal your pace. Don't destroy now the very relationships you might have to rebuild later should you take my place."

A. Discuss: Was Ted's exasperation justified? Or did his supervisor have a good point?

B. Expand Your Understanding: Develop a "Winner's Strategy" paper that provides several recommendations for developing a good work skills balance. Emphasize human relations and productivity. Use the Internet and other sources such as the *Wall Street Journal* to develop and support the premises you select for your paper. Draw some conclusions that would be useful for anyone, including suggestions for Ted and his supervisor.

CHAPTER 8
Your Most Important Working Relationship

"I understand my supervisor perfectly."

Thought for the Day: The quality of any relationship is dependent upon the quality of communications.

PERFORMANCE COMPETENCIES

- Appreciate the role of your supervisor and how you can learn from her (or him).

- Identify the types of working climates supervisors create and ways to work within them.

- Understand the two basic supervisor styles and how you can be productive in different environments.

- Recognize ten tips for maximizing your relationship with your supervisor within the climate he (or she) creates.

- Practice good ethical behavior, especially to make your most important working relationship—working with your supervisor—as strong as possible.

The most important working relationship you have is the one between you and your immediate supervisor. This single relationship can speed up your personal progress or slow it down to a discouraging crawl. It can make going to work a joy or a drag. It can prepare you for greater responsibilities or it can frustrate your desire to learn. And there is just no way to avoid the human-relations fact that, good or bad, you must learn to cope with your boss.

What kind of person will you get as your supervisor?

It is impossible to predict. However, he (or she) will be basically the same person he used to be when he held a job similar to yours, except that now he has much more responsibility. He may or may not have been given some special training to help him become a good supervisor. He may be easy to get along with or he may be very difficult. He may be sensitive to your needs or he may be insensitive. He may be feeling his way along and making many mistakes, or he may be highly experienced and a real pro at his job.

Three things are certain about your supervisor:

1. She (or he) probably has a strong personality that gave her the confidence to become a supervisor in the first place.
2. The responsibilities of being a supervisor probably weigh heavily on her shoulders.
3. She has work authority over you.

YOUR SUPERVISOR'S ROLE

What Is a Supervisor?

- *Teacher.* He (or she) is a teacher. He will not only teach you the routine of your new job, but he will also have a great influence on your attitude toward your job and the company. He has a reservoir of knowledge, skills, and techniques that you need to learn. You will be most fortunate if he is a good teacher. If he is not, you will have to learn from observation.

- *Counselor.* He is a counselor coach. His job is to see that you live up to your potential. He may need to correct errors you are making. He may need to give you tips on improving yourself as an employee. He may feel the need to have a heart-to-heart talk with you at times.

- *Leader.* He is a leader. More than anything else, your supervisor must provide the leadership your department requires. He must provide a motivational setting for all employees. He must earn your respect—not by being soft and easy, but by being a strong leader who will help you build a long-range career.

ACTIVITY

My Investment in My Most Important Working Relationship

In the space provided below, use the first column to describe at least three ways or areas you work well with your supervisor. Then, in the second column, describe how you contribute to your working relationship for each of the items.

Ways or areas in which I work well with my supervisor	Contributions I make to my relationship with my supervisor
1.	
2.	
3.	

Now, in the first column below, suggest three areas of improvement for creating a better working relationship with your supervisor. In the second column, describe how you could contribute to improving the working relationship for each of the items. Hint: If you have difficulty completing the second column, you may want to finish reading this chapter before completing it.

Areas in which my working relationship with my supervisor could be improved	Suggestions or ways I can contribute to improving my relationship with my supervisor
4.	
5.	
6.	

Once you have completed the chart, review the responses you added to the second column for each of the six items. In the space that follows, summarize what you can do to build and maintain a strong, open, and productive relationship with your supervisor.

To build a better relationship with my supervisor, I should:

Do not be surprised if your summary included some recommended action that includes applying good human-relations skills. Also, if your recommended action is not as positive as it should be, modify and rewrite your summary. What can you do right now to put your recommended action into practice? How will what you do make both you and your supervisor's job easier? If your answers to both questions are positive actions and you put your suggestions into practice, your actions will contribute to your investment in your career success.

And, remember, *Your Attitude Is Showing!*

Avoid Stereotyping. It would be a mistake to attempt to type supervisors. They cannot be clearly classified into different groups. Each supervisor has a unique personality. Each has her (or his) own style.

Do you recall your early school days, when you discovered the differences between teachers? You may have had one who expected much more from you than the others. You may not have liked that person at the time, but years later you came to realize how much that one teacher taught you. The same can be true with supervisors.

If you are ambitious, you don't want an easygoing supervisor who does not care and, as a result, hinders instead of helps your progress. You will be better off with a more concerned, more demanding supervisor who will help you reach your potential. With an easy supervisor, you may develop some poor working habits and eventually become unhappy with yourself. With a strong supervisor—one who will take time to train you—you will become a better worker and improve your future. But no matter what kind of boss you encounter, it is up to you to learn to understand him (or her) and work efficiently under his type of leadership.

Remember, too, you should do some of the adjusting. You should provide some of the understanding. Also, you should help build the relationship that must exist between the two of you.

WORKING CLIMATES

Each individual supervisor creates her (or his) own special climate, or atmosphere, under which you must operate. The following analysis of three kinds of climates may give you some indication of the adjustments you might have to make in the future.

1. *The structured climate.* Some supervisors are **more strict** than others. They operate a tight department by keeping close, and sometimes restrictive, controls. They frequently expect employees to be precisely on time, orderly, and highly efficient. They permit foolishness only when a special occasion calls for it. Ninety-eight percent of the time, they stick strictly to business.

   The supervisor who creates this kind of atmosphere often appears cold, distant, and unfeeling to the new employee. He (or she) seems unreachable. As a result, the new employee may begin to fear this person.

   Some jobs force supervisors to be autocratic. Some kinds of work require very high safety standards and efficiency. For example, a producer of a television program may have to be autocratic in order to maintain the split-second efficiency required. Work of a highly technical nature, in which certain precision standards must be met, will call for a different climate than work in a service field.

Although the supervisor who establishes a structured atmosphere may appear cold and unapproachable, the opposite is often true. The supervisor is probably more interested in you and more willing to help than you suspect.

2. *The permissive climate.* The direct opposite of the structured climate is the permissive atmosphere. Some supervisors have a free-and-easy leadership style. There is no apparent intervention, and there are few controls or restrictions.

The permissive climate can be the most dangerous of all, especially for the inexperienced employee because her (or his) need for self-discipline is so great. The employee who does not feel the presence of a leader may not make good use of time. The employee may find it difficult to develop self-motivation. If things are too easygoing, the employee may relax too much and become too friendly with fellow workers. All of this can create bad habits that will ultimately lead to mutual dissatisfaction. Instead of being an ideal situation, then, the permissive climate becomes a trap that can destroy the desire to succeed and eventually cause great unhappiness.

A permissive environment can be so relaxed it is unproductive

Whether we like to accept it or not, a structured climate often gives us more job security and forces us to live closer to our potential. Beware of a climate that is too relaxed unless you are a self-starter and can discipline yourself. You might discover that too much freedom is your downfall.

3. *The democratic climate.* The goal of most supervisors in modern organizations is to create a democratic climate. A democratic atmosphere is the most difficult of all to establish. In fact, purely democratic action is often a goal rather than a reality.

A democratic climate is one in which employees want to do what the supervisor wants done. The supervisor becomes one of the group and still retains his (or her) leadership role. The employees are permitted to have a lot to say about the operation of the department. Everyone becomes involved because each person works from inside the group rather than from outside. The supervisor is the leader and a member of the group at the same time. As a result, a team feeling is created. Many isolated cases of research indicate that most people experience greater personal satisfaction and respond with greater productivity if the supervisor can create and maintain a democratic atmosphere.

A democratic environment encourages involvement

Difficulty of Achieving an Ideal Working Climate. So why can't more supervisors achieve a democratic climate? There are several reasons.

First, the democratic climate is the most difficult climate to create and, once created, the most difficult to maintain. It requires a real expert, an individual with great skill and sensitivity. One should not expect to find a large number of supervisors with this ability.

Second, not all workers respond to a democratic climate, ideal as it may seem. You may like it best, but others in your department may like a more autocratic approach. This is especially true when there are young workers in a department where many more experienced and older employees work. You will often hear employees say: "I wish he would quit fooling around and tell us what to do" or "I wish she would tighten up things around here—people are getting away with murder" or "He is too easy. I can't enjoy working for someone who doesn't set things down clearly and specifically from the beginning."

Third, the supervisor who aspires to build a true democratic climate always exists somewhere between the structured and the permissive. The supervisor may approach the ideal situation for a while, only to find that a few employees are taking advantage of the situation. When this happens, it is necessary to tighten up again and become more structured.

All supervisors must create and maintain what some people refer to as a discipline line. A discipline line is an imaginary line or point beyond which the employee senses she (or he) should not pass lest some form of disapproval and possible disciplinary action take place. It is important to keep a consistent discipline line. Some supervisors claim that keeping a firm, but comfortable, line is a tightrope they walk each day on the job.

Each type of working climate presents supervisor-worker challenges

BASIC SUPERVISORY STYLES

Theory X versus Theory Y. You may hear your supervisor or a college professor discuss Theory X and Theory Y, what Douglas McGregor identified as assumptions that mold behavior. What are they?

- *Theory* X (representing a more structured climate) supports management by control. It states that the worker should be directed and controlled in order to achieve high productivity. A basic assumption is that most employees are not self-motivated. Leaders with a Theory X orientation often reach consistently high productivity levels in their departments. They also have the reputation of doing an excellent job in training their employees.

- *Theory* Y (representing a more democratic/permissive climate) encourages participative management. It states that workers will achieve greater productivity if they can set their own goals and direct their own efforts through involvement. The theory assumes that under the proper working climate, workers will motivate themselves. A discipline line is maintained at a lower level. Theory Y leaders who are sufficiently skillful to achieve high productivity demonstrate a high level of leadership talent that often attracts the attention of upper management.

Every supervisor creates an individual climate. Some supervisors come up with a workable blend of the structured and democratic. Others come up with a blend of the permissive and democratic. We call this blend their management, or leadership, style.

Learn to Be Productive in Any Working Environment. Whether we personally like a supervisor or like his (or her) style is not as important as whether we can learn to be productive in the climate the person creates. A new worker should not be too quick to judge, however, because it is often true that what appears to be a difficult climate at the beginning may turn out to be a comfortable and beneficial one later on. So whatever style your supervisor has, it will be your responsibility to build the best possible relationship with him. Your career progress may depend upon it.

Practice good human relations in all your interactions

MAXIMIZING YOUR RELATIONSHIP WITH YOUR SUPERVISOR

To help you meet the challenge of building the best relationship you can with your supervisor, here are ten tips that should assist you.

1. *Avoid transferring to your supervisor the negative attitudes you may have developed toward other authority figures in your life.* Some people who have had problems with other supervisors, parents, teachers, and similar authority figures make the mistake of transferring their feelings of hostility to their new supervisor. This is unfair. Wipe away any previous negative feelings you may have and give your new (or present) boss an opportunity for her (or him) to build a healthy relationship with you. If you give her a fair chance, she will almost always earn your respect instead of your hostility.

2. *Expect some rough days under your boss's supervision.* Everyone, including a supervisor, is entitled to a few bad days. Your boss is only human. If she should boil over on a given day, don't let it throw you. If she seems to be picking on you for a while, give her time to get over it. More important than anything else, try not to take personally anything she does that you don't like. There may be times when you do not understand your boss's behavior, but if you can float along with it, chances are that it won't last long.

3. *Refuse to nurse a small gripe into a major issue.* A small gripe, when nurtured, can get blown out of proportion and can lead to a confrontation with your supervisor that will hurt your

relationship. If you have a legitimate gripe, try to talk it over with her as soon as possible so you can get it out of your system before it builds up. Remember, she won't know you have a complaint unless you tell her.

4. *Select the right time to approach your supervisor.* Whether you have a complaint or a positive suggestion to make, try to approach your supervisor at the right time. She may be too busy or under too much pressure on a given day to talk to you. If so, wait it out. When the pressure is off, chances are that she will give you a fair opportunity. However, if you do try to talk to her at a bad time and are turned away, wait until another day and try again. If it is important to you, she will no doubt want to talk to you about it. Give her another chance.

Communication is key to good supervisor-worker relationships

5. *Never go over your supervisor's head without talking to her first.* The easiest and quickest way to destroy your relationship with your supervisor is to go over her head on a problem that involves her unit or department. Always talk to your supervisor first. If you are not satisfied with the results, you can then take other action. At least this way your supervisor will know that you consulted her first.

6. *Try not to let your supervisor intimidate you.* Keep in mind that she may not be a professional. She could be guilty of playing favorites and other forms of nonprofessional behavior. Such behavior could cause you to fear your boss. Fear is a strong emotion. If you become so fearful of your boss that you cannot approach her, you should talk to someone in the human resources department, consider a possible transfer, or if necessary, resign. You will never be happy working for a person you fear, and a supervisor will seldom respect you if you are afraid of her.

7. *It can be a human-relations mistake to make a buddy of your supervisor.* Your relationship with your supervisor is a business relationship. Keep it that way. The distance between you and your boss may often appear to be a fine line, but she is still your boss. If you get too personal, it will almost always turn out badly.

8. *In case you make a mistake, clear the air quickly.* If you make a serious goof and injure your relationship with your boss, why not clean the slate with an open discussion? It is a good idea to leave work every day with a pleasant feeling toward your job and your supervisor. If you have had trouble with her on a given day and truly believe that it is partly your fault, the mature thing to do is to accept your share of the blame. You will feel better and so will your supervisor.

9. *Not all supervisors enjoy their roles.* A surprising number of supervisors would really prefer to be workers. Some may have accepted their promotions because management has pressed them to do so. Others may feel they can contribute more as supervisors because they can make more money to help their families. As an employee, you should view this as a possibility. It will give you more insight into the role itself and perhaps help you tolerate your supervisor more easily. Try to remember that being a good supervisor is difficult. Sometimes those who try the hardest to win the respect of their workers never fully succeed because of personality traits they cannot change.

10. *When possible, convert your supervisor into a mentor.* A mentor is a person in a key position who takes a personal interest in your career and acts as an advisor. Your present supervisor may be on her way up in your organization. If you build the right relationship with her, she may counsel and guide you over a period of time, even though she may no longer be your supervisor. You may even ride her coattails to the top.

IS THIS ETHICAL?

Ethical Behavior Is Essential. Ethical behavior on the part of both you and your supervisor is essential if the relationship is to be strong and lasting. To maintain your side of the bargain, consider the following suggestions.

- *Maintain open and honest communication.* Tell the whole story regarding any problems that develop. The moment deception appears, the relationship is permanently injured.

- *Do not discuss your supervisor in a negative way with coworkers.* It communicates an absence of loyalty and is considered by many to be unethical. You need not approve of everything your supervisor does, but it is best to keep your attitude to yourself.

- *Refuse to be influenced by either your supervisor or coworkers to perform unethical acts.* A good way to take your stand on any questionable situation is to ask openly: "Is this ethical?"

Keep your ethics at the highest possible level

Summary

Building and maintaining a strong, warm, productive relationship with your boss can be a real human-relations challenge. It isn't always easy partially because your supervisor's role as teacher, counselor, and leader may not meet your expectations.

Yet, nowhere is a positive attitude more appreciated than on the job—mainly because, for many people, work is not what they prefer to be doing. Performing tasks next to a positive person makes what they are forced to do more enjoyable. Consider, too, that some workers may have extremely difficult private lives; the only place they may find positive people is near their workstations. Supervisors depend upon the positive attitudes of their employees to establish a "team spirit." Your positive attitude makes your supervisor's job easier.

You also may get used to one supervisor's style in one type of working climate, only to discover that you have been transferred to another department and have to start from scratch. Learn to be productive within the climate your supervisor creates and within the style that he (or she) demonstrates. If you do, your career progress will be headed in the right direction.

Every relationship you have will offer you a unique challenge. That is why it is critical for you keep a positive attitude if you hope to ensure your relationship success. As you are confronted with the many challenges in your work environment, use the tips provided in this chapter for developing and maintaining good human relations with your supervisor. And, above all, practice good ethical behavior and make the most of every experience.

Test Your Understanding

Respond to the following items to test your understanding of the chapter.

Part A: Circle the correct answer (T = True; F = False) for each of the following statements.

T F   1. Employees who do not go partway in building a good relationship with their supervisors hurt their career progress.

T F   2. Supervisors establish working climates primarily through the use of discipline lines.

T F   3. A Theory X supervisor usually demonstrates behavior that represents a structured, controlling leadership style.

T F   4. There is no evidence that employees who transfer negative attitudes toward other authority figures also will do so to their supervisors.

T F   5. Discussing your supervisor in a negative way with coworkers is often considered to be unethical.

Part B: Circle the letter of the correct answer for each of the following items.

6. A working atmosphere characterized by employees wanting to do what the supervisor wants done can be referred to as a (a) structured climate, (b) permissive climate, (c) democratic climate, (d) socialistic climate.

7. To foster a good working relationship with your supervisor, avoid (a) becoming a buddy with your supervisor, (b) making your supervisor your mentor, (c) approaching your supervisor to clear up a misunderstanding, (d) keeping a positive attitude around your supervisor and coworkers.

Part C: Write a short response to demonstrate your understanding related to the following item.

8. Discuss why open communication not only is important to a good relationship with your supervisor but also is linked to ethical behavior.

Turn to the back of the book to check your answers.

> Positive relationships are built
> from positive behaviors
> transmitted
> by a positive attitude.

Think and Respond

Respond to the following items with two or three complete sentences.

1. Describe two of the primary roles of a supervisor.

2. Contrast two working climates of supervisors and the characteristics representing each.

3. How does a Theory X supervisor differ from a Theory Y supervisor?

4. Suggest two or more tips for creating a good employee-supervisor relationship.

5. What are some actions or behaviors that would "pass" the test: "Is this ethical?"

Relationship Self-Assessment

Your most important and delicate working relationship is the one between you and your immediate supervisor. This exercise is designed to help you evaluate and improve this vital relationship through the process of self-assessment. When you evaluate the relationship in private without any communication with your supervisor, you will need to be honest about the contribution you have made and what improvements you may be willing to make in the future.

Read both statements associated with each of the following items. Circle the number that indicates where you fall in the scale from 10 to 1 on each factor.

1. I believe I have done everything possible to develop a sound relationship with my supervisor.

   10 9 8 7 6 5 4 3 2 1

   I admit I have done almost nothing to develop a sound relationship with my supervisor.

2. I have always taken advantage of opportunities to communicate with my supervisor.

   10 9 8 7 6 5 4 3 2 1

   I have been stubborn and have never taken advantage of opportunities to communicate.

3. I have been 100 percent fair with my supervisor.

   10 9 8 7 6 5 4 3 2 1

   I admit I have not been the least bit fair with my supervisor.

4. I keep my personal productivity as high as possible to improve my relationship with my supervisor.

   10 9 8 7 6 5 4 3 2 1

   I produce only as much as I must to keep my job.

5. To keep a better relationship with my supervisor, I do everything possible to keep good relationships with my coworkers.

   10 9 8 7 6 5 4 3 2 1

   I am not making any effort to keep good relationships with coworkers.

6. I have never bad-mouthed my supervisor.

   10 9 8 7 6 5 4 3 2 1

   I bad-mouth my supervisor every day both at work and at home.

7. I seldom nurse a small gripe that could hurt my relationship with my supervisor.

   10 9 8 7 6 5 4 3 2 1

   I am currently nursing a number of small gripes.

8. I respect the need for a formal working relationship with my supervisor.

10 9 8 7 6 5 4 3 2 1

My supervisor is stuffy and unapproachable. I can't respect such authority.

9. I have earned the respect of my supervisor and have been aboveboard on all matters.

10 9 8 7 6 5 4 3 2 1

I have taken advantage of every opportunity to undermine my supervisor.

10. I have given my supervisor every possible chance to build a good relationship with me.

10 9 8 7 6 5 4 3 2 1

I have never given my supervisor a chance to build a good relationship with me.

Total Score _____

Total your score for the ten items. If you rated yourself 80 or above, you are probably doing your part and more to build a good working relationship with your supervisor. If you rated yourself between 50 and 80, you may need to initiate some positive action to improve your current status. If you rated yourself under 50, you may not be doing your part to strengthen your most important working relationship and need to strive hard to improve your working relationship with your supervisor.

Although your supervisor, as a manager, has the primary responsibility to build a good relationship with you, your own responsibility is considerable. If you do not go partway in building such a relationship—perhaps because of a personality difference or breakdown in communication—you are hurting your career progress.

CASE 8 ————————————————————

Choice

"I'm a Theory Y person myself."

Carol is a customer service representative with an e-commerce organization. For the last sixty days she has been training for a new position and assignment. She has just received word to report to the human resource department to discuss her new role in the company.

The director gives her a choice of assignments. She tells Carol that two departments have requested her services. The departments are identical in their operations. The only difference is the type of climate created by each supervisor.

One department has a rather demanding supervisor who has a leadership style that leans in the direction of Theory X. He is an old-timer and has been in charge of his department for many years. He expects and gets high productivity and loyalty from all his employees. Everyone admits that he has trained more people who are now in top management positions than anyone in the company.

The other department is run by an up-and-coming younger supervisor who adheres to Theory Y. She tries to get everyone in the department to participate in decisions and get involved. She prides herself on her democratic leadership style and feels she has been very successful. People appear to be very happy working for her. The personnel turnover is lower in this department than in the other. Productivity is slightly higher.

A. Discuss: Which department would you select? On what basis?

B. Expand Your Understanding: Interview three or more supervisors or managers to identify the characteristics of their management styles. Start your research by (a) identifying several elements associated with Theory X and Y styles and (b) finding other management styles (and their elements) that managers practice today. Develop a survey instrument for conducting your interviews. Summarize your findings and revist your recommendation for Carol, noting why you supported (or did not support) your original recommendation for her.

CHAPTER 9

Understanding the Nature of Relationships

"People are easy to figure."

Thought for the Day: Don't confuse your assumptions (biased or not) with facts—ingrained assumptions have wrecked many potentially good relationships.

PERFORMANCE COMPETENCIES

- Understand the importance of the mutual-reward theory in creating, maintaining, and repairing relationships.

- Recognize that every person has his (or her) own value system.

- Appreciate how diversity and ethnic demographics have contributed to the changing international workplace.

- Recognize the dangers and implications of sexual overtones and harassment.

- Appreciate the value and significance of building relationships with people of all age levels.

- Learn to develop tolerance, but also correct irritating habits and mannerisms that can damage relationships.

As we delve more deeply into the nature of working relationships, there are several characteristics that have a considerable influence on the quality or tone of the relationship. In a sense, they constitute the ingredients, or components, of the relationship itself. The first of these characteristics (presented in the first major section of this chapter) is the mutual-reward theory. The remaining five characteristics (also discussed in separate sections) represent human-relations challenges you should consider as you study the nature of past, present, and future working relationships.

A RELATIONSHIP IS A TWO-WAY PROPOSITION

The idea of a relationship may be easier to understand if you visualize it as an invisible tunnel between two fellow employees. Disregard the personalities involved and concentrate on the relationship itself. The following illustrations may help you do this.

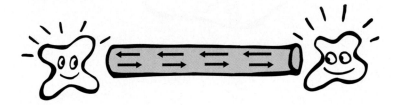

The two-way arrows between the amoebas remind us that verbal communication is the lifeblood of the relationship. Good input and good reception are necessary at both ends. The following illustration adds to the relationship the six factors we discuss in this chapter.

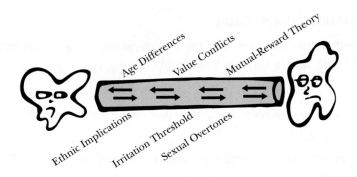

Of course, not all of the elements in this illustration are likely to be present in any single relationship. Some relationships may have only one or two. Others may have four or five. An investigation into each of them, however, will give you additional insight into the nature of all working relationships.

THE MUTUAL-REWARD THEORY

With proper care, you can create working relationships that will turn out to be mutually rewarding. The mutual-reward theory (MRT) states that a relationship between two people is enhanced when there is a satisfactory balance of rewards between them. In a good MRT relationship, both parties come out ahead.

In fact, if a working relationship is to remain healthy over a long time, it must contribute something of value to both persons. When one individual suddenly discovers that she (or he) has been contributing substantially more than she has been receiving, the relationship can quickly weaken. However, when there is a balanced reward system between people, the working relationship can thrive. The cases of Gina and Molly illustrate this theory.

The mutual-reward theory is biased toward a win-win outcome

Gina. Gina was a quiet, timid, serious worker with outstanding job knowledge. A coworker, Joe, however, was a very outgoing person with great personal confidence but less job knowledge. They worked next to each other in identical jobs and, despite their differences, they slowly built a strong relationship.

How did it happen? Gina made a patient effort to teach Joe as much as possible about the job and took care of some mistakes he made without their supervisor finding out about them. What did Joe do in return? He helped Gina develop more self-confidence and become a more outgoing person. He paid her well-deserved compliments, introduced her to coworkers from other departments, and generally gave her a feeling of acceptance that she had not been able to develop by herself. Because each party contributed to the success of the other (both eventually became supervisors), their relationship became strong and permanent.

Molly. Molly worked for Ms. Gonzales for three years before taking over her job as division manager. During that period, MRT was constantly in effect. Molly provided high productivity, loyalty, and dependability to the division and to Ms. Gonzales. Ms. Gonzales, as the supervisor, provided a good learning environment for Molly and gave her the recognition she needed. For example, Ms. Gonzales often introduced Molly to upper-management people and related the progress she was making. This exposure eventually gave Molly the edge she needed to achieve a promotion.

The term *bonding* is frequently used to signify a close, emotionally important relationship. Bonding can take place between two coworkers, between an employee and an immediate supervisor, and especially between an employee and a mentor. A working relationship that involves bonding needs to have two characteristics. First, it is important that the relationship not become overly personal to the point at which the present productivity and future career of either individual are placed in jeopardy. Second, it is vital to the longevity of the relationship that it be mutually rewarding so both parties benefit somewhat equally.

Contribute to Your Relationships. Relationships can almost always be mutually rewarding because people can strengthen each other in many different ways. Obviously, however, when one person does all the giving, deterioration sets in quickly. As you build new relationships and protect old ones, look for things you can do to contribute to the success and happiness of the person next to you. When you help others, you will almost always receive something in return that will make life better for you. If you weave MRT into your behavior, you demonstrate a significant human-relations competency.

─ACTIVITY ─

My Plan: Mutual-Reward Theory

In the space provided, describe at least one way you can apply the mutual-reward theory toward understanding and building better relationships.

VALUE CONFLICTS

Differing Value Systems and Lifestyles Are Natural. Everyone has his (or her) own value system. And everyone has his own priority list of what is really important in life. Different people seek different lifestyles. It is only natural that value conflicts exist between people who are forced to associate with each other closely in the world of work. Here are two typical examples.

Tony. Tony was assigned to work next to Mr. Henderson, who was more than twice his age. Tony was single, energetic, and enjoyed a rather flamboyant social life. It was no secret that Tony did not want to assume family responsibilities too soon and he was determined to have a lifestyle different from that of his parents. Tony's foreign sports car and fashionable clothing reflected this attitude. Mr. Henderson, however, was a family-oriented, religious person.

How did they learn to work together gracefully? At the beginning, they both played it cool and built their relationship exclusively on the basis of job factors. Tony learned to respect Mr. Henderson for his many years of job experience and his willingness to share it. Mr. Henderson learned to respect Tony for his willingness to learn and contribute a full day's work. After six months, they could even discuss their value differences. A better mutual understanding resulted.

Banefa. Banefa was brought up in a strict home environment and was taught to respect discipline. She was considered fairly square by her contemporaries. Her coworker, Trish, however, was very happy-go-lucky and undisciplined. Trish considered herself very much ahead of others of her generation. How did Banefa and Trish get along when they were forced to work very closely together? At first, the sparks of conflict were rather obvious. But slowly they built a sound working relationship based upon their mutual desire to do a good job for the company and further their careers. They did not become close personal friends, and they did not go out together socially. However, they learned to respect each other, and both benefited from the working relationship despite their value differences.

It is a mistake, perhaps even an invasion of privacy, to impose one's own values on another, especially in the work environment. What a fellow worker does with her (or his) private life is her own business and should have nothing to do with the relationship you build with her on the job. To react to an individual in a negative way for what she does on the outside should be avoided. Common interests on the job should provide a sufficient basis for a good working relationship. You will be surprised how many good working relationships you can build with people who think and live differently than you do.

Don't impose your values on others

ACTIVITY

My Plan: Value Conflicts

In the space provided, describe at least one way you can avoid and/or address factors associated with value conflicts and move toward understanding and building better relationships.

ETHNIC IMPLICATIONS

International business, e-commerce, and the increased awareness of the critical need to promote diversity in the workplace have contributed to the world becoming a "great mosaic" of different cultures working together. Most businesses have made concerted efforts to truly address the diverse issues associated with this change. Many opportunities have opened up for women and other minority groups, especially in positions of authority that traditionally have been dominated by males. More and more companies are involved in international e-business. As a result, businesses have become much more concerned with employing and meeting the needs of the growing diverse populations that make up our culture.

Not only are more women and young people in the workforce, but they also are a segment of the significantly increasing numbers of Asian, African, East Indian, and Latin American workers, especially in American and multinationally owned and operated businesses.

Depending on your organization, you can react to this demographic workplace change in three different ways:

1. If you are in the dominant culture, you can maintain a negative attitude toward others, but you may never learn to work with others successfully. In turn, your career may suffer.
2. If you are in a minority culture, you can try so hard to be one of "them" that you lose your own identity at great expense to your own positive attitude and job productivity.
3. Regardless of the position you occupy, if you adapt to all cultures in your organization, you will become a better person; you will be more productive, and your career will be enhanced.

Accepting the last premise, an "international" or "mosaic" view of diversity may assist you in building strong and lasting relationships with the many different people you have will meet in your workplace. It will also help you maintain your positive attitude.

Respect the Uniqueness of Others. A basic human-relations competency is to respect and treat every person as a unique, special individual. Look beyond outward appearances, ignore how he (or she) might resemble someone with whom you have had an unfavorable experience, and accept each person as a unique individual.

Respect is a fundamental human-relations skill

If everyone could sincerely adhere to this one fundamental practice, relationships would have a good chance of functioning harmoniously. Each person—and each relationship—would stand on its own, without reference to ethnic background. Unfortunately for all of us, not enough people practice this principle. Here are two short cases to illustrate the point.

Jean. Jean, a middle-aged Anglo who grew up in an ethnically diverse community, had always believed she was free of prejudice but had never worked with anyone other than coworkers from her own ethnic background. When Hobart, a young African American man, joined the department, Jean realized she felt a bit uneasy and apprehensive as to how she and Hobart would get along.

Jean found Hobart to be a very easygoing, friendly person and everything started out fine with their working relationship. However, when Hobart began making mistakes and, in Jean's opinion, began asking stupid questions, Hobart definitely was not living up to her expectations. Jean became so frustrated over the matter that she was tempted to go to her supervisor.

Look for positives in others and you'll find them!

In thinking about what she would discuss with her supervisor, Jean realized that she was expecting more of Hobart than she was of her other coworkers. Without a doubt, she seemed to be looking for things to complain about with Hobart's work instead of being understanding. To try to get the relationship back on a fair footing, Jean called Hobart aside and admitted her mistake. It was a good move because Hobart had felt Jean's negative attitude and wanted to build a better relationship himself.

Yao. When Yao, a bright young Asian man, went to work for a moving company, he was assigned to work with José on a moving van. Yao was a community college graduate who hoped eventually to get into management. José was a high-school graduate with over three years' experience in the moving and storage business.

Yao learned quickly that José was an outstanding worker with excellent skills, but he didn't like to talk much. In fact, José communicated only when it was necessary to get the job done.

After two months of working as a team, Yao could stand the silence no longer. Having made many attempts to get a light conversation going, Yao concluded that José did not like him and had a lot of deep-seated hostility toward Asian people. Yao's need to converse just made him bitter about the situation. Should he ask for a transfer? Should he resign?

As Yao thought about what he could do to get José to talk with him, he decided to ask José to join him after work at a small Latino pub near José's home. Yao learned a lot about José that night. José had been pushed around by many people. He did not feel accepted. His silence was more a defense than anything else. But what got to Yao was the fact that José felt that Yao was against him, and not the other way around.

The discussion was a revelation for both Yao and José, and much of the tension that had been present on the job was gone the next day. They had learned how to communicate and, as a result, became a better team. Yao and José didn't become personal friends, but they gained a high degree of mutual respect.

Communication enhances understanding

Avoid Judging Others. There are many relationships ahead of you that will involve people from different ethnic backgrounds. These relationships will not always be easy to build and maintain. Sometimes they may demand more perception than you possess. Yet, if you are open, honest, sincere, and willing to talk, your chances of building sound MRT relationships are excellent. Keep in mind, though, that discussions of religious, political, and cultural differences do not belong in the workplace. If you judge others in ways they do not wish to be judged, they may do the same to you.

ACTIVITY

My Plan: Ethnic Implications

In the space provided, describe at least one way you can avoid and/or address factors associated with ethnic implications and move toward understanding and building better relationships.

SEXUAL OVERTONES AND HARASSMENT

Working relationships between employees frequently contain sexual overtones. For the most part, this sexual tension is not dangerous and has little important influence on productivity one way or the other. But not always. Take the case of Judy.

Judy. Judy was attracted physically to her supervisor from the moment he was transferred to her department. A perceptive observer would have noticed that immediately she started wearing the best clothes in her wardrobe. She became more particular about her makeup. She started working harder to win the favor of her new boss and to create more opportunities to talk with him on business matters.

The other women in Judy's department quickly sensed the sexual overtones to the relationship, and their positive attitude toward Judy began to cool. They became more distant, less willing to help her, and less tolerant of her mistakes. It didn't take long for a certain strain to develop among all the employees in the department, and productivity began to suffer.

Judy's case raises a very difficult question: What are the human-relations dangers involved in dating someone where you work?

There is little danger involved, provided that the individual is not your supervisor, she (or he) works in a section separated from yours, and you are smart enough to keep your business and personal worlds separate. Under these circumstances, management will probably be very understanding.

Personal relationships at work can impact productivity

Be Cautious of Personal Relationships at Work. There are some real dangers, however, when working relationships have sexual overtones. Most will occur in the following ways: (1) when a supervisor dates someone in his (or her) own department, immediate cries of favoritism are raised and productivity is lost; (2) when two people—especially if they are in the same division—do not keep their business and personal worlds separate, relationships with others are hurt and eventually productivity is lowered; and (3) when one or both parties become involved or get married, a sticky situation is created that can produce harmful gossip, reduce productivity, and sometimes make it necessary for management to intervene.

Before you create or engage in a personal relationship where you work, you should also consider the chance of a later breakup between the two of you. Even a friendly breakup could be awkward, but worse, it could hurt both people involved and leave bad feelings among fellow employees who were in on the matter and took sides.

Sexual harassment involves something beyond natural overtones. Sexual harassment in the workplace is behavior of a sexual nature that causes a coworker to be uncomfortable and has a negative impact on productivity. In most cases, sexual harassment is more than one isolated incident. Rather, it is behavior pursued in a deliberate way over a period of time.

There are three forms of harassment:

- *Verbal.* Examples are telling risqué jokes, commenting on one's sexual anatomy, pursuing an unwanted relationship, and asking for sexual favors.

- *Visual.* Examples are wearing suggestive attire, staring at someone's anatomy, flirting nonverbally, and sitting in a revealing position.

- *Physical.* Examples are touching, standing too close, giving a "too lengthy" handshake, and excessive hugging.

Sexual Harassment Is Unacceptable Behavior. Sexual harassment violates the law in many countries and inhibits work performance. Victims can be male or female, a manager or subordinate, a vendor or customer. When an individual believes she (or he) is being sexually harassed, the following steps are recommended: (1) take your complaint to your immediate supervisor; (2) provide the specifics and dates involved; (3) document any further harassment while waiting for the supervisor to correct the situation; (4) if further action is necessary, file a formal complaint with the director of human resources or a superior other than your immediate supervisor; and (5) if the source of the harassment happens to be your supervisor, the first step should be to speak to your supervisor's superior.

ACTIVITY

My Plan: Sexual Overtones and Harassment

In the space provided, describe at least one way you can avoid and/or address factors associated with sexual overtones and harassment and move toward understanding and building better relationships.

AGE DIFFERENCES

The new employee who is young, capable, and ambitious is faced with a peculiar challenge in most organizations—and it doesn't take long for the challenge to occur. You hear it expressed in many ways:

"I could have had that last promotion if I had had more seniority."

"Everyone in this company has age, seniority, or experience beyond mine. I'll never get a chance. I'm wasting my time and ability. I won't get a chance to show what I can do until I'm thirty."

"I think I'll grow a mustache, so I'll at least appear older."

Young Employees Sometimes Feel Handicapped. Many employees between the ages of eighteen and thirty consider their youth a handicap. Some feel that they must put in time to reach a certain age level before they will be given a chance to demonstrate their ability. In a few cases, the situation becomes aggravated because the employee appears younger than he (or she) actually is.

It is easier to understand having a youth-discrimination attitude if you put yourself in the place of a young employee. When she (or he) sees older, more experienced employees everywhere, she may begin to feel that the generation gap is wider inside a business organization than outside. Because she wants to make progress to enhance her career, and doesn't want to wait, the pressure builds.

Yet, it is not unusual today to find young supervisors in charge of employees many years their senior. No doubt, some young people have the human-relations skills to compensate for their youth.

Take the cases of Laurel and Leonardo as examples.

Laurel. Laurel manages a trendy fashion department in a major department store. The department had sales of over $1 million last year. Laurel, who just turned twenty, supervises nine full-time people, all of whom are at least twice her age. The problems are constant and the pressure is great. But, without exception, the older workers consider her an excellent manager, and her boss feels she has a great future.

Leonardo. Leonardo, twenty-three years old with one year of college behind him, is the manager of a large, popular restaurant. Two of the three managers who work under him are much older than he, and one is old enough to be his father. In fact, most of the regular employees are older than Leonardo. The establishment is open twenty-four hours a day, and the problems never end. Under all this pressure, Leonardo still seems to be on top of everything. The president of the chain feels that Leonardo is just getting started.

Good human-relations skills go a long way to bridge employee age gaps

How do young people like Laurel and Leonardo do it? They demonstrate early that they can accept and handle responsibility. They demonstrate that they can make mature decisions. They demonstrate great personal confidence. But most of all, they demonstrate skills in human relations. They show that they can build strong MRT relationships with older and more experienced employees and management personnel, as well as with people their own age. The fact is that your more mature fellow workers will not resist your progress if you go about it in the right way. Rather, they will want you to succeed and will be willing to help you.

Appreciate and Respect Mature Workers. Your decision, then, is a simple one. If you are ambitious, you can either drift along until you are older and have more experience or you can face the human-relations challenge now and speed up your progress. If you decide to make the effort, there are, among others, two important rewards you should provide in building a relationship with a more mature, experienced person: 1) appreciation and 2) respect.

Everyone, regardless of age, likes to be noticed. Older employees, especially, like to receive compliments (even if the compliments border on flattery). They like to feel that they are still important as employees and as people. They need to feel appreciated and respected. They like to receive credit when due.

A more mature person often likes to keep a young image. Any action that tends to make a mature person feel out of touch or out of date is a mistake. Try to make him (or her) feel that he still has a lot to offer, that he is part of today's world, not yesterday's. Make a big effort to keep the communication lines open at all times. Do not isolate yourself from this person. Seek his advice. Always include him in your plans for any job-related social activities. Remember, you cannot expect a good vertical relationship with him—should you become his supervisor later on—unless you build a good horizontal working relationship with him now.

Perhaps the most important aspect of building good relationships with mature employees is learning how to gain their respect. Thus, demonstrate your ability, hard work, and reliability on a day-to-day basis. Deeds will do more than words. Statistics will do more than promises. Performance will do more than flattery.

Appreciation and respect have no age limitations

More than anything else, learn from this person. Her (or his) additional years of experience have taught her many things that you can learn without having to experience them. You can learn through osmosis. Then, if the time comes for you to move ahead of her, give her credit for making it possible. Let her have the satisfaction of calling you her protégé. Let her take pride in your success.

It will be wise of you to keep your relationship on a formal basis until she gives you the signal to be more relaxed and personal.

Generation Differences Present Challenges. It is also an important responsibility of older employees to help newer workers. How can the mature worker build better relationships with the new, younger employee? It is a difficult question to answer, especially because of generation differences that affect relationships on and off the job. Differences in generations (which include one's values as well as the way one implements goals and interests) frequently change. And to complicate the generation differences are the gaps that exist between generations. For example, the under-twenty-five age group is much more concerned with individuality and a "shorter-term" future than are people in groups representing fifty-plus generations. In general, older generations are more "we" oriented and have "longer-term" goals.

Even with such vast differences in generations, there are many steps that can be taken to build strong relationships across generational gaps. Here are three that will be greatly appreciated: (1) be patient with new employees' adjustment problems; (2) learn from them and help them learn from you by sharing your experience with them; and (3) initiate communication, and, if needed, give them the confidence to communicate with you.

ACTIVITY

My Plan: Age Differences

In the space provided, describe at least one way you can avoid and/or address factors associated with age differences and move toward understanding and building better relationships.

IRRITATION THRESHOLD

Relationships are frequently endangered because one of the individuals has an irritating habit or mannerism that bothers the other. Here are some common ones:

- Harsh or loud voice
- Irritating laugh
- Overbearing manner
- Constant name dropping
- Constant talk about money
- Constant reference to sex
- Telling dirty or unfunny stories
- Overuse of certain words or expressions
- Constant discussion of personal problems
- Constant bragging about successes off the job or the successes of their children
- Having an opinion on everything
- Dominating conversations, especially in meetings

Whether or not a habit or mannerism becomes an irritant depends upon the threshold or tolerance level of the second party. If one party has a high enough threshold, he (or she) may not even notice something that might bother someone else. However, it is possible for an individual to have a very low threshold for a certain mannerism. In the case of a low tolerance threshold, the habit can do considerable damage to the relationship.

Tolerance is a valuable human-relations skill

Diann. Diann is an excellent example of a young employee who hurt her relationship with a few fellow workers because of a nervous giggle that followed almost every sentence she uttered. Unfortunately, Diann had no idea what was happening. She was not conscious of the habit or of the fact that it was hurting her relationships with certain people who had low irritation thresholds. One day, after getting a complaint from a good employee who worked next to Diann, the supervisor had a talk with Diann about her nervous giggle. Thanks to some very hard work on Diann's part, the irritating mannerism all but disappeared in a few weeks.

Once the individual knows about them, bad habits usually can be modified and sometimes eliminated. But the person at the other end of the relationship must not expect too much too soon. In some cases, it may be necessary to learn to live with certain irritants by making an attempt to raise one's tolerance level. Seldom do such irritants come from only one side of the relationship. Almost all of us have at least a few mannerisms or habits that bother other people. The individual, even in the business environment, retains the right to remain pretty much the way she (or he) is. Some adjustment on your part to such factors will be necessary in most relationships. Tolerance, obviously, is a human-relations skill that must be developed.

ACTIVITY

My Plan: Irritation Threshold

In the space provided, describe at least one way you can avoid and/or address factors associated with irritation thresholds and move toward understanding and building better relationships.

Summary

Work relationships present considerable challenges primarily because of the various characteristics associated with each unique relationship. While there are many relationship characteristics, some can be isolated. Focusing attention on understanding the major characteristics that represent human-relations competencies can provide greater objectivity in creating, maintaining, and repairing relationships. The following six characteristics or areas deserve your attention for greater human-relations competency:

1. The mutual-reward theory should be practiced on a regular basis to maintain healthy relationships.

2. Because value conflicts can impede a relationship, appreciate the values others hold.

3. Relationships built on trust will maximize diversity and minimize ethnic implications.

4. Avoid being caught up in sexual overtones and harassment that can harm otherwise good relationships.

5. Capitalize on the opportunities that age differences can bring to a productive work relationship.

6. If you have habits that are irritating to others, make the necessary adjustments to change them.

No doubt you will be most successful, over the long term, in creating, maintaining, and repairing relationships if you consistently practice the premises of the mutual-reward theory. Also, it is extremely important to develop a keen appreciation that your human-relations success depends on how you view other people—that is, respecting all people regardless of their values, ethnic origin, age, and similar factors. Giving others respect is basic to how you will be treated.

Test Your Understanding

Respond to the following items to test your understanding of the chapter.

Part A: Circle the correct answer (T = True; F = False) for each of the following statements.

T F   1. The relationship between two people can often be better understood if isolated from the personalities who create it.

T F   2. For the most part, mutually rewarding relationships do not include the benefits people get from each other.

T F   3. With the increased focus on international business, the world has become a "mosaic" of diverse cultures working together.

T F   4. Many relationship overtones can exist without having any negative effect upon productivity.

T F   5. There are certain dangers involved when it comes to dating people at work; one is when a supervisor becomes personally involved with someone in his (or her) department.

Part B: Circle the letter of the correct answer for each of the following items.

6. One of the basics of a good relationship lies in (a) sharing common interests, (b) imposing your values on others, (c) discussing lifestyles, (d) aligning your cultural and political views with others.

7. The most important aspect a young person can develop to build a relationship with a more mature person is (a) promise favors, (b) talk about personal interests, (c) flatter the person, (d) gain the person's respect.

Part C: Write a short response to demonstrate your understanding related to the following item.

8. Discuss what you should do to maintain a good relationship with a coworker who has a habit or mannerism that bothers you.

Turn to the back of the book to check your answers.

> Your attitude,
> like the small flame
> of a candle,
> can have an illuminating effect.

Think and Respond

Respond to the following items with two or three complete sentences.

1. Define and describe the significance of the mutual-reward theory.
2. Describe one of the most fundamental of all human-relations skills.
3. Discuss two forms of sexual harassment.
4. How can you build a working relationship with someone much older/younger than you?
5. What is meant by an "irritation threshold"? Give an example.

Evaluating a Personal Relationship

It is extremely difficult for two people to discuss and evaluate the relationship between them. There are many reasons that this is true. (1) It takes a high degree of personal confidence to initiate such a sensitive conversation. (2) It is difficult to evaluate the relationship without being overcritical about personalities. (3) Sensitive points from the past might surface. (4) Damage might occur if one or both persons take the results too personally.

Carefully select a person with whom you already have a healthy relationship. Close friends, spouses, and children seem to work best. Also, select an individual who has the time and will take the evaluation procedure seriously. Once the second person has agreed to participate, give a copy of this form to the individual to complete. While she (or he) is doing this, complete one yourself.

Relationship Evaluation Form

Using the scale of 10 to 1, circle the number that indicates the state of the factor under consideration.

1. There is a high level of humor in this relationship.

   10 9 8 7 6 5 4 3 2 1

   This relationship needs more humor.

2. There is 100 percent two-way communication in this relationship.

   10 9 8 7 6 5 4 3 2 1

   There is almost no communication in this relationship.

3. There is a total absence of tension in this relationship.

   10 9 8 7 6 5 4 3 2 1

   There is considerable tension that needs to be eliminated.

4. There are no irritating mannerisms involved.

   10 9 8 7 6 5 4 3 2 1

   There are a number of irritating mannerisms that need to be discussed.

5. I feel free to go to this person to discuss mutual problems.

   10 9 8 7 6 5 4 3 2 1

   I cannot discuss mutual problems with this person.

6. The mutual-reward theory (both parties going partway) works 100 percent in this relationship.

   10 9 8 7 6 5 4 3 2 1

   I feel I am doing far too much of the giving in this relationship.

7. There are no listening problems in this relationship—both parties listen.	10 9 8 7 6 5 4 3 2 1	There are some real listening problems in this relationship.
8. This relationship has shown substantial improvement recently.	10 9 8 7 6 5 4 3 2 1	This relationship has deteriorated recently.
9. There is no conflict because of age difference.	10 9 8 7 6 5 4 3 2 1	There is something of a generation gap.
10. All previous misunderstandings have been resolved.	10 9 8 7 6 5 4 3 2 1	There are still some misunderstandings to be resolved.

Total Score_____

When both of you have completed the form individually, sit down and discuss the differences openly. Through the discussion, insights can be gained and improvements made. Those who have completed this exercise have rated its value highly. In fact, most stated that their relationships improved as a result of the exercise. The statement "we learned to understand each other better" was common.

> *"Appreciation is like an insurance policy—it needs to be renewed now and then."*
>
> Anon

CASE 9

Currency

"What's in it for me?"

When it comes to his career, Sam deals in only one currency, and that is money. Sam, in his late twenties, wants big bucks, and he wants them fast. Human relations and compassion (other forms of exchange) have no appeal to Sam.

You can read Sam's attitude in his movements. He appears totally confident, and he seems to know how to be aggressive at just the right time. As a result, many of his friends and coworkers envy him for the job opportunities that he is bound to have offered to him.

A quiet dissenter is Ralph, a forty-year-old coworker and good friend of Sam. Ralph feels money is important, but that financial rewards come to those who select career paths that contribute to the lives of others as much as to those who take a direct, megabucks approach. Ralph made this comment to Sam yesterday: "You're going to make it fast, Sam, but I think I will be happier getting to where I'm going. And, who knows, I might wind up with as much money as you while my personal values remain intact. I think you are sacrificing human-relations values for the dollar, and in real life this is not necessary."

Sam replied: "It's a jungle out there, Ralph. It may be possible that you end up rich and happy, but it seems like a slim chance to me. You and your values will get pushed around so much that you will be sidelined as far as money is concerned. I can worry about values after I have it made!"

A. Discuss: How would you reply if you were part of this conversation? Would you side with Sam or Ralph? How do you intend to maintain your personal values and still enjoy monetary success?

B. Expand Your Understanding: Identify two prominent, successful individuals who seem to represent the differences in thinking similar to Sam and Ralph, respectively. Research their backgrounds to identify the elements and characteristics of their lives that have contributed to their success. Pay particular attention to the way each has developed his (or her) human-relations skills and how age differences (and generation differences) may be influencing each person's perspective. Back up your research with documentation (sources from magazines, books, the Internet, etc.) and draw some conclusions that will be of benefit to you as well as to Sam and Ralph.

PART III

Maximizing Your Relationships

CHAPTER 10

Your Success as a Team Player

"I cooperate with everybody."

Thought for the Day: Believing in yourself and others is the best faith one can have to achieve realistic goals.

PERFORMANCE COMPETENCIES

- Understand the importance of teams and the three essential requirements for team membership.

- Identify the elements that contribute to harmony and success of teams with diverse membership.

- Appreciate the value of the mutual-reward theory in creating effective, productive work teams.

- Evaluate the attitude factors needed by team members and the ways team membership contributes to relationship building.

In another chapter we took a close look at the various elements often found within a working relationship. We gave recognition to the possible presence of value conflicts, irritating mannerisms, sexual overtones, age differences, and ethnic implications. We also introduced the mutual-reward theory (MRT) as a way to build and maintain healthy relationships under all conditions.

In this chapter, we focus on how these elements take on more importance for you as a member of a working team. In the typical, traditional department, the supervisor is at the top of the pyramid. She (or he) manages or controls the operation from that position and assumes responsibility for results. Hopefully she welcomes suggestions and often involves employees in decision making, but adheres to the philosophy that most employees need frequent, steady supervision.

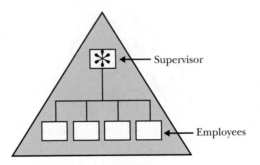

Under the team concept, the supervisor operates within the team itself. He (or she) takes time to involve members in the formation of goals. He delegates authority and considerable responsibility to the team. He communicates frequently and assumes that team members like to, or at least will, manage themselves.

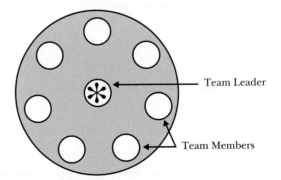

Anyone who participates in a team sport learns that success depends upon the contributions of all members. It is one for all and all for one. The pressure to produce comes more from other team members than from the coach. Most important of all is the way individual members work together. A good team member is anxious to make another member a star, providing that the team itself wins. Mutual-reward theory operates at a higher level in a successful team than it does in a traditional department.

The team concept in industry is more popular today than ever before. There are volumes of books on the subject, and team-building seminars are prevalent all across the country. Many corporations are retraining traditional supervisors to become team leaders. Why all this emphasis? Because there is evidence that work teams often achieve greater productivity than that of traditional departments.

Teamwork and work teams are essential to most organizations

TEAM MEMBERSHIP ESSENTIALS

As a team member or potential team member, what should you learn so you will be an outstanding team player? Here are three basic requirements for you to follow.

Promote the Four Cs of Teamwork

A successful, highly respected team member accepts and promotes the four Cs of team membership.

- *Conform to all decisions made by team members.* While you should actively participate in team discussions and decision making, it is extremely important to a team's success that you give your support to the final solutions and recommendations that are identified and agreed upon by the team. Team members may not always agree on the team outcomes, but the most successful teams are those whose members support the team's final decisions.

- *Cooperate with other team members without undue conflict.* Cooperation doesn't mean that there won't be disagreement. But because you have a responsibility to contribute to your team's success, your cooperation is critical to both the team's outcomes and the relationships you build with fellow team members.

- *Contribute talents without holding back for selfish reasons.* That is, your contribution should always be focused on the success of the team. Taking a win-win approach to your team's charge leaves no place for selfishness.

- *Collaborate with another member on a creative idea regardless of who receives more recognition for success.* When team members share and expand upon each others' ideas, team synergy occurs. An effective team is usually one with a high degree of synergy that has resulted from collaborative efforts and a good exchange of ideas among team members.

The four Cs of team membership communicate how team members can control their behavior so that all actions are in the best interest of the team as a whole. The four Cs of team membership also need to be accomplished with enthusiasm, self-discipline, and little supervision. It is not always easy to be a productive member of a work team, but it will be to your advantage to learn to be a good team player.

Be Sensitive to Team Member Needs

To be effective, a team must have a leader who is sensitive to the needs of the team members. It is the team leader who can create a working environment in which everyone wants to contribute. That is, as a team member, you must understand the role of your team leader and give her (or him) your full support even when mistakes are made. If you complain about your leader, you may also be criticizing your team, which means you are criticizing yourself.

Use the Team Approach Appropriately

Not all work environments are suitable for the team approach, nor can teams accomplish all work outcomes. You may be preparing for a career in which only parts of the team concept are applicable. For example, fast-food operations may have such frequent turnover of personnel that there is not enough time to form a group into a team. In contrast, in a research department in which a high level of creativity is needed, the team approach may be almost mandatory. Both examples point to some of the advantages and disadvantages of teams—but neither example ultimately may offer the best approach. That is, in fast-food operations, many job responsibilities are independent of each other and the team approach is critical for each person to carry out his (or her) job responsibilities for a successful outcome. However, a research department may not be productive if too many creative people (on a team) try to focus on identifying an appropriate, timely course of action.

Productivity relies on worker interrelatedness

Most organizations expect employees to be productive both as individuals and as team members. Employees who learn how to be successful team players will better appreciate the interrelatedness of worker productivity. Whether employing a traditional approach, a team approach, or some combination approach, management's goal usually is to maximize working together for high productivity.

Each work environment and situation should be studied by management to determine which approach—the pyramid, the circle, or a blend of both—will produce the best results. Regardless of where you might wind up as an employee, the more you learn about both traditional and work-team styles the better.

How would you rate yourself as a team member? Completing the activity that follows may provide you with some insights.

ACTIVITY

Rate Yourself as a Team Member

This exercise will give you an idea of just how good a team member you are or may become. Simply place a check (✓) in the appropriate box opposite each question and total your points at the end. Give an "Excellent" rating five points, a "Good" rating three, and a "Weak" score one.

Question	Excellent	Good	Weak
1. How willing would you be to accept the fact that another team member might be stronger than you in a certain area?			
2. What would be your chances of maintaining a more positive attitude in a team versus working in a regular group or alone?			
3. What would be your chances of quickly resolving a human conflict in which you are involved?			
4. How good would you be at conforming, cooperating, and contributing when, in some cases, others may enjoy personal gain more than you?			
5. What would be your patience threshold in working with a team member who is slower than you?			
6. How receptive would you be to support a goal developed by your team when you hold a minority position?			
7. How would you rate yourself in terms of working effectively with team members from ethnic groups different from your own?			
8. How understanding would you be of members with a point of view different from yours?			
9. How well do you think you would accept a team leader who always takes time to see that all members participate in the decision-making process?			
10. How successful do you think you might be in keeping your ego from getting in the way of full cooperation with the team?			
Total Score _____			

If you scored 40 or more points, you show indications that you are or would be a sensitive and productive team member. A high score suggests you probably would like being on a team. If you scored between 30 and 40 points, you probably could adjust to team membership without great difficulty. If you scored below 30 points, you might be happier and more productive working in a traditional group or working alone. However, since teamwork is so important in a productive business environment, it may be in your best interest to work on improving your "weak" areas to develop good team skills.

WORKING ON A DIVERSE TEAM

We often hear that the right combination of talent among a team of people can produce synergy. That is, when everyone is working together, the team can produce a sum greater than the total of each individual operating alone. This is true.

Diversity can expand team perspectives

Good Relationships Promote Team Harmony. Teams that work in harmony (the best possible horizontal relationships) are those that win the awards. Also, teams made up of culturally diverse people frequently have broader perspectives than teams of employees who all have the same background.

Have you stopped to think about how culturally diverse your environment is? If you haven't, you may want to make some observations the next time you are standing in line on a campus, at a bank, at a fast-food restaurant, or at a post office waiting your turn. Recently, for example, at a post office, a line with the following six people was observed: a young Latin American mother with a baby, a middle-aged African American male, an Anglo male teenager, an Asian American female, and an elderly East Indian male. While you may find your experience very different, what is described here is very commonplace in many geographical areas of the world.

Now, let's consider such a scenario as a work team. Note from the following graphic that there is a high cultural mix of team members among the females and males that make up this work group.

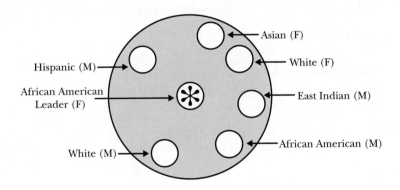

If you were to join this team, how comfortable would you be? What would you want to learn from the various members of this team?

Now assume, for a moment, that you are a team member and a new individual from another culture is assigned to your team.

How would you go about helping the new team member make the transition? What things might you do to help the new member become comfortable and contribute at a high level? For the following statements, check (✓) those that fall within your comfort zone:

❑ Explain the meaning of some of the common slang expressions, jargon, or idioms in your culture and how they may differ from those of other cultures.

❑ In a sensitive way, explain why a mannerism in another person's culture may differ from yours (e.g., handshake versus a hug).

❑ Discuss little things the newcomer can do to fit in and contribute to a team.

❑ Assist the individual in understanding how workers in your culture generally view leaders and supervisors. For example, explain when and how the newcomer should approach a leader for advice and guidance.

❑ Help a person understand business protocol where you work, and be generous in giving compliments when progress is made.

Your Goal Should Be to Build a Strong Team. Assist others, especially culturally diverse newcomers, to learn the work customs where you work. In so doing, you will enrich your own life because new employees never forget those who give them a helping hand when they need it most. You should, however, be aware of some pitfalls in over-identifying with new members. Your primary goal should be to strengthen the team, not just to build an enjoyable relationship with a person who has an intriguing foreign background. Further, if you go too far, one of two things may happen. First, the newcomer may become overly dependent on you or may not foster relationships with others. Second, if you spend too much time with a new team member, you may turn other team members against you or against the new team member.

Learn how to be effective on a culturally diverse work team

APPLYING THE MUTUAL-REWARD THEORY

The application of MRT is a successful way to create and maintain harmonious relationships in any environment. Its contribution to the success of a work team, when properly understood, can be exceptional. In many cases, work team rewards may be unevenly distributed at the beginning. But when the team wins, everything is balanced out. For example, a new team member may need to back up more experienced team members at the start, as in the case of Gregg.

The mutual-reward theory contributes to team rewards

Gregg. When Gregg was invited to join a special team with a great reputation within his company, he was excited. Experienced members were most helpful during his transition period. But it didn't take them long to discover that Gregg was more interested in his own ideas than in listening to or helping others. As a result, he started to isolate himself.

When a senior member of the team invited Gregg to lunch, it became obvious to Gregg that he had violated an important team rule. The team member explained it to Gregg this way. "Gregg, it is my understanding that you were on the varsity football team in college and that you played the position of guard when your team was in possession of the ball. In short, you did the blocking for your quarterback and for those who carried the ball. As a newcomer on our team, your primary job is to block for others by helping them with their ideas. This doesn't mean you can't carry the ball now and then. You can! And when it happens, others will block for you. Your big job at this point is to help the team become a winner. You see, when the team wins, everyone shares in the rewards. When this happens, it doesn't matter what position you played."

Sometimes new team members forget that when they have an idea that needs support from others, the kind of blocking they receive may depend upon the quality of blocking they did for others when they were new to the team.

Strong work teams add value to an organization

Teams Provide Individual Rewards. There is little doubt that teamwork provides many advantages and opportunities to team members. Team members learn more about their coworkers. Teamwork provides a good opportunity for each individual team member to expand his (or her) expertise as a result of working with the other members of the team. Work units that otherwise may function well through isolated individual efforts can become cohesive work groups (e.g., teams) to give added value to their departments and organizations. Work teams that develop good camaraderie usually are happier workers than other groups that do not realize that there are many rewards associated with team building. Members of strong teams also are more likely to find satisfaction with their work environment and they frequently outperform other units by completing highly successful projects.

The fact is that, there are rewards in teamwork for everyone. Because every team member has a stake in the outcome, the accountability of the team depends on the contributions of each of its members. A team member who has contributed her (or his) best effort to the team should be proud of the outcome of a team's work. Satisfaction comes because a single individual's effort usually is enhanced with all members of the team contributing and building on the ideas and expertise of each other to achieve success.

In the long run, MRT works.

Work Teams Are Expected to Be Productive. Anyone who has been a member of a sports team of any kind probably has some valuable insights into what makes a work team successful. The more these insights are applied, the better. The comparison, however, can only go so far. Sports teams operate for only one season; then they can start over with some new members and a built-in goal of winning a conference. A work team, however, frequently does not have the luxury of starting over.

Work teams are expected to be productive. A team is established to accomplish a work project or set of tasks.

Just as an individual is responsible for his (or her) own personal productivity, a team also has responsibility for an outcome that will contribute to a department or unit—and to an organization. Teams that are not focused on their charge will not be successful in the long run. For this reason, an organizational team must create goals from within and provide its own rewards. While team autonomy offers a challenge to be responsible and to head in the right direction, the team assumes considerable power and authority in its ability to manage itself. No doubt, such teams can experience the thrill of winning because they have charted their own destiny.

TEAM ATTITUDE FACTORS

A Positive Attitude Promotes Team Success. Success as a team member depends heavily upon the attitude of each of the team members. That is, each individual's attitude toward the team is critical to the way a team works together.

All teams are different. They may work on creative matters, production, service, and so on; but no team can function at its highest level if even one member has a consistently negative attitude. Regardless of the type of team, its composition, and its leadership, there are attitude factors that must be present among all team members. Here are a few:

A work team's success is only as good as its weakest member

- *Enthusiastically accepting the team concept as an organizational form.* If you support such ideas as supervising yourself and working un selfishly for the team, you do so not because you are expected to contribute your best, but because you want to do your best.

- *Accepting the four Cs (conforming, cooperating, contributing, and collaborating) of team membership.* As a team member, you will achieve because you will achieve more for your firm than would be true if you were an independent worker.

- *Undertaking the responsibility of self-discipline.* By using self-discipline, you recognize that your team leader has a less demanding style than would be the case in a traditional department.

- *Keeping your own attitude positive and upbeat.* Your good attitude will help your other team members to be positive. Team spirit can do wonders for productivity.

- *Being willing to put your career temporarily in the hands of the team.* Your future is somewhat determined by how other team members perform. Many a professional sports star has had a modest career because she (or he) was a member of a nonwinning team.

- *Realizing that the contributions of other team members may be different from yours.* It is the blending of talent and abilities that can give a team power.

- *Maintaining an open attitude toward people of diverse cultures.* An unprejudiced attitude toward all team members, regardless of cultural and other differences, is essential for effective teamwork.

- *Realizing that a good team leader has some of the attributes of a successful coach.* Your attitude toward your team leader—a key individual—is crucial.

Teamwork Contributes to Relationship Building. Any time a person becomes a part of a team effort, that individual has an excellent opportunity to expand and reinforce his (or her) good human-relations skills. Team processes lend themselves to greater interaction that is otherwise not possible in a work environment. That is, individuals who come together as a team can establish ground rules for how they will work together. Team members can tap the expertise of each of the members to form themselves into a productive, cooperative team. A team can generate ideas that can be discussed, expanded, reduced, and focused into a workable plan for solving problems. A team can assess its progress and successes throughout the life of a project. No doubt, the potential for building relationships throughout the entire team process is excellent!

Relationship building is a team value-added factor

The merits of teamwork, especially from a perspective of building relationships, cannot be overemphasized. That is, each time a team comes together, team members build upon past relationships they have created. Each time a team meets, new relationships are created among the members of the team. Because it's up to each team member how those relationships are built, what a great opportunity a team provides for you to become better at projecting your positive attitude while building strong, healthy work relationships!

Summary

Teams and teamwork are becoming increasingly important to organizations because management knows there are benefits associated with group project management and productivity. To promote team effectiveness and bias success for the team, it is essential for team members to understand the three basic requirements of team membership—(1) the four Cs of teamwork, (2) a sensitivity to member needs, and (3) appropriate use of a team.

Management also knows that being a team member can present many challenges both to a supervisor and to team members, especially in a diverse workplace. The rewards, however, of building strong, diverse teams based on the mutual-reward theory can be extremely beneficial to all. With a greater understanding of human relations and attitude factors, workers can be more successful as individuals (including supervisors and workers) and as team members. It follows that the more successful you become as a team player, the more successful you will be at building good relationships. No doubt, your positive attitude will be reflected in your increased skill in human relations; and, as your positive attitude shines through, the more valuable you will be to an organization.

Test Your Understanding

Respond to the following items to test your understanding of the chapter.

Part A: Circle the correct answer (T = True; F = False) for each of the following statements.

T F 1. Those who prefer the traditional leadership approach feel that most employees prefer and require frequent and steady supervision to produce at their highest levels.

T F 2. Management's focus on utilizing teams is based on the promise of higher productivity.

T F 3. Usually, it is more difficult to be a team member than to be a regular employee.

T F 4. Those who have played team sports have insights that can give them an edge when it comes to being a member of a work team.

T F 5. Teams of employees with culturally diverse backgrounds usually have broader perspectives than teams made up of members with similar backgrounds.

Part B: Circle the letter of the correct answer for each of the following items.

6. The successful team member practices four essential Cs of team membership, which include the willingness to conform, cooperate, collaborate, and (a) compensate, (b) concentrate, (c) contribute, (d) control.

7. No team can function at its highest level if one team member (a) has a consistently negative attitude, (b) is focused on the team versus on individual productivity, (c) has a different cultural background, (d) is a higher producer than another team member.

Part C: Write a short response to demonstrate your understanding related to the following item.

8. Discuss some of the important attitude factors that team members should understand.

Turn to the back of the book to check your answers.

> Attitude is the rock
> upon which
> the foundation of team spirit
> is built.

Think and Respond

Respond to the following items with two or three complete sentences.

1. Discuss two of the basic requirements or essentials for teams to operate successfully.

2. Suggest at least two questions you can ask yourself to determine how effective you may be as a team member.

3. Explain the action you should take to help a team member of a culture other than your own successfully join your work team.

4. What does MRT mean in relation to team membership?

5. Discuss two "attitude factors" that every team member should practice.

Orientation of Employees from Cultures
Other than Your Own

The top management of your firm strongly supports the team approach and has highly qualified employees from all cultures. Your eight-member team serves customers both in person and by telephone. Recently when one of your team members was appointed to lead another area, you were assigned a young Japanese man who is new to this country. His educational background and job skills are excellent, but his use of the English language is weak. List the steps you would take to make sure he becomes a strong and respected team member within ninety days. Compare your suggestions to those at the bottom of the page.

1. _____

   _____

2. _____

   _____

3. _____

   _____

4. _____

   _____

5. _____

   _____

Here are five suggestions you can use to help orient a new member to your team as quickly as possible.

1. Introduce him (or her) at a special meeting where refreshments are served. Coach him ahead of time to give a short talk on his background and special skills.

2. Provide him with a weekly "sponsor" until he has worked closely with all seven members.

3. Meet with him on a daily basis to discuss any special problems he may be having.

4. Encourage him to take an "English-as-a-Second-Language course" (or you learn his language, especially if you will be working with others from the same culture).

5. Follow your company's policy manual on team reviews. For example, let him know he will have a progress review (and what it will entail and when it will take place). In thirty days, review his progress with him and, as appropriate, with other team members.

CASE 10

Controversy

"I treat everyone as an individual."

Justine and Zeke are two of the most vocal students in their university's organizational communication class. Although other members make significant contributions during discussions, everyone, including the professor, enjoys it when Justine and Zeke square off on controversial topics. Take yesterday as an example.

Justine stated that the essence of good human relations is to treat everyone as a separate and unique individual. "Each person deserves the same high level of treatment and respect given to others. It really doesn't matter about ethnic origin, religious preferences, sex, age, or education. All we need to do is to accept this one basic principle, and the world will immediately become a better place. What do you do if after giving a person fair and dignified treatment, he scorns you? Well, you can turn your cheek once or twice and then politely back away without changing your basic attitude. It is *continuing* the way you look at people from the start that counts."

Zeke replies in a quiet, patient voice. "I think it is wonderful that Justine is an idealist and believes that the more we treat people as individuals, never grouping them together, the better. But Justine's idea that one basic premise will change the world is simplistic. What we really need to do is evaluate people on their performance as producers and human beings, not on the color of their skin or background. It is what people do that is important, not what they look like or the way they dress. The real criterion is to treat people as individuals based upon what they are doing to make the world a better place for all of us."

A. Discuss: Assume that you would like to add a few sentences to either Justine's or Zeke's comments. What would you say?

B. Expand Your Understanding: Conduct the research needed to expand upon the three basic requirements for team members to understand and practice for team success. Find several Internet articles, as well as other resources from books, magazines, newspapers, and so on to support your premises relating to successful teams. Create a checklist of successful team elements, characteristics, and practices. Ask two or more human-relations directors, team leaders, or project managers to help you develop and refine your list. Once you have a solid list, rate yourself on the factors; then strive to improve any weak areas you identified.

CHAPTER 11

Emotional Intelligence: Managing Stress, Frustration, and Aggression

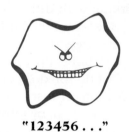

"123456 . . ."

> Thought for the Day: Permitting yourself to get upset, frustrated, angry, or aggressive is a condition that only you control.

PERFORMANCE COMPETENCIES

- Understand the causes of stress and frustration as well as appropriate ways to harmlessly release tension.

- Determine the roots and forms of aggression as well as the factors to help you avoid the pitfalls of aggressive behavior.

- Explain the frustration-aggression hypothesis and how you can put the hypothesis into practice.

- Appreciate the value of developing good emotional intelligence.

Minimizing the stress in your life undoubtedly contributes to your overall well-being and happiness. Because it is possible to learn techniques to manage your stress, it is a popular belief that stress reduction is inversely proportional to maintaining a positive attitude. That is, as your stress levels go down, your attitude becomes better. If you can identify and understand the elements that are causing your stress, and if you take appropriate action, you should be better able to avoid burnout.

This chapter introduces you to stress, frustration, and aggression. You will learn ways to help you to release tension caused by stress and frustration and ways to help you avoid aggressive behavior. You will also learn about the frustration-aggression hypothesis and the importance of good emotional intelligence, both of which can greatly assist you in understanding your own behavior and that of others.

STRESSED OUT? NOT ME!

Stress Affects Everyone. In this fast-paced world we live in, everyone faces tension and stress at some time or another. Stress can be viewed as the fever that comes with overwork, trying to reach too many goals at the same time, and working with difficult peers and superiors.

When you learn to release your tension harmlessly, you are lowering the fever by reducing the stress that has accumulated within you. For example, assume that you build up your stress to a level at which taking action is required. What do you do? You release the stress through some form of activity, recreation, or just getting away for a short time. Releasing stress lowers the fever. Then, by rebuilding yourself physically (through more activity), you also recover your positive attitude. In other words, one answer to burnout is being able to manage stress by releasing your tension without having to cut back on your productivity.

Stress and frustration cannot be avoided altogether

Frustration Is Normal. Everyone encounters frustrations in life. We learn to adjust to most of them easily without hurting our relations with others. Sometimes, however, a major frustration or series of frustrations may cause our feelings to heat up or even boil to the point at which we lash out verbally and seriously injure or destroy a relationship we deeply treasure.

Naturally, many disturbing experiences occur on the job. In fact, most of your frustrations may be job oriented. The mechanic who climbs under a car to do a repair job only to discover that he (or she) took the wrong wrench with him becomes frustrated. A supervisor who must get a report in before going home to an important dinner engagement must cope with feelings of frustration. Or your phone won't stop ringing when you need uninterrupted time to work on other things. You're asked to do "yet another" task when you are the busiest. Or a deadline is closing in on you just as the copier breaks down—the list of daily and frequent frustrations goes on and on.

Frustration is the feeling of disturbance or anxiety you experience when you meet a temporary block to your immediate goal.

The more important the goal is to you, the more intense is the disturbance. Major frustrations come about when something happens to keep you from reaching a goal that means a lot to you. While small frustrations can usually be eliminated quickly, major frustrations must often be controlled for days or weeks before an adjustment can be made. Controlling major frustrations may mean replacing one goal with another.

Blocked goals may result in frustration

Tension-Reducing Techniques. There are many acceptable ways a person can release inner tension due to frustrations. Here are a few.

On the Job

Regroup your thoughts (e.g., silently "take a step back").

Focus on a happy thought; relax and breathe deeply.

Clean up your desk.

Take a break; walk down the hall for a snack or water.

Talk things over with another person.

Make a list of office supplies you need.

Rearrange your work area to curb interruptions by passersby.

Listen to classical or relaxing, soothing music while you work.

Do some disagreeable or stacked-up paperwork.

Make a list of "to do" things you want/need to accomplish.

Off the Job

Do some physical exercise (e.g., workout at a gym; or clean a closet or the garage).

Play a computer game.

Go shopping, even if it's window shopping.

Prepare an exotic meal.

Rearrange some furniture.

Update your photo album.

Talk to a friend on the phone.

Trim some house or yard plants.

Read a magazine or book.

Play golf or go running.

Do some laundry.

Plan your next vacation.

Take your dog for a walk/run.

Sometimes just by "stepping back" and reflecting for a moment, some tension can be reduced. For example, take a short time-out to relax your tense muscles and think of someone you love (a child or other family member). Or think of something pleasant you enjoy doing (a favorite sport or lying on a sunny beach). Many people find that relaxing one's posture and taking some long, deep breaths—thinking only about breathing in and out, especially with your eyes closed—is an excellent tension reducer. Such an activity, done several times a day, can help you prevent tension buildup. Also, by doing something physical, you can release inner tensions and no one is hurt.

Frequently, it is more difficult to find acceptable ways to release inner tensions on the job than it is off the job. Let's say a worker became frustrated on the job and she (or he) was discourteous to a fellow worker. Such action demonstrates an unacceptable release of frustration. If, however, she walked away and calmed down, she would be releasing her frustration in an acceptable manner to avoid hurting her human relationships. Calming down when your tensions or frustrations are high is not an automatic response. Thus, it is to your distinct advantage to find some ways that can help you release your tensions and frustrations. When you use your good judgment and apply your tension-relieving strategies, especially in stressful situations, you mobilize some highly valuable tools to help you manage your stress. In so doing, you extend your ability to keep a positive attitude.

Find acceptable ways to release tension

ACTIVITY

My Tension-Releasing Strategies

In the space provided below, list several specific things you can do to release your tensions and stress. In the first column, suggest the tension-reducing action. In the second column, indicate where you can take the action—at work, at home, at both home and work, in particularly stressful social settings, and so forth. If you need more space than provided, add your ideas on a separate sheet of paper.

To help you get started on your list of stress-reducing strategies, consider this example: To release some tension at both work and home, just stop what you are doing, smile (no matter how forced your smile may be), and count to 10 (or 20). Count silently or even out loud (quietly or loudly) if you make sure nobody hears you. Also, refer to the list provided earlier for more tension-reducing ideas.

Tension-Reducing Strategy or Action	Where Action Can Be Helpful (Work, Home, etc.)
1.	
2.	
3.	
4.	
5.	
6.	
7.	

In addition to completing this activity, you may want to keep a list of your "Work Tension Relievers" at work (and a similar list at home) where you can access and review your list when you are calm as well as when you may be upset. In fact, in times of stress, you may find that you become calmer in the short time it takes you to take out your list—a good tension reliever in itself. Identify a strategy or action to reduce your tensions, stress, or frustrations. Include actions both for your "little frustrations" and also for when "your attitude really heats up." Good luck!

AGGRESSION AND ITS PITFALLS

Aggression Can Give Off Lethal Steam. Managing stress is not an easy task because you know you can't eliminate or always successfully address *all* frustrations that are part of life. So, now we must ask ourselves the big question: What happens when we become *really* frustrated?

Almost always, frustration leads to aggressive behavior, especially if frustration is not checked quickly or is not "tackled" in appropriate ways. When a steam boiler builds up too much pressure inside, some of the steam must be released. If there is no safety valve, the boiler will explode. Just as the steam boiler must release some of the pressure after it reaches a certain point, so must the individual. When a person releases pressure, it is usually in some form of aggressive behavior.

Aggression takes many forms. Take the case of the driver who becomes frustrated when he (or she) meets a slow-moving car on the highway. He may curse (verbal aggression) and drive on. Or he may pound on his horn and speed around the slow car (physical aggression). Or he could be so disturbed that when he returns to his office, he may refuse to speak to his assistant or coworkers (passive aggression).

Another example of aggressive behavior may be seen in a parent who becomes frustrated because of her (or his) small child. If frustration turns to anger and aggression, the mother may be tempted to slap her child, which would be an unacceptable release of aggression. However, if the parent releases her aggression physically by energetically shampooing the carpets or mowing the lawn and then disciplines the child in some other manner, it would be more acceptable. If the parent takes out her aggression on the carpets or lawn—not on the child— she has found a good release for her aggression.

Verbal aggression also can get a person into serious trouble. Lashing out at someone—no matter how much you do not really mean it—can do untold damage to your relationship with that person. Telling off a fellow worker or supervisor at the wrong time and place can destroy a relationship and cripple a person's progress toward career success.

Aggression of any kind frequently has damaging effects. Physical aggression, especially if it involves another person, is serious. It can be assault and battery and could mean a police record. So, learn to release aggression in acceptable ways without hurting relationships with others. There are acceptable forms of physical aggression and acceptable forms of verbal aggression.

It is necessary to release your anxious feelings occasionally. It is not always healthy for a person to keep his (or her) tensions bottled up. Some release is necessary and healthy. You would do well, however, to refrain from any kind of verbal aggressiveness on the job. It would be wiser to unburden yourself to someone you can trust outside the organization—your spouse, other family member, or a good friend.

Frustration can lead to many kinds of aggressive behavior

Aggressive behavior can quickly destroy strong relationships

Avoid Self-Victimizing.
Learning to live with frustrating experiences is not easy, but it can and should be done without being verbally aggressive on the job, without damaging our relations with others, and without victimizing ourselves.

Aggressive behavior resulting from inner disturbances and hostilities takes many strange forms. It's not always physical or verbal. It may be passive. In extreme cases, passive aggression takes the form of silence. Deliberate and planned silence on the part of the person who has been frustrated is a most potent weapon. Nothing is more uncomfortable to your fellow workers than your silence. Nothing destroys relations faster. No one can interpret your silence. All anyone can do is to leave you alone and wait; productivity usually suffers.

Silence is a form of passive aggression which is difficult to interpret

When a person takes out her (or his) inner aggressive feelings in silence, who is on the receiving end? Fellow employees? The supervisor? Although everyone suffers from silence of this nature, the silent person herself suffers the most. She is, in fact, taking out her aggressive feelings on herself. It is a form of self-victimization. Naturally, self-victimization is most destructive to the human personality. It is also juvenile. Many normal, mature people, however, temporarily react to a series of frustrations in this manner.

Avoid Corporate Aggression.
Another form of aggression—aggression toward your company—can be subtle and sinister. Aggression on the part of an employee toward the company for which he (or she) works has been the downfall of many career-minded persons. There is rarely anything personal about such a person's aggressive behavior. Such a person seems to get along well enough with fellow workers and immediate supervisors. Instead, the aggression always seems to be directed toward the company itself. Often, one hears expressions like these from such an individual:

"This organization does nothing but chew people up and spit them out."

"This company is so large that the only thing that keeps us from getting lost altogether is the computer."

"I'd put in for a transfer, but by the time it got through channels I'd be ready to retire."

Company aggression can severely damage your attitude and career

In a very real sense, it is frustrating to work in any organization. Some rules must be followed. Some degree of conformity is expected. Yet, an employee who nurses minor frustrations into aggressive behavior toward a large corporate structure is fighting a hypothetical monster, and it is counterproductive. When a person attacks the company, she (or he) starts to lose loyalty to it. And it begins to show in the employee's attitude—not overnight, of course, but in subtle ways that begin to hurt that person's progress in the company.

THE FRUSTRATION-AGGRESSION HYPOTHESIS

Hypothesis Damage Control. You may already have identified the premise of the frustration-aggression hypothesis from what you've read. However, a simple definition is in order: If you let frustration get out of hand, aggression usually will follow; and, if you let it intensify or if you "feed it," your aggression can grow in such magnitude that it will cause serious damage to you and your career.

To help you to understand the importance of the frustration-aggression hypothesis, read the following story about Shaneika, an intelligent, highly motivated person who let stress affect her life.

Shaneika. A well-educated young person, Shaneika joined a large utility company as a management trainee. She liked her job, and for two years her productivity and human relations were very good. She took advantage of every opportunity to learn. She received four salary increases.

One day, in talking to the director of human resources, Shaneika mentioned that she would like to qualify as an employment interviewer. The director, pleased with her success so far, encouraged her. He told Shaneika that she would be considered if an opportunity came along. Shaneika, more highly motivated than ever, continued to do an outstanding job and set her goal for the next opening as an interviewer.

Two weeks later, another person was promoted to the position of interviewer. Shaneika was not informed about the change. Not thinking that the plans for the personnel change might have been set before her initial talk with the director, Shaneika permitted herself to become deeply frustrated. She had set a goal for herself, and now they had selected another person.

"At least they could have talked to me!"

"Why should that person get the breaks?"

"So that's the way they keep their promises!"

Shaneika, without thinking it through, permitted her frustration to grow. Indeed, she set out to feed it by talking it over with a few fellow employees, which only intensified her feelings. What happened? Shaneika released her frustrations through verbal aggression. For the first time in her career, she sounded off in a highly emotional manner at a weekly staff meeting. She voiced more than her share of gripes during coffee breaks. And all of this found its way back to the department of human resources. The result was what you might expect: Shaneika, through her verbal aggressiveness, displayed her temper and immaturity; and she hurt her previously excellent relationships with others. Six months later, another position as an interviewer opened up and Shaneika was passed over.

What should Shaneika have done from the outset of her frustration until she learned the reason why she didn't get the promotion? Shaneika should have released her aggressive behavior outside her job until she discovered or rationally sought out the truth of the situation.

She could have spent more time playing her favorite sport or talking her problem over with a close friend. Or she could have vented her frustration by putting it into writing without showing it to others, a mechanism that seems to help a number of people. None of these actions would have injured her relations with others.

As a mature, mentally healthy person, you must seek and find acceptable releases for your inner aggression. You should conduct yourself in a manner that eliminates many of the frustrations of life. The fewer frustrations you have, the fewer times you will have to seek acceptable releases.

Take quick action so your frustrations do not turn into aggressive behavior

Putting the Hypothesis into Practice. It is hoped that the preceding discussion has given you a good understanding of the frustration-aggression hypothesis. To summarize, how can you put the frustration-aggression idea to work for you?

1. *Admit that your frustrations often produce aggressive behavior of some kind and learn to recognize them.* Once you recognize the frustrations that cause your aggressive behavior, you should work on ways to channel aggressive actions into acceptable outlets. Be careful to release your aggressions in the right way and in the right place. Keep from releasing them on the job in a way that will hurt relationships and your future.

2. *Recognize aggressive behavior in others (including executives).* Keep in mind that aggressive action by others is usually not directed toward you personally. You may just happen to be at the wrong place at the wrong time and the best available target for verbal abuse. You should try to accept such behavior as a natural outcome of uncontrollable frustrations and not overreact to it. An accepting attitude should make for all-around better human understanding. As a result, your relationships with people who express their aggression probably will not suffer as much as if you were neither aware nor sensitive to the factors that prompted their frustration-aggression behaviors.

3. *Be sensitive to your own verbal aggression, and be very cautious in group discussions and staff meetings.* When you need to release feelings verbally, do so to a friend outside the company and not to a fellow employee, thus protecting your work relationships.

4. *Don't let aggressive behavior keep you from reaching your ultimate goal.* When a detour is necessary, you should take it. When an unexpected block to your plans appears, accept it for what it is. If frustration occurs, release it in an acceptable way and come up with an alternative goal. Do not allow aggressive behavior to victimize you on a permanent basis.

BEING EMOTIONALLY INTELLIGENT

Understanding yourself and keeping your positive attitude have practical significance for maintaining good stress management. That is, the more you understand yourself, the better you will be at controlling and directing your emotions in positive directions. The result is that you are both aware of and able to manage your emotional intelligence, frequently referred to as EI or EQ.

Simply stated, emotional intelligence is how aware you are of yourself and how you interact with people. It is also how well you manage your emotions and social interactions. Because your self-awareness and interactions are linked to your behavior, your positive attitude plays a significant role in the success of your relationships.

Your EQ is important to positive relationships

EQ More Important than IQ? It may come as a shock to you that, today, many companies consider emotional intelligence (EQ) more important than both innate intelligence (IQ) and work knowledge (experience) combined. Why is EQ (or EI) so important and sought after by employers? Because EQ is critical to a person's well being, and it is directly related to your human-relations competency.

Over the decades, management has continued to assess employee behavior. The conclusion that comes from such assessments is this: the main reason people are hired, promoted, and fired is because of their human-relations skills—skills that reflect a person's EQ. Emotional intelligence has been proven to be a good predictor of employee success. In fact, many employers now require new hires to complete EQ assessments to assist them in the management-selection process. It is a costly endeavor to hire, train, and promote an employee for a management position; however, with EQ as a predictor of success, many employers realize that employees who demonstrate a high EQ are those who increase profitability for a company.

People who have a high EQ usually are good at identifying and understanding what causes their stress and frustrations. They are also better at managing their stress and frustrations than those who have not given attention to developing their human-relations skills. Because EQ can be learned and practiced, your EQ offers considerable value to your daily interactions with people. It is your EQ that helps you keep your attitude from heating up when obstacles get in the way. It is your EQ that helps you identify the things that cause stress in your daily life. It is also your EQ that helps you to understand the cause of your frustrations, to choose appropriate ways to reduce tension and stress, and to control your emotions that otherwise might turn into aggressive behavior.

Biasing Your Human-Relations Success. Developing a healthy EQ will help to increase your self-image and help you to become more aware of others' needs. Your EQ will help you maximize your interactions

Developing high EQ is an admirable goal

and relationships on and off the job. Your EQ also will contribute to your productivity because high producers frequently are happy people with positive attitudes and good emotional control.

Because your human-relations skills are directly related to your EQ, it makes sense to strive to achieve higher and higher levels of self-awareness. As you give attention to your self-management, you will get better and better at releasing your frustrations in ways that will not hurt you or others. The overall outcome, with practice and hard work, can be significant because you bias your chances of success in all your relationships.

Summary

This chapter has attempted to show you the importance of managing stress and why you should try to release your frustrations and tensions harmlessly. You learned four important facts:

1. Stress and frustration are part of everyone's daily life.
2. You can enhance your positive attitude and improve your relationships by identifying and practicing tension-reducing strategies.
3. You can make the frustration-aggression hypothesis work for you if you understand and ascribe to the underlying ideas and premises upon which it is based.
4. Good emotional intelligence needs to be a top priority or primary goal in your life for you to be able to meet your daily pressures head-on.

Continue to practice and periodically review your tension-reducing strategies (see activity, "My Tension-Releasing Strategies"). Frequently modify or add more strategies, especially strategies that can help you ward off potential aggressive behavior, and don't wait for a reason to take action. Finally, if you avoid aggressive behavior, self-victimization, and corporate aggression at all costs, you will have gained the emotional intelligence to create and maintain the positive, productive relationships that will further, not hinder, your career progress.

Test Your Understanding

Respond to the following items to test your understanding of the chapter.

Part A: Circle the correct answer (T = True; F = False) for each of the following statements.

T F   1. Every person experiences some degree of tension and stress at one time or another.

T F   2. Frustration is the feeling of disturbance or anxiety you experience whenever a personal goal is interrupted.

T F   3. It is easier to find harmless ways to release your frustrations (and aggressive behavior) on the job than it is at home.

T F   4. Self-victimization often occurs when you are mistreated by others.

T F   5. Understanding the frustration-aggression hypothesis helps a person avoid taking things personally.

Part B: Circle the letter of the correct answer for each of the following items.

6. Tension and frustrations caused by coworkers can frequently be reduced harmlessly if you (a) avoid contact with them for a considerable period of time, (b) redirect frustration to your supervisor, (c) become more aggressive, (d) do some physical activity.

7. Human relationships among coworkers can be harmed very quickly if a person (a) is sensitive to their needs, (b) tries to find ways to eliminate frustrations, (c) exhibits verbally aggressive behavior, (d) helps them get their work completed.

Part C: Write a short response to demonstrate your understanding related to the following item.

8. Describe what is meant by emotional intelligence.

Turn to the back of the book to check your answers.

> A positive attitude
> is the enemy
> of stress, frustration,
> and aggression.

Think and Respond

Respond to the following items with two or three complete sentences.

1. Contrast the differences and similarities between stress and frustration.

2. Give two general summary suggestions to release tension both (a) on the job and (b) off the job.

3. Discuss the meaning of aggression and ways to avoid and control it.

4. Describe two ways to put the frustration-aggression hypothesis into practice.

5. Why is good emotional intelligence so important?

Choosing Appropriate Ways to Release Your Frustrations Harmlessly

In this activity, you are to assume that your frustration-aggression level (threshold) has almost been reached and that you need a harmless way to let off steam. The idea is to release this steam without hurting or injuring your relationships with others. In short, you always have options. You can, at the "point of release," select a harmless (rather than harmful) form of behavior.

On the next two pages are two lists of possible things you might do at the "point of release":

(1) *if you are at work* or

(2) *if you are at home or away from work.*

Place a check (✓) in column 1 if you feel the action would be dangerous. By doing this, you automatically eliminate the possibilities in the other two columns.

If you do not place a check mark in column 1, then you should place one in column 2 to indicate that as far as you are concerned, the action is harmless; that is, it would not hurt relationships with others.

Next, check column 3 if you feel the action described is appropriate for you. In other words, this action would be natural and comfortable for you to do.

If you check both columns 2 and 3, you appear to have found a suitable and harmless way to release aggression caused by frustration.

Once you have completed the activity review your responses. Then come back to this page and write a summary about ways you believe are appropriate for you to release your frustrations without being harmful to you or others.

_____

_____

_____

_____

_____

Now, begin practicing your suggestions as soon as they are needed. Good luck!

Things to Do to Release Your Aggressions "On the Job"

RELEASES	(1) HARMFUL TO HUMAN RELATIONS	(2) HARMLESS TO HUMAN RELATIONS	(3) APPROPRIATE FOR ME
Slam a door where it can be heard.			
Slam a door where it cannot be heard.			
Blow up in front of your supervisor.			
Let off steam in front of a coworker.			
Count to ten under your breath.			
Move around physically.			
Take an unauthorized thirty-minute break.			
Go home sick.			
Swear so others can hear.			
Swear under your breath.			
Steal some company property.			
Make some personal phone calls.			
Rave about the good old days to anyone who will listen.			
Go to the restroom.			
Take an unauthorized coffee break.			
Tell your supervisor you feel faint, then go lie down.			
Write a personal letter on company time.			
Go to a bar and have a drink.			
Clean out your desk or do a task you don't like.			
Sulk silently where you are.			
"Dream" about something pleasant.			
Talk to yourself.			
Sing to yourself.			
Do a crossword puzzle.			
Let off steam to a coworker who sometimes uses you for the same purpose.			
Ask your supervisor for a raise.			
_____			
_____			
_____			

Things to Do to Release Your Aggressions "Off the Job"

RELEASES	(1) HARMFUL TO HUMAN RELATIONS	(2) HARMLESS TO HUMAN RELATIONS	(3) APPROPRIATE FOR ME
Listen to some music.	_____	_____	_____
Turn the music up and scream.	_____	_____	_____
Curse and swear.	_____	_____	_____
Slam doors all through the house.	_____	_____	_____
Cook a favorite dish/meal.	_____	_____	_____
Get drunk.	_____	_____	_____
Spill out your frustration to a neighbor.	_____	_____	_____
Spill out your frustration to a close friend.	_____	_____	_____
Yell at someone.	_____	_____	_____
Go jogging.	_____	_____	_____
Eat more than you should.	_____	_____	_____
Wash your car or clean your house.	_____	_____	_____
Throw rocks at the moon.	_____	_____	_____
Go shopping and buy some things you can't afford.	_____	_____	_____
Call someone on your cell phone and complain.	_____	_____	_____
Work in your garden.	_____	_____	_____
Do something nice for another person.	_____	_____	_____
Throw a party.	_____	_____	_____
Take a long drive.	_____	_____	_____
See a friend who is a good listener.	_____	_____	_____
Relax with a cup of tea and a good book.	_____	_____	_____
Get mad at yourself for getting frustrated.	_____	_____	_____
Give your pet some special attention.	_____	_____	_____
Play the piano.	_____	_____	_____
Take out your frustration on a family member.	_____	_____	_____
_____	_____	_____	_____
_____	_____	_____	_____
_____	_____	_____	_____

CASE 11

Frustration

"Me and my big mouth!"

As Allen thinks about the last two years of his life, it makes him angry. He's tired all of the time. In fact, it's a chore just to get up in the morning. He is bored with his programming job and he despises his Ms. Know-It-All boss. His coworkers aren't any better. And friends? Of course, he doesn't have any, thanks to his bitter divorce.

While riding the train to work, Allen thinks about what he has to do after work. That makes him angry too since he'll rush home and probably have to discipline his two kids for their falling grades, not doing their chores, and so forth. Miring down in self-pity about how things can't get worse, the little girl leaning over the seat in front of him spills her orange juice on his suit. That's it! He immediately jumps up and yells at the child and mother. The little girl starts crying. Even though the mother is very apologetic, Allen continues to give them both a piece of his mind—not an unusual behavior these days for Allen.

When the little girl cries "I want my Grandma," tears well up in the mother's eyes. The mother, looking extremely sad as if the weight on her shoulders is very heavy, tries to console her daughter. What Allen does not know is that the grandmother passed away last week and the little girl had been living with her grandmother for the past six months while the mother was recuperating from surgery.

A. Discuss: Was Allen justified in his outburst (with or without knowing the situation of the mother and little girl)? Besides his divorce, what is "growing" Allen's frustration? What can he do to get into a better frame of mind and reduce his stress?

B. Expand Your Understanding: Research the topic of emotional intelligence (EQ or EI). Include in your inquiry an understanding of Daniel Goleman's EQ four-quadrant model relating to awareness and management of yourself and your relationships. Back up your research with additional facts about various companies that use EQ measures in their hiring, management selection, and training practices. Draw some conclusions about your research and offer some additional suggestions (including a list of recommended reading and resources) that will be useful for you and Allen.

CHAPTER 12
Restoring Injured Relationships

"Some relationships are not worth saving."

Thought for the Day: Negative thoughts and actions are like toxic waste. Unless they are recycled into something positive, they can be detrimental to you and to everyone around you.

PERFORMANCE COMPETENCIES

- Appreciate the power and significance of communication in restoring a damaged relationship.

- Understand both the importance of repairing an injured relationship as quickly as possible and the negative consequences of not doing so.

- Identify four basic principles that can assist you in restoring a damaged relationship.

- Identify why relationship restoration strategies are based on "rebuilding willingness" and why there still may be challenges and risks associated with repair efforts.

No matter how skillful one becomes at building healthy and rewarding human relationships, a relationship can easily be damaged through insensitivity and misunderstanding by anyone in the relationship. Human relationships are fragile. Once an injury occurs, the restoration process can be like walking barefooted on broken glass; it can be difficult—even challenging—but not impossible.

In the work environment, damages occur when there is a misuse of power by leaders—for example, or when the behavior of one person toward another is less than honest; when there are breakdowns in communication; or for a host of other reasons, many of which are highly personal and unintended. The important thing to remember is that all relationships—both on and off the job—occasionally become damaged and need repairing.

THE POWER OF COMMUNICATION IN REPAIRING RELATIONSHIPS

Take responsibility to repair an injured relationship

Because communication is the lifeblood of any relationship, reopening communication lines should be the first step in restoring relationships. Which party initiates the communication is unimportant. Communication, in this sense, can be compared to using ointment to help heal a cut. The ointment (communication) by itself may not solve the problem, but it enhances the healing process. If neither party is willing to supply or apply the ointment, the wound may fester and eventually destroy the relationship.

Regardless of who may be at fault (often both parties are responsible), it is an effective human-relations practice to restore the relationship as soon as possible. Any lapse of time may seem to deaden the pain, but it can make restoration more difficult—and sometimes impossible. Those who move from one job to another, leaving a wake of broken relationships behind them, often pay a high price in many directions.

When a relationship is in need of repair work and nothing is done about it, everyone loses. That is why it could be to your advantage to initiate restoration even when you are not primarily responsible for the injury.

Nadia. Without intending to do so, Nadia let her emotions spill over last Friday and became testy with June, her favorite coworker. June, wounded emotionally, reacted with a huffy silence for the rest of the day. Nadia worried about the situation all weekend but failed to make repairs Monday. Early Tuesday, June initiated a discussion on the incident that gave Nadia an opportunity to apologize, and the relationship was restored. Although she was not at fault, June was not content to work in an uncomfortable climate, so she used her human-relations skills to restore the relationship.

Gilbert. Last week, Gilbert came down too hard on Harry over a minor work rule infraction. Harry, knowing Gilbert (his supervisor) would find it difficult to apologize, took action himself. On the following day, he said, "Gilbert, our relationship is important to me, so I want to keep communication lines open and eliminate any differences that may occur between us. I want to be relaxed and comfortable under your supervision. Is it a deal?"

WHY REPAIR DAMAGED RELATIONSHIPS QUICKLY?

The Toxicity of Unrepaired Relationships. Unfortunately, when a minor falling out between two people occurs, both parties may have a desire to nurse the hurt and pull farther away from each other. If an injured relationship is allowed to continue, some dangerous side effects may develop. For example, the possibility exists that the relationship between them may become more toxic and spill over into bad relationships with others.

Jillian. The rift that developed between Jillian and Jessie pushed Jillian into a negative rut. Some of Jillian's other relationships also seemed to turn sour with her negative change in attitude. Jillian started to ask herself such questions as: "Why should I work hard to build healthy relationships when others could care less?" "Why should I permit myself to be vulnerable to the hurts of others that are carelessly imposed upon me?" Unfortunately, the road selected by Jillian was to withdraw into her newly designed shell and become less of a team member on the job and less socially accepted in her personal world. Jillian made the classic human-relations mistake of permitting a repairable rift to develop into a major problem.

Communication is essential to relationship restoration

Can You Afford the Consequences of Slow Damage Control? Consider the following possibilities and consequences of not quickly repairing a damaged relationship:

- *Constructive "mind time" is lost.* Preoccupation with a relationship left unrepaired is self-defeating. Living day in and day out with an unhealthy relationship, especially with a supervisor, causes you to mentally reprocess the conflict over and over, thus stealing your "mind time" from more constructive pursuits. Those who permit conflict preoccupation to happen often put their career progress on hold or in jeopardy.

- *An already stressful situation is compounded.* Emotional conflicts in the workplace can be more stressful than long hours, heavy concentration on a special project, or other heavy job demands. Worst of all, emotional stress makes everything else more difficult. To maintain peace of mind and high personal productivity, restoration of broken relationships should receive top priority. When not given immediate attention, false inferences often compound the stress. Statistics continue to tell us that over 50 percent of all resignations come from unresolved human conflicts.

■ *Chances of becoming a victim increase.* In some work environments, a broken relationship left unattended can convert you into a victim. For example, a coworker with whom you previously enjoyed a healthy relationship suddenly begins to fear you may replace him (or her). As a result, this individual deliberately creates a conflict situation in the hope that you will be unable to deal with it effectively. If the supervisor does not step in as a mediator/counselor or if you refuse to take action yourself, you could easily wind up a victim. Your refusal to take action (even going to the supervisor with the problem) could give the coworker the upper hand he seeks; and, eventually, management could misinterpret the situation in favor of the other employee. Your failure to remove the feeling of fear through communication and restore the relationship to its previous state could cause you to become a victim.

Such possibilities, although remote, should motivate you to set the difficult goal of creating, maintaining, and repairing relationships, even when you would prefer to ignore the individuals involved or to carry out a vendetta against them. In many cases, your career may depend upon how effective you are in practicing good human-relations skills.

BASIC RELATIONSHIP-REPAIR PRINCIPLES

There are four principles or guideposts that may assist you in repairing a damaged relationship.

1. *See the connection between repairing relationships and career success.* A damaged relationship left unrepaired between you and a coworker or superior may reduce support you need at a later date. As a result, your upward mobility may be impeded. You have victimized yourself.

2. *Try to see behind the cause of the falling out.*   When one takes the time to study the causes of breaks in human relationships, it becomes obvious that often one party was under unusual pressure which precipitated the rift. It is easier to forgive when such causes can be identified. Through your own perception, try to see behind misunderstandings. Once you see why misunderstandings occur, your attitude toward rebuilding damaged relationships may be more positive.

A positive attitude maximizes the repair of an injured relationship

3. *Develop a willingness to rebuild damaged relationships.*   The more you nurse a resentment, the less effective you are in restoring a relationship. Some give-and-take from both sides usually is necessary for a satisfactory repair job. If one person is unwilling to listen, the process may never get off the ground. That is why some relationships are never repaired. Until you reach a point where your mind is open to the possibility of repair (regardless of

who did the damage), you have not reached the effective level of willingness.

4. *Design your own rebuilding techniques.* As you ponder just how you might initiate a rebuilding process, many questions will emerge. Can both people save face? If hostility and resentment are present, can they be dissipated through open communication so that the repair job is permanent? As you consider such factors, ask yourself these additional questions:

- Can you insert some humor into your approach?

- Can you be a better listener than a talker?

- Can you "give" as much as you expect from the other person?

- Can you accept some of the blame, even if you're not at fault, so the other person can save face?

ACTIVITY

"Breaking-the-Ice" Expressions

In restoring a previously healthy relationship, taking the first step is the most difficult. Assume that you and a coworker had a misunderstanding yesterday, and you *want* to clear it up quickly regardless of who might be at fault. Following are some expressions for "breaking-the-ice" that may lead to an open discussion that could help to restore the relationship. Select the three you like best by placing a check mark in the appropriate box. Then, write out two expressions you prefer over those listed.

- ❏ "Look, Marge, you have my apology for what happened yesterday."

- ❏ "Hi, Rolf. I just want you to know I am willing to forgive and forget the little incident yesterday. It really doesn't matter to me how or why it occurred."

- ❏ "Marge, our relationship is very important to me. I don't want what happened yesterday to come between us."

- ❏ "Rolf we've become a little irritable with each other recently. I think it is time we review our relationship. How about a cup of coffee?"

- ❏ "Our relationship isn't what it used to be, Marge. I think it is time to sit down and discuss the rewards we should be giving each other."

- ❏ "We've been rather short with each other recently, Marge, and yesterday things got out of hand. I'd like to take you to lunch and forget it. Okay?"

- ❏ _____

- ❏ _____

- ❏ _____

RELATIONSHIP-REBUILDING STRATEGIES AND RISKS

Are you willing to state openly that a relationship is important to you—important enough to forgive and forget what or who caused the damage?

Relationship-Restoration Strategies Once you feel your "willingness factor" is sufficient, consider these rebuilding strategies:

Rebuilding Strategy 1. If you were fully or partially responsible for the damage, swallow your pride and take the direct approach. Say you are sorry and say: "I would like to get our relationship back to its previous healthy state as soon as possible. You and our relationship are important to me, and I intend to be more sensitive in the future."

We all make human-relations mistakes. We always will. Unless we accept the premise that now and then we need to initiate a repair job, we will lose many significant relationships well worth keeping.

Rebuilding Strategy 2. If you were not responsible for the damage, give the responsible person some room to make repairs. That is, when the person at the other end of the relationship line makes the mistake (the reason is not important), give the person the opportunity to approach you to restore the relationship. Be accessible! Have an open mind! If the other person does not approach you in a reasonable length of time, take the initiative yourself. Taking the first step may sound like asking too much, but keep in mind that you may be getting hurt more than the person responsible. Why should you become a victim? Why not restore the relationship for your benefit? One way to employ Strategy 2 is to say: "That incident last week really got to me, Mia, and I'm bringing it up for discussion so that hopefully it won't happen again. If we don't work harder at maintaining our relationship, we will both wind up losers."

Rebuilding Strategy 3. When no one is clearly responsible for a rift, initiate a MRT (mutual-reward theory) discussion so that the rewards both people receive from the relationship can be reviewed. A MRT approach can help each person recognize how important the relationship has been in the past and can continue to be in the future. Only when rewards are somewhat equal do both people come out ahead. The win-win premise is the significance and the promise of MRT.

Exercise your willingness to rebuild a damaged relationship

If you show a willingness to restore an injured relationship, even though it may not have become damaged by any fault of your own, you are demonstrating a very important human-relations skill. Your willingness to "bury the hatchet" shows you value relationships that are strong and healthy. By taking a positive approach to relationship building, your rebuilding strategies are bound to be much more successful than if you tried a less positive alternative.

Initiating Restoration Is Not without Risk. Restoring a damaged relationship, however, is not without its challenges and risks. You may, for example, gather up your courage in a sincere effort to restore an important relationship, only to be rebuffed for your initiative. Consider what happened to Vijay.

Vijay. After two days of increased silence and tension on the job, Vijay approached his boss, Erin, to reconcile a communications misunderstanding. Erin responded by walking away. However, the following morning, Erin invited Vijay to lunch with her, and the relationship was fully restored. With time to think over Vijay's gesture, Erin had a change of attitude. The risk had been worth taking after all.

Why So Many Challenges? So why does relationship building present so many challenges? Because people differ and people change. And because relationships are built (and can become damaged) in so many different ways. For example, consider the array of differences in individual personalities, values, and preferences. There are vast differences, too, in the goals, wants, needs, strengths, and weaknesses of people. Also, there are significant age and generation differences as well as wide differences in ethnic and cultural morés that factor into relationship building. Many other differences in people relate to their communication styles, performance and productivity, and personal ideals, not to mention differences between various people's background, education, expertise, experience, and other factors. All in all, most people don't view things from exactly the same perspective—and thank goodness for that! Otherwise, the world would be rather dull!

Both relationship building and restoration are critical to our social nature. Yet, it is unfortunate that some people refuse to restore a relationship even if the alternative means finding a new job. To those who understand the importance of having quality relationships, the challenge of relationship restoration can be rich and rewarding. Of course, this points to the need for learning as much as you can about human relations—and making sure your attitude is positive.

Individual differences and change affect relationship building

Summary

Everyone benefits from relationships that are strong and healthy—and there is no better way to keep relationships strong than through good communication. Communication also is a powerful and critical factor in restoring injured relationships. Regardless of who initiates communication toward restoring a damaged relationship, the first step should be taken as quickly as possible.

Making needed repairs quickly can go a long way to restore an injured relationship. The consequences of not doing so will steal your "mind time," compound a negative situation, and possibly turn you into a victim. Using the four basic repair principles you have in your tool kit of good human relations will take effort on your part, but they will help you maximize your success in restoring damaged relationships. The principles also will help you to see why it is important to forgive and forget what or who caused the damage.

Mobilize your "willingness factor" to restore a relationship. Your willingness to initiate relationship restoration is the underlying premise of the rebuilding strategies presented in this chapter. Use the strategies whenever they are needed to give your career a needed boost.

Finally, keep in mind that a professional technician needs just the right tool to repair a sensitive instrument. Yet repairs are not without challenges and risks—there are no guarantees a repair will be totally successful. Neither are there any guarantees for mending life's injured relationships, but using the right tools bias the odds for success. The right tool to repair a damaged relationship is communication—in fact, it is the only tool available. When you use communication in a sensitive manner, you will be more than pleased with all of your relationship-repair jobs.

Test Your Understanding

Respond to the following items to test your understanding of the chapter.

Part A: Circle the correct answer (T = True; F = False) for each of the following statements.

T F   1. All human relationships occasionally become damaged.

T F   2. Fortunately, minor fallouts between workers seldom hurt productivity.

T F   3. Most damaged relationships are left unrepaired because neither party is willing to "break the ice" and initiate communication.

T F   4. Accepting some of the blame is a poor approach to help another save face and restore a relationship.

T F   5. A discussion centered around MRT is a weak way to restore a severely damaged relationship.

Part B: Circle the letter of the correct answer for each of the following items.

6. Damage to relationships in the workplace usually is *not* caused by (a) a misuse of power, (b) good human relations, (c) dishonesty, (d) a communication breakdown.

7. If you were not responsible for damaging a relationship but you take the initiative to restore it, you are (a) exercising poor judgment, (b) practicing the "willingness factor," (c) setting a dangerous precedent, (d) being unrealistic.

Part C: Write a short response to demonstrate your understanding related to the following item.

8. Discuss why communication is the essential ingredient to the restoration of an injured relationship.

Turn to the back of the book to check your answers.

> If your present attitude
> were broadcast
> in stereo surround sound,
> how would you be received?

Think and Respond

Respond to the following items with two or three complete sentences.

1. What role does communication play in relationship rebuilding?
2. What makes a relationship so susceptible to damage and why should a damaged relationship be repaired as quickly as possible?
3. Discuss two of the principles that are basic to relationship restoration.
4. Describe two strategies you can use to repair a damaged relationship.
5. What are some of the challenges and why are there risks associated with relationship rebuilding?

SUMMARY ACTIVITY

My Relationship-Rebuilding Process

In the space provided identify the questions you should ask yourself to help you restore a damaged relationship. Keep in mind that relationship restoration is a "process" and not frequently just a "one-time deal." That is, you'll need to consider some of the risk factors (such as a person not immediately accepting your approach) that you may encounter as you implement your rebuilding process. The time you spend on this activity will be well worth your while to strengthen just *one* relationship, let alone many. Good luck!

1. _____

_____

_____

2. _____

_____

_____

3. _____

_____

_____

4. _____

_____

_____

5. _____

_____

_____

6. _____

_____

_____

CASE 12

Restoration

"I'm willing if you are."

Noreen and Krystal are highly competent supervisors. They both possess outstanding computer skills, do quality work, and receive high productivity from their employees. There is only one problem. As supervisors, they must work closely together, and *they do not get along well with each other.*

Noreen is a single, highly competitive, and assertive person who presents a "flashy and trendy" appearance. She sets a fast pace; and, as far as management can tell, those who work in her section accept her leadership with enthusiasm. Krystal, however, is a family-oriented person with two children. She has a far more conservative approach to her job and lifestyle. Although her approach and management style are different from Noreen's, Krystal also gains high productivity from her staff.

Mrs. Raji, their superior, is tired of the many personal conflicts that arise between Noreen and Krystal. She is fearful that they are drawing so much attention to their conflict that the productivity of her division (she has nine supervisors under her control) will suffer. Yesterday, she called both of them into her private office and stated: "I respect both of you and appreciate your contributions, but it is obvious to everyone that your personal conflict is beginning to disturb the productivity of my division. I'm giving you three hours for lunch today, courtesy of our division. For the good of everyone, resolve your conflict and be back here at three o'clock to tell me what progress you have made. If you can't work it out, I will assist one of you in getting a transfer to another division."

A. Discuss: What are the chances of the plan working? Will they resolve their differences?

B. Expand Your Understanding: Interview three or more supervisors or managers and three or more nonsupervisory employees in different organizations; if possible, select a private, public, and government organization for your interviews. Find answers to questions relating to (a) types of conflicts that exist among workers and (b) solutions that work (and mistakes to avoid) to restore relationships. Consult several resources from the Internet and other sources to support or reject your findings. Summarize what you believe are the best suggestions for resolving conflict and restoring injured relationships—suggestions you can give to Noreen, Krystal, Mrs. Raji, yourself, or, for that matter, to anyone.

CHAPTER 13

Attitudes among Culturally Diverse Coworkers

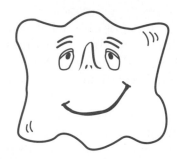

"The more diversification, the better."

> Thought for the Day: If you can't honestly expose the dialogue you have with yourself, maybe you need to make some serious adjustments in your thinking.

PERFORMANCE COMPETENCIES

- Recognize that team synergy is dependent, to a large degree, on the cultural comfort zones of the individual team members.

- Identify three ways in which you can improve your attitude toward *all* coworkers, including culturally diverse coworkers.

- Understand that attitudes are mental sets either for or against those from cultures other than your own.

- Suggest several ways cultural diversification in the workplace can contribute to productivity.

Living in a culturally diverse environment has become a vitally important aspect of today's society. The United States, in particular, has become a culture of people bonded together by ethnic backgrounds as well as by values, preferences, attainments, beliefs, religion, traditions, generation ideals, and even age, gender, and career choices. Similarly, as a department or a corporation integrates employees into the workplace, a "culture" of its own eventually develops.

YOUR CULTURAL COMFORT ZONE

Building Team Synergy. A healthy work culture is one that can be created by drawing positive elements from each of the individuals who make up a department or unit. That is, teams and teamwork rely heavily on maximizing the synergy that can be created from the combined team. Team synergy frequently is enhanced by the expanded ideas that come from the interaction occurring as a result of the contributions of individual team members.

We have learned that it is not only what you produce yourself but how well you work with others that determines how much you contribute to your organization. Your contribution, no doubt, is significantly impacted by your overall attitude as well as your attitude toward your coworkers.

When team members have diverse backgrounds, a team can greatly benefit from the contributions that each member brings to the team effort. Yet, team synergy among culturally diverse coworkers also depends, to a significant degree, on how comfortable you and your coworkers are with each other.

What is your attitude toward cultural diversification? Are you comfortable working with coworkers from cultures other than your own? To give you an indication, complete the following exercise. The "Cultural Diversity Comfort Zone Scale" will give you an idea of how comfortable you are in a culturally diverse working environment.

ACTIVITY

Cultural Diversity Comfort Zone Scale

Read and respond to each of the following questions relating to cultural diversity. Then, place a check mark (✓) in the appropriate box to reflect your opinion about each question and total your answers at the end of the scale.

Cultural Diversity Factor	Yes	No
1. Do you sometimes unknowingly favor coworkers from one culture over another?	❏	❏
2. Do you find yourself spending more social time during breaks and lunch periods with coworkers from your own culture?	❏	❏
3. Do you give full acceptance to new employees from one culture more slowly than another?	❏	❏
4. Would you feel unmotivated and at a disadvantage if, for the first time, your new supervisor was from a different culture than your own?	❏	❏
5. When working near coworkers from other cultures, are you outwardly "cool" but inwardly resentful?	❏	❏
6. Do you find that coworkers who have trouble with your native language irritate you?	❏	❏
7. Are you less tolerant with coworkers who maintain aspects of their own cultures than those who fully adopt your culture?	❏	❏
8. If you needed a coworker to take your place while on a vacation, would you prefer to train someone from your own culture?	❏	❏
9. Would those who know you best say you need more time to be fully free of cultural prejudice?	❏	❏
10. Do you think it is more difficult for you to accept coworkers from a different culture than it is for them to accept you?	❏	❏
Total	☐	☐

The more "No" answers you gave yourself, the more comfortable it should be for you to work in a culturally diverse workplace. However, you may wish to go back over the questions to see how many "Yes" answers you could, with effort, move into the "No" column. This exercise may give you some idea of how easy or difficult it may be for you to work effectively with a more diverse cultural mix of workers in the future.

ATTITUDE-ADJUSTMENT SUGGESTIONS

Can Your Attitude Be Altered? What might you do to change or improve your attitude toward all coworkers regardless of cultural background? Here are three suggestions:

Your attitude toward all workers is critical to relationship building

1. *Build strong relationships with all coworkers.* As a permanent employee, take the initiative to build equally good relationships with all coworkers—especially those who are new and from a culture different than your own. Go about building relationships slowly. Translated, this means you should play the role of the friendly, helpful host, but not to the extent that you might put your relationships with your regular coworkers in jeopardy.

   Shirley. Shirley is extremely friendly and outgoing. In fact, when a new employee arrives in her department, she tries so hard to build a warm and friendly relationship that she makes it uncomfortable for the new arrival. Why is this? Because the new employee needs to win acceptance from all members of the team. Thus, when Shirley dominates the new employee's orientation, other employees may withdraw somewhat. You may even hear other employees say, "There goes Shirley again, trying to be a one-person welcoming committee."

   Try to be a comfortable coworker to know, but do not move too quickly. Give the new employee a chance to adjust slowly and build equally good relationships with all team members.

2. *Appreciate the skills offered by all coworkers.* Give those from different cultures the opportunity to demonstrate their special talents. Nothing will make new workers feel more comfortable than to gain acceptance through their own performance. Their greatest need is to know that they can contribute. It is natural that newcomers in a work team or department feel shy or reluctant to express their special talents.

   Sue Lin. Sue Lin was raised and educated in Korea where she acquired unusually high computer skills. When Sue Lin took her first job in Australia, she decided, however, to soft-pedal her skills until she found a high degree of personal acceptance. Fortunately for Sue Lin, her team leader knew of her special abilities and brought them into play in a sensitive manner so that Sue Lin was able to win acceptance based on her skills as well as her personal qualities.

   Martino. A large Canadian investment firm recruited Martino from Mexico City immediately upon his university graduation. In addition to his accounting degree, he had unusual artistic talent that would be helpful to the advertising department. His bilingual communication skills would be particularly effective with the company's growing market of Mexican customers. Because Martino's supervisor did not bother to identify Martino's strengths and talents, she assigned him to dull work tasks. As a result, his coworkers underestimated the contribution he could make. Had it not been for Jeanne, who made a special effort to know Martino and discover his background, Martino might have become discouraged and left the company.

Obviously, when a new employee becomes a member of a work team, adjustments must be made by all members of the team. If the work setting is not culturally diverse, a new employee from a culture other than the dominant culture of the team may offer additional challenges for everyone.

Assist new employees in adjusting to your team

For example, let us assume that you work in a department in which three cultures have already formed a highly productive team. The team, made up of mostly males who are African American, Anglo, and Hispanic, have molded together into a single productive unit with little evidence of cultural conflict or disharmony. Then, for the first time, an energetic young Japanese woman is introduced as a new team member. While group members, regardless of their cultural background, have already made the adjustment, the new Japanese woman must, in effect, adjust to three different cultures—as well as to the predominantly male team. The group's challenge is much easier than that of the newcomer.

3. *Apply the mutual-reward theory (MRT).* Mutual reward means that all individuals involved benefit from a relationship. The more equally the rewards balance out, the stronger and more permanent the relationship becomes. Frequently, MRT performs best when each participant is from a different culture because each person has more to learn from each other than probably could be gained from a less diverse relationship.

Strong relationships with all coworkers yield mutual rewards

Jahal. After being educated in India, Jahal went to England to work for an export business—a firm eager to expand the market for its products in Jahal's native country. Initially, Jahal was very uncomfortable in the strange environment. Nearly a month passed before he felt at home and was willing to contribute ideas. Much of this was due to Sonja, a coworker in the marketing department who tutored Jahal in British marketing concepts. When the marketing director decided to send Jahal on a promotional trip back to India, Sonja was invited to go along; and Jahal had the opportunity to repay Sonja for her training. As a result, both employees came out ahead and the win-win philosophy of the mutual-reward theory came strongly into play.

Nothing erases differences and prejudices faster than two people from different cultures who build a strong working relationship between themselves. Sooner or later, the rewards balance out.

MUTUAL UNDERSTANDING AND ACCEPTANCE

We do not always recognize our own prejudices toward those from cultures different from our own. Sometimes, the only way to eliminate such prejudices is to get to know and understand each other by working closely over a long period of time.

Fernand. When Fernand went to work for a furniture company right out of high school, he had a real drive to achieve. It took him only two years to work himself up from a warehouse worker to the top delivery person. Fernand seemed to get along well with everyone. Then came the day his assistant, also of Filipino descent, resigned and Cedric, an African American man, was assigned to him. Immediately, Fernand recalled the many fights between the two cultures in high school and figured he might have a challenge ahead of him. Cedric also was nervous about having a Filipino boss, wondering if he would receive fair and equitable treatment.

How did the relationship turn out? For a month, there was little communication, but slowly the two came to know and understand each other's culture. Fernand talked a lot about his family. Cedric talked about his interest in sports and why he was going to college at night. Eventually, a strong relationship developed. When Fernand was given a promotion to the head of the shipping department, he strongly recommended Cedric as his replacement. The fears based upon old high-school conflicts had dissipated, and a mutually rewarding relationship had been built.

Cultural attitudes are mental sets for or against those of diverse cultures. Often, they are biases created from family values or information transmitted by the media. Many people have negative mind sets against another culture when they have never had the opportunity to work closely with a person from that culture.

Try to put yourself in another's place

How Can You Avoid Stereotyping?
If an individual who has English as a primary language has been raised to stereotype everyone from Mexico as weak in English skills, then that person needs to "exchange places" in her (or his) thinking. Also, she should try to build a close relationship with a person of Mexican descent who has excellent English skills. Similarly, if an individual has stereotyped women in the workforce to be less capable than men or has characterized a specific culture as unwilling to accept work responsibilities, then the individual needs to seek out work relationships that dispel these stereotypes. A good way to eliminate your stereotyped feelings is to put yourself in the other person's place. Ask yourself how you would feel if you were characterized by your coworkers as having poor communication or human-relations skills; being inflexible, pompous, or aloof; or being lazy and unhelpful—just because of a cultural bias they may have.

CULTIVATING CULTURAL CONTRIBUTIONS

Fairness Contributes to Cooperative Endeavors. Everyone in the expanding global economy faces the challenge of judging people fairly and on their individual performances regardless of cultural background. Unless performance is judged fairly, mutually rewarding relationships cannot exist. The best place to learn this vital human relations lesson is in the workplace. The more opportunities you receive to work closely with those from other cultures, the greater your personal growth can be.

The benefits of culturally diverse work teams should not be underestimated

Consider, too, that when several individuals from culturally diverse backgrounds contribute to a work team, the result can produce a wide range of ideas. Ideas provided by such a work team can help departments find creative solutions and alternatives to problems that a more homogeneous team might not discover. The synergy of creative people working together probably will contribute to greater productivity and more positive outcomes.

Learn about Other Cultures. Also, because most prejudice comes from fear of the unknown, those who attempt to understand another person's way of life will be less prejudiced and less likely to stereotype him (or her). To expand your perspectives, consider the multitude of excellent media and print resources for exploring the cultures of the world as well as your own culture. The more you learn about the geography and customs of diverse cultures, the more you will be valued in the workplace. Your value comes from expanding your horizons. Learning about cultures other than your own undoubtedly will make you more knowledgeable—and, as a result, you probably will become a better conversationalist and a more interesting person all around.

Summary

The work environment within a company, unit, department, or even a project team can be strengthened with people of diverse cultures working together. Because most companies are entering into, or at least are concerned about, international markets, the more diverse approach to problem solving also makes good business sense. To ensure that your attitude is "on the right track" in a culturally diverse environment, consider the following points that were stressed in this chapter.

1. Your cultural comfort zone with other employees—and especially in your own work team—is important for creating a positive, productive work environment. You and your team can greatly benefit from the ideas that come from the interactions among culturally diverse team members.

2. Your attitude toward all cultures can be improved if you practice three attitude-adjustment suggestions: (a) build good relationships

with *all* workers, (b) encourage others to express their talents and expertise, and (c) practice the mutual-reward theory.

3. Your mind-set toward others from a culture different than your own will influence your working relationships. Avoid stereotyping. To improve your mental set, put yourself in the place of the other person and ask yourself how you would feel if your coworkers had prejudices against you.

4. Your cultural awareness can be improved by exploring the many cultures and ethnic groups that represent our world. If you take advantage of the prevalent information and many types of media to learn about and appreciate diverse cultures, you are bound to cultivate your own cultural contributions as well as those of others.

Remember, too, that to maximize the benefits of working with culturally diverse people, your mental set or attitude toward *all* coworkers needs to be open, unbiased, flexible, and nonstereotyping. Work toward that important goal. If you strive to improve your attitude and build good relationships with *all* people, there is little doubt that mutually satisfying rewards will be enjoyed by everyone.

Test Your Understanding

Respond to the following items to test your understanding of the chapter.

Part A: Circle the correct answer (T = True; F = False) for each of the following statements.

T F 1. Your total contribution to your firm is a combination of what you produce yourself plus how well you work with coworkers.

T F 2. The sooner you rush in and build a strong relationship with a new employee, the better.

T F 3. A new employee from a culture not already represented in a work team is often at a double disadvantage.

T F 4. A prejudice is, in effect, a mental set or attitude.

T F 5. Most prejudice comes from understanding other people's way of life rather than from a fear of the unknown.

Part B: Circle the letter of the correct answer for each of the following items.

6. When working with culturally diverse coworkers, especially in the beginning, you may need to go outside your comfort zone to (a) adjust your attitude, (b) become more stereotyped, (c) create a less flexible acceptance level, (d) establish a firm tolerance level.

7. Cultural attitudes for or against those of diverse cultures usually are *not* created by (a) family biases, (b) translations by the media, (c) stereotyping, (d) being flexible.

Part C: Write a short response to demonstrate your understanding related to the following item.

8. Discuss some of the attitude adjustments that contribute to building good relationships with *all* coworkers, regardless of cultural background.

Turn to the back of the book to check your answers.

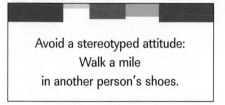

Avoid a stereotyped attitude:
Walk a mile
in another person's shoes.

Think and Respond

Respond to the following items with two or three complete sentences.

1. What is meant by a cultural comfort zone?
2. Discuss two of the suggestions to improve your attitude toward culturally diverse coworkers.
3. What is the greatest value you can achieve by applying MRT in any situation?
4. What is a cultural attitude and how can a cultural attitude be changed?
5. Why do cultural prejudices occur and how does one reverse negative thinking?

SUMMARY ACTIVITY
Orientation Exercise

Assume that you are the supervisor or team leader of a group of high-tech employees in a science laboratory. A new employee from a culture other than that of the majority of team members has been assigned to your team. You wish to assist her in getting off to a good start so she can make her best possible contribution. You have had a preliminary interview with the new employee. You find her to be quiet, intense, and fearful as to how she will be accepted by coworkers. She possesses many skills important to laboratory work.

List three suggestions you would make to the new employee prior to her first day in her new assignment.

1. _____

2. _____

3. _____

As her supervisor, list three suggestions you would make to members of your team to help the new employee find the acceptance she will need.

1. _____

2. _____

3. _____

Now, check your responses with the following suggestions that could be helpful to both the new employee and your other team members:

Suggestions to the new team member: (1) Provide her with the names of team members and a few positive comments about each individual. (2) Give her a copy of her job description, but stress her overall responsibilities as a team member. (3) Take time to personally introduce her to each team member. (4) Assign her a sponsor to give her any special assistance that might be appropriate. (5) Take her to lunch so she will feel comfortable with you as her superior.

Suggestions to team members: (1) Ask for a volunteer to act as her sponsor for the first thirty days. (2) Present a brief background on the new employee's skills and a small amount of upbeat information on her background. (3) Mention the special contributions she can make to team productivity. (4) Give her ample time to make her adjustment. (5) Welcome any suggestions from team members as to what they and you, as her team leader, might do to assist her during the first thirty days of her employment as well as what everyone can do to help her become an integrated member of your team over the long term.

When a new employee joins your work unit, always put yourself in the place of the new employee because he (or she) must learn a new job and establish new relationships. Keep in mind that his transition is difficult enough without encountering potential road blocks that may be attributed to assumptions associated with cultural biases.

CASE 13

Communication

"Everybody has a problem these days."

Ariele, a US-born, European-educated biochemist, was disturbed emotionally after a late afternoon meeting. Why? Because the CEO just announced that Yoshio was appointed manager of their biotech research team. It isn't that Yoshio has not earned the promotion through his contribution to the team. Everyone recognizes his skills. Besides, Yoshio also has seniority. However, Ariele was angry and rationalized his negative reaction on the premise that Yoshio is not a good communicator and everyone on the team will suffer because of it. In Ariele's opinion, Yoshio has not fully adapted to American ways that Ariele believes are absolutely necessary for working in their US-based firm. Besides, Ariele feels that, at times, Yoshio is insensitive to the needs of coworkers, is a poor speaker in front of a group, and has an overpermissive leadership style.

What is fortunate for Ariele is that he recently received an offer from a competitive firm at a high salary with a more comprehensive benefit package. He could make the move at any time. The problem in accepting the new job is that it would necessitate a geographical move—a move that would make his wife and children unhappy. His wife is a medical doctor who is happy with her assignment at a fine local hospital. His two daughters are in high school and are doing well with many friends. It would be unwise to disrupt such a good educational environment.

A. Discuss: How should Ariele view his choices? Is he upset emotionally because of some hidden prejudice? If Ariele made the effort, could he build a mutually rewarding relationship with Yoshio, one that would give both parties a better future? Assume you are Ariele's best friend and he comes to you for advice. How might you counsel Ariele to make the right decision for himself?

B. Expand Your Understanding: Make a list of diversity issues that are important to today's multicultural society. Then, develop your list into a company manual that offers information, suggestions, and solutions for each of the issues. Your manual should be valuable for new employee orientation as well as be a good resource for all employees. Consult several company Web sites to complete your manual. If possible, make some additional suggestions to Ariele and Yoshio for helping them forge brighter futures.

PART IV
Building Your Career

CHAPTER 14
Succeeding in a New Job or Assignment

"There's more here than meets the eye."

Thought for the Day: A good reason for giving your best effort in everything you do is to enjoy the many benefits of "effort ownership."

PERFORMANCE COMPETENCIES

- Understand the value of having organization and balance in your life for making a smooth and effective transition to a new work role.

- Recognize the importance of the learning factor for success in your new job or assignment.

- Understand why organizations develop manuals of work policies and procedures.

- Realize that taking a "good common sense" approach to your job assignment is smart on your part—and is expected by your employer.

- Appreciate how much a commitment to your positive attitude contributes to the success of all your interactions.

189

Undoubtedly, you want to succeed on any new job or assignment you undertake. First, you want to prove to your family, friends, and management that you are a winner. Second, you want to prove it to yourself. Undoubtedly, there is a lot at stake when starting a new endeavor.

This chapter is devoted to ten tips that can help you in reaching your goal. If you take these tips seriously and apply them conscientiously, you can avoid many of the mistakes others make.

A BALANCED AND ORGANIZED LIFE

Tip 1: Balance Home and Career. When you accept a new work challenge, it is vital that all home demands be under complete control. Your on-the-job concentration needs to be at a high level, and any home worries, especially those connected with small children or other relatives, can be distracting to both you and your coworkers. Balancing home and career so that you can be a winner in both areas is never easy to accomplish and maintain. The time to start reorganizing is before you accept a new job or assignment. Once things are out of balance, it may be too late for you to reach your full job potential. Give your career a break and get things organized at home first.

A balanced, productive person is an asset to everyone

When it is necessary to call in ill, make every effort to talk with your supervisor or another management person. A direct contact, especially about being absent from work, shows that you respect your supervisor. It is unfair (possibly even against the company procedures) to ask a coworker to relay such an important message to your boss. If a coworker tells your supervisor you won't be in, doubts may be raised about the "real reason" for your absence. Your supervisor may even call you for verification, and such a contact could be embarrassing to both you and your supervisor.

Value trust, integrity, and ethics

Further, if the relayed message raises some doubt, questions of trust, integrity, and ethics may become issues between you, your supervisor, and even your coworkers. Trust, integrity, and ethics are basic to strong and healthy relationships; they are hard to "repair" once damaged. Thus, don't do anything that could jeopardize your relationship and future interactions. Also, it never hurts to bring in a physician's statement to document an extended absence.

Tip 2: Use a Calendar Notebook to Help You Get Organized. An abundance of important information—rules, regulations, and procedures—will be thrown at you at the beginning of a new job. The first days are days of adjustment and excitement, so don't trust yourself to remember everything. Rather, buy an inexpensive calendar notebook or day-to-day organizer and use it to record some of the instructions and hard-to-remember information you get from your supervisor or fellow workers. Jot these data down as they are given to you.

Do not hesitate to take notes when receiving a complex answer to a question involving considerable detail. The notebook itself (if not overused) will create a good impression. It will help show that you are organized, methodical in your approach to learning, and serious about your career. In the evening, use the notebook to review certain facts and procedures. You can also use it to record appointments, ideas, names, and so on.

THE LEARNING FACTOR

Tip 3: Ask Questions, but Learn to Ask the Right Ones. Fear of being considered inadequate is the reason most people in a new work situation do not ask more questions. A genuine concern about making mistakes in a new position is understandable, but it is better to ask questions than to suffer the serious results of continued mistakes. If you don't understand something, ask questions until you do. Asking questions may be necessary because those responsible for your adjustment and training do not always take enough time to explain things fully. Because old hands tend to forget that they, too, had trouble learning at the beginning, they often talk so fast that only a genius or a psychic could get the message the first time around.

There is a right time and a wrong time to ask a question. One should not, for example, interrupt a person who is concentrating on getting a job done or who is communicating with others. There are also right and wrong questions. A right question is one you need to ask to be effective; a wrong question is one that does not apply to the task being explained. One should not, for example, ask questions that are answered in the orientation literature you have been given to read on your own time.

In asking questions, keep in mind that you must listen to the answers with your eyes as well as your ears. Sure, you receive the auditory impressions with your ears. But you should also look at the person who is speaking. Most people, in fact, feel it is discourteous when someone they are talking to lets his (or her) eyes wander. You will understand the importance of attentiveness if you have ever seen someone look at his watch, shuffle papers, stare at the floor, or look out a window while you were talking to him. You will make a better impression on people if you form the habit of listening with your eyes as well as your ears. You also stand a better chance of receiving any hidden—but vital—meaning that may lie under the message.

Active listening is a critical communication skill

Tip 4: Don't Flaunt Your Education or Previous Experience. You may have had more formal education than many of the people you will work with on your new job. But these people probably have far more on-the-job experience and practical know-how than you do. That being the case,

*Use good judgment
to mesh relationship
building and productivity*

you would be wise to let them discover your educational background and experience gradually.

The job you are assigned may be more difficult than you expect. If you try to impress people with your experience or intelligence, they may not want to give you any help when you need it most.

If you are an experienced employee, you may have received your job training in another company. You will probably find that things are done differently in your new firm. Perhaps your way of doing things is better. But until you are sure, be safe and do it the way people at your new job do it. Give your coworkers the satisfaction of explaining how they do things. You will have plenty of time later to make changes that can result in improvement for your work environment, products, or services.

It is also a good idea to keep your salary to yourself. It is possible that another employee, doing work similar to yours as you start out, has yet to reach your salary level. Misinterpretation and resentment may occur. If so, both you and the other employee could lose.

FOLLOWING ORGANIZATIONAL POLICIES AND PROCEDURES

Tip 5: Read Your Employee Handbook and Other Materials Carefully. Many organizations publish handbooks and other pamphlets for their employees. These materials usually contain vital information. Yet many employees, especially those with experience elsewhere, never read them.

*Company manuals can be
valuable employee
resources*

Don't be casual in your use of company literature. Where else can you learn company policies that can keep you out of trouble? Where else can you discover important data that will prevent you from asking unnecessary questions? Take home all of the literature you are given and devote some time to it. Understanding your company, its expectations and safety rules, and the benefits it provides will not only help you start on the right foot but will further your career.

Tip 6: Many Organizations Have Personal Appearance and Grooming Standards. A few organizations, like factories, may have few or no personal appearance or grooming standards. They are interested primarily in your work performance and your human-relations ability.

Other companies, especially those that do business directly with customers, set minimum dress standards that are usually easily met by most employees. Still other companies, like department stores, have rather high personal and grooming standards that may be difficult for some people to accept.

When you join an organization, carefully assess its standards and decide what is best for you and your future. You have a right to be yourself and protect your individuality. In doing so, however, you should weigh all factors and take into consideration that most people, including management, feel that a little conformity won't hurt you. You are responsible for meeting minimum dress standards. Managers quickly tire of those who try to slip by with unacceptable attire. They often interpret such behavior as immature.

GOOD COMMON SENSE

Tip 7: Use Good Judgment in Working Extra Hours and Taking Work Breaks.
Some employees with a new opportunity attempt to secure their jobs and attract management's attention by working more than the normal number of hours at the beginning. They arrive first in the morning and make a point of leaving last at the end of the day. They often skip their breaks. A zealous work attitude, if sincere, is to be admired.

However, overzealousness can get you into trouble on two counts. First, there are usually regulations governing hours to be worked. On certain jobs, unauthorized overtime work and failure to take breaks can involve you and your employer in labor difficulties. It is important, therefore, always to abide by the instructions given to you by management.

Second, your fellow employees may misinterpret your motives and make life more difficult for you and your supervisor. Working extra hours (and eliminating breaks) when an important deadline must be met and when you are asked to do so by your supervisor is one thing. Working extra hours only to impress others is quite another.

As a rule, it is better to make full use of the time you spend on the job rather than to try to impress others with your willingness to work extra hours.

Many employees, especially those who are closely monitored by management, feel they need to immerse themselves in work as soon as they enter the workplace. It is often better to circulate around and send out a few friendly signals before digging into a day's work. Some people call this "doing a figure 8."

Tip 8: Look Energetic, but Don't Be an Eager Beaver.
Some people start their careers with a great burst of energy and enthusiasm that cannot possibly be sustained. These people frequently create a favorable impression to begin with but later on are reclassified by both management and their fellow workers.

It is easy to be overeager at the beginning. You are new to your job, so you have a fresh and dynamic approach. You have a lot of nervous energy to release. You are interested, and your interest motivates you to achieve. Your desire to succeed, however, might cause you to reach too far too fast.

Be consistent in demonstrating good work habits

The best way to make progress inside an organization is to make steady progress.

Goal setting is a good idea and may help you achieve an even work tempo. Daily goals, written down and accomplished according to a priority system, make you a more productive and valuable member of the team. The practice will also help you in preparing for a supervisory role.

BUILDING POSITIVE RELATIONSHIPS

Tip 9: Make Friends, but Don't Make Close Friends Too Soon. There are many little human-relations traps you can easily fall into in a new work environment. One of these is building one or two very strong friendships at the expense of all others. For example, suppose you discover that one of the employees in your department is extremely friendly the first day. Such friendliness is usually more than welcome the first few hours in a strange setting.

But beware. What if you spend all your time with this one employee and neglect being friendly to the others? What if this friendly person is not respected by the others? What if she (or he) has earned a poor reputation in the department and is offering you friendship for purely selfish motives?

Sometimes people who have failed to earn respect from others at work try desperately to win the friendship of a new employee. Remember that it is only natural that the other employees (including management) will quickly identify you with any employee or employees with whom you spend excessive time.

If one employee clings to you as you start your new job, you obviously have a difficult situation to handle. Of course, you should not be rude to this person. You will do well, however, to back away and be somewhat reserved toward this individual for the first few weeks and concentrate on building relationships with everyone.

Tip 10: Send Out Positive Verbal and Nonverbal Signals. There are many verbal signals you can use to create a good first impression. "Good morning" and "thank-you" are examples. Such easy signals of friendship should be transmitted with sincerity at every opportunity to acknowledge the presence of others and to recognize any courtesies they have extended to you, however small.

A friendly person—one who creates a good first impression—is also one who uses nonverbal signals. For example, a person with a ready smile is easily interpreted as a friendly person. The smile seems to break any psychological barriers that might exist in a meeting of strangers. You immediately feel adopted by the person who smiles. A smile, then, is a friendly, nonverbal signal.

Attitudes can be highly communicated through body language

There are many effective nonverbal signals in addition to the smile. Shaking hands, gesturing positively with the hand or head, opening doors for people—these are all signals you send that make it easier for people to meet and know you. When you send out such signals naturally and in good taste, others do not feel awkward about approaching you. You have made it easy for them, and they like you for it.

In communicating a positive attitude to coworkers or clients, body language is most important. You probably have heard people say, "That's no problem," while their attitude (communicated through their body language) demonstrated that it, indeed, was a problem.

ACTIVITY

Succeeding in a New Assignment

Review each of the ten tips needed to succeed in a new job or assignment. Identify at least one human-relations skill (or characteristic) that is important for four of the ten tips. Write that skill or characteristic in the numbered spaces on the grid that follows. Once you have four human-relations skills identified, write a summary statement about how important each of these skills is to you (regardless of whether you are starting a new job or continuing your present status).

Human Relations Skill	Importance of the Skill to Me
1.	
2.	
3.	
4.	

The human-relations skills I identified are of significance to me because

Note: If your summary included (or implied) the importance of your positive attitude, give yourself a pat on the back because you are aware that, no matter what you do, *Your Attitude Is Showing!*

People who develop confidence in sending out strong signals of friendship make excellent first impressions. They quickly increase their sphere of influence and build many lasting working and personal relationships. Have confidence in yourself and your ability to communicate such signals. Take initiative. Send out your own brand of signals in your own style, and be a comfortable person to meet.

Remember, too, that the better you become at sending out sincere signals of friendship, the better prepared you will be for any job interviews you may face in the future.

Summary

After studying this chapter, it may be rather obvious to you how important good human-relations skills and a positive attitude are to your success on the job, especially in a new job or assignment. The ten pragmatic tips presented in this chapter also provide good suggestions to follow for making a smooth and effective transition to a new work role in a new environment.

Most of the tips, too, offer good practical advice to guide you in your everyday life. To be more specific, realize that a balanced and organized life will lead to your being in better control of your job responsibilities and your personal life. Continue to learn, regardless of how much you already know, as you'll be rewarded with a better understanding of your job as well as the jobs of others—and your relationships will benefit, too. To get an accurate perspective of your organization, read the company manuals. The materials your company provides to employees will tell you what policies and procedures are important to the organization.

No doubt, you benefit from taking a common-sense approach to your job. That means you should practice good judgment in your work habits. For example, being overzealous can be misinterpreted by your coworkers. Finally, practice good communication skills—verbal, nonverbal, written, and, of course, listening skills—to build strong and healthy relationships with *all* workers. Earning the respect of your supervisor and coworkers will go a long way in enhancing your confidence and self-image as well as in succeeding in your job and career.

Practicing these tips and committing to them will take you a long way on and off the job. If you make your positive attitude central to building and maintaining strong relationships, it is without question that you will have the propensity to achieve success in *all* your interactions.

Test Your Understanding

Respond to the following items to test your understanding of the chapter.

Part A: Circle the correct answer (T = True; F = False) for each of the following statements.

T F   1. To balance home and career, it is best to reorganize yourself after, rather than before, you start a new job assignment.

T F   2. Fear of being considered "stupid" is a prime reason that many new employees do not ask more questions even though it would be better if they did.

T F   3. People don't care how much you know until they know how much you care.

T F   4. When arriving at work, it is good to circulate and make contact with coworkers before immersing yourself in your assignment.

T F   5. The main reason people do not send more positive signals is that they lack the confidence to send them.

Part B: Circle the letter of the correct answer for each of the following items.

6. Good advice about asking questions on the job, especially for a new employee, is to ask questions (a) at every opportunity you can even if you have to interrupt another person, (b) that clearly reflect company orientation materials, (c) without regard to body language of others, (d) and listen to answers with your eyes and ears.

7. The best way to make progress inside an organization is to set goals and (a) show bursts of energy, (b) release nervous energy with great enthusiasm, (c) try to impress your boss, (d) achieve at an even work tempo.

Part C: Write a short response to demonstrate your understanding related to the following item.

8. Explain why human relations and attitude are so important (and included in so many suggestions) for succeeding in a new job or work assignment.

Turn to the back of the book to check your answers.

Success can depend on luck;
to increase your propensity for luck,
seek out opportunities
and work hard.

Think and Respond

Respond to the following items with two or three complete sentences.

1. Suggest one way you can organize your life and describe how it can help you on and off the job.

2. Give two reasons active listening is important for every person.

3. Why is it important to read and follow company manuals?

4. What does common sense have to do with job success? Give an example.

5. Provide and describe a good reason for building positive relationships.

SUMMARY ACTIVITY

Behavioral Change Commitments

Although you may have adjusted successfully to one or more previous jobs, this activity is designed to help you make measurable improvements in the future. Many psychologists claim that the ideal time to make behavioral improvements is during a job or assignment change. One of many reasons for this is that you probably will be motivated to win the acceptance of your new coworkers.

This activity will help you identify those specific areas in which you feel you need to make the greatest improvement. Here are four tips you are urged to follow.

1. Place a check mark (✔) in column A only if you honestly intend to make a personal contract with yourself to show a measurable improvement. Limit yourself to no more than three commitments in this column.

2. Limit yourself to no more than five check marks in column B because it is better to concentrate on a few important changes than to spread yourself so thin that nothing happens.

3. Circle the one single check mark in column A or B where you feel you need to make immediate improvement and you intend to start today. Then do it!

4. Once you have made significant progress on one improvement, move to your next commitment. Periodically revisit this exercise to reorder areas for continued improvement.

Although the exercise is designed primarily to assist you in adjusting to a new job or work role, whether inside or outside your organization, you may decide to make some behavioral changes in your present situation. If you do not start making improvements now, you may forget your commitments to yourself before your next work environment change occurs.

POSSIBLE AREAS OF IMPROVEMENT	(A) I HEREBY MAKE A PERSONAL CONTRACT WITH MYSELF TO IMPROVE SUBSTANTIALLY IN THIS AREA	(B) I INTEND TO MAKE MORE EFFORT TO IMPROVE IN THIS AREA	(C) AT THIS TIME, I DO NOT NEED TO MAKE IMPROVEMENT IN THIS AREA
1. Learning more about the organization; reading available materials	_____	_____	_____
2. Sending out more positive, friendly signals	_____	_____	_____
3. Adhering to appropriate dress standards	_____	_____	_____

4. Doing a better job of building a good relationship with my supervisor _____ _____ _____

5. Learning to do a better job of asking the right questions at the right time _____ _____ _____

6. Making friends with all coworkers on an even basis; not showing favorites _____ _____ _____

7. Balancing home and work demands _____ _____ _____

8. Becoming more assertive without being aggressive or militant _____ _____ _____

9. Using a calendar notebook to improve my efficiency _____ _____ _____

10. Improving my reliability; not being absent or late to work _____ _____ _____

11. Making friends, but not so quickly with one person that I neglect other work relationships _____ _____ _____

12. Setting a better productivity tempo; achieving a better balance between work and human relations _____ _____ _____

13. Refusing to bad-mouth others in the organization _____ _____ _____

14. Becoming a better listener _____ _____ _____

15. Having a more positive attitude _____ _____ _____

Attitudes are caught, not taught. In the classroom, teachers' attitudes frequently are "picked up" by their students. In the work setting, attitudes (especially positive ones) frequently are caught to a lower degree; however, most people prefer being around people who are positive.

We may transmit our negative attitudes on one wavelength and our positive attitudes on another, but both seem to travel at the same speed and within the same perimeter. This principle sends us two signals: (1) it is almost impossible to teach another (child, employee) to be positive; (2) setting a good attitude example is more important than we may have thought.

CASE 14

Nonprofessional

"Whom can you trust?"

Tyrell is the Webmaster for a division of a company that is a major distributor of electronic components. Tyrell is normally an honest individual. For example, he would never think of taking office supplies for home use, but he seems to feel that ideas are fair game. In practice, Tyrell believes he is creative and resourceful. He thinks nothing of embellishing an idea created and introduced in casual conversation by a coworker or fellow Webmaster and submitting it to his superior as if it were his own. Tyrell is extremely good at e-mailing ideas to his boss. While many of his written suggestions are ideas discussed informally with other Webmasters and coworkers in the organization, Tyrell is not very good at giving others credit for their ideas.

Two weeks ago, Helen, one of Tyrell's counterparts in another division, shared a layout idea at an informal luncheon meeting at which Tyrell was present. Yesterday morning, after a discussion with their common supervisor, Helen discovered that Tyrell had submitted her layout idea as his. As a result, Tyrell will receive a commendation at this Friday's staff meeting.

A. Discuss: If you were Helen, what would you do? Where does ethics (or ethical behavior) fit into the practice of human relations at work? How is Tyrell hurting himself by stealing other people's ideas?

B. Expand Your Understanding: Discuss this case with three or four employed individuals you know, at least one of whom is a supervisor. Have them tell you what they believe it takes to be successful on the job. (Hint: Share and have them comment on the ten tips presented in this chapter.) Draw some conclusions about your findings and give some additional advice to Tyrell. It is highly recommended that you also back up your conclusions and advice with research you glean from other sources, including Internet references, pertaining to work success factors such as trust, integrity, and ethics.

CHAPTER 15

Initiation Rites—
Coping with Teasing
and Testing

"Seniority counts for something."

Thought for the Day: No one understands better than you when you successfully negotiate one of life's difficult hurdles.

PERFORMANCE COMPETENCIES

- Appreciate that teasing and testing frequently are ways of helping a new employee to become an accepted member of the group.

- Recognize that the purpose of organizational testing usually comes with the territory of being a new employee.

- Understand the purposes and consequences of personal testing.

- Identify several acceptable ways to address prolonged or negative testing.

Getting started in a new job or assignment, for which the setting is strange and the employees are strangers, is bound to give you a few psychological challenges. Rather than magnify these challenges, this chapter will help you understand why such problems sometimes develop and, even more importantly, show you how you can handle them.

ACCEPTANCE IN YOUR NEW ENVIRONMENT

You may be assigned to a department as a replacement for someone the others hated to lose. They will need time to get used to you. You may not have the experience of the person you replaced; and, as a result, others may have to work harder for a few days to get you started. It is even possible that someone in your new department wanted another person to have your job and, as a result, there may be some resentment toward you.

Transitioning to a New Job. It is never easy to be the newest member of a group. You cannot expect to go from being an outsider to being an insider without making a few adjustments. In the first place, you and your personality were forced upon the group. Probably they were not asked whether they wanted you. You have been, in effect, imposed upon them. Because they were there first and because they probably have strong relationships among themselves, they may feel that you should earn your way into their confidence. It may not seem fair, but it is only natural for them to look at your arrival in a somewhat negative way.

Did you ever go through an initiation into a club? If so, you will understand that teasing or testing the new member is often a tradition. To a limited extent, the same can be true when a new employee joins a department or division in a business organization. There is nothing planned or formal about it, of course, but you should be prepared for a little good-natured teasing or testing. Let us look at the psychological reasons behind these two phenomena.

Teasing usually is nonthreatening and helps a new person feel welcome

Teasing—An Initiation Rite That Can Benefit a New Employee. The teasing of a new employee is often nothing more than a way of helping the person become a full-fledged member of the group. It is a form of initiation rite that will help you feel you belong. Sometimes it is a group effort in which everyone participates. More often, however, it is an individual matter. *Teasing, for the most part, is harmless.*

The shop foreman who never had the advantage of a college education but who has learned considerably from practical experience may enjoy teasing a recent graduate of an engineering school. If the graduate engineer goes along with the teasing, a sound relationship between the two should develop. If, however, she (or he) permits it to get under her skin, the relationship could become strained.

The shop foreman's motive may be nothing more than a desire to help the new engineer build good relationships with the rest of the gang. There may be nothing resentful or personal about it.

A small group of employees who work together closely in a branch bank, lawyer's office, or other work-team environment can usually be expected to come up with a little harmless teasing when a new person joins the staff. He (or she) may be given the oldest equipment with a touch of formal ceremony or the dismal job of keeping the stockroom in order.

Usually, good-natured teasing is based upon tradition and human nature. People who like to tease in a harmless manner are generally good-natured. They enjoy people. They mean no harm. In fact, they usually do it to make you feel more—not less—comfortable.

If you are on the receiving end of some good, healthy teasing, you have nothing to worry about so long as you do not take it personally. Just go along with it and you come out ahead. It is much better to be teased than to be ignored. If by chance the baiting should go a little too far and you find yourself embarrassed, the very fact that it is embarrassing to you will probably make you some friends. A little good-natured teasing that is handled well by you will help you get off to a good start on your new job. It will also help break down any communication barriers that may exist.

Testing—Understanding Is Key. Testing is different. It can have more serious implications, and testing will take more understanding on your part.

Because testing related to new employee initiation is commonplace in most organizations, the discussion that follows will give you some insight into why new employees frequently experience different kinds of initiation rites. You will learn about various ways to cope with testing that comes with new employee initiation. You will also learn how your reactions can help or hinder you during testing situations. Study the examples and suggestions that are provided; they will give you a good background on how you can get through testing experiences successfully.

Testing can present some challenges

Testing Modes a New Employee May Encounter. There are two kinds of testing. One is *organizational testing*. Organizational testing comes from the organization (management, personnel, or your supervisor) and is a deliberate attempt to discover what kind of person you really are and whether you can adjust to certain conditions. The other kind of testing—*personal testing*—comes strictly from individuals. Personal testing is one person trying out another because of personality conflicts or inner prejudices.

┌─ **ACTIVITY** ─────────────────────────────────

Understanding Initiation Rites

In the spaces that follow, (a) define the term related to initiation rites, and (b) give an example of a workplace action that represents the term. If you have difficulty with this activity, continue reading about the topic. Then, once you have a clear idea of the difference between teasing, organizational testing, and personal testing, return to complete this exercise.

Teasing	
a.	b.
Organizational Testing	
a.	b.
Personal Testing	
a.	b.

──

ORGANIZATIONAL TESTING

Organizational Testing Should Be Expected. Organizational testing is one of two major testing modes that should be expected by an employee who is starting a new job. Organizational testing usually is done so your employer can find out more about you. In a way, it is an initiation rite. Organizational testing frequently involves the fact that you are "the new kid on the block," and management wants to see how you handle and react to various situations.

Almost all kinds of organizations—especially the smaller ones—have certain unpleasant tasks that must be done. Frequently, these tasks are handed to the newest employee. The new salesperson in a department store may be given excessive amounts of stock work at the start of her (or his) career. The factory worker may be given unpleasant cleanup jobs until another new member joins the department. The clerical employee may be given a dreaded filing assignment as a way to get totally acquainted with the new position.

Organizational testing has a purpose and usually doesn't last long

The important thing to recognize is that these tests have a purpose. Can the new worker take the assignment without complaining? Can he (or she) survive without developing a negative attitude? Will he accept the assignment as a challenge or show resentment and thereby destroy his chance of gaining the respect of the other members of the department?

The old phrase "starting at the bottom of the ladder" sometimes means exactly that. Many top management people started at the bottom, and they feel that "starting at the bottom" is the best way for you to start, too. If you can't take the mundane or "grunt" work at the onset of a new assignment, you may not be able to assume heavier responsibility later. It is the price you pay for being a beginner.

Management sometimes feels that "starting at the bottom" is the best way for the manager of the future to appreciate fully the kind of work that must be done by the entry-level employee. Many college graduates find themselves beginning their careers by doing the most uninviting tasks the company needs to have done. If they are human-relations smart, they will take it in stride, using the time to size up the situation and learn as much as possible about the organization.

React Positively to Organizational Testing. During testing periods, you are being watched by management and by your fellow employees. *The better you react, the sooner the testing will end and the better your relations with others will be.* In other words, although getting the job done is important, your attitude toward it may be more important. If you react in a negative manner, three things can happen:

- You may be kept on the assignment longer than you otherwise would have been.

- You may hurt your chances of getting a better assignment later on.

- You may damage relationships with people involved in or observing the testing.

If you can take the long-range perspective and condition yourself to these tasks with an inner smile and an outward grin, you'll do well for yourself. Roll up your sleeves and get the job done quickly. If you finish one job, move on to another. Don't be afraid to get dirty. If you must take a little abuse, don't complain. It is part of the initiation rite, and someday you will look back on the experience as those ahead of you look back on it now. It is foolhardy for the new employee to fight any of the many forms of organizational testing, as long as it doesn't seriously damage her (or his) personal dignity.

PERSONAL TESTING

Personal Testing Goes beyond Teasing. Organizational testing (discussed in the previous section as one of two primary testing modes for new employees) may appear to have some similarities to personal testing (the second main testing mode that can be part of initiation rites for new employees). Personal testing, as contrasted with organizational testing, can be a very different matter. Personal testing could give you more trouble, especially if you fail to recognize it for what it is. It may come from someone your own age or from someone much older or someone younger. It may come from a fellow worker or from someone in

Recognize personal testing for what it is

management. You may be wise to start out in your new job with a very "open" attitude that everything is teasing rather than testing. Then, if the teasing doesn't last long, you have automatically solved the problem.

However, if the teasing continues for a long period of time, you will know that it is personal testing and that it is probably the product of prejudice or genuine hostility. When this happens, you have a real challenge ahead of you. For example, one of your fellow employees may refuse to accept you. She (or he) may harass you at every turn and may not give you a chance to be a normal, productive employee. The needle will be out at every opportunity.

■ *Example: Serious Testing #1*

Rayleen. When Rayleen was assigned to a maintenance crew with a gas and water company, she knew she was on a very strict ninety-day probation period. The job was extremely important to her, especially since it had taken her a long time to get it. She decided she would go all out to keep her personal productivity high and still build good relationships with the rest of the crew.

Everything would have been great if it had not been for Art. Art started out the very first day using every technique in the book to slow Rayleen down and get under her skin. Art constantly came up with comments like "What are you trying to do, Rayleen, make us all look bad?" "Who are you trying to impress by working so hard?" "If you slow down a little, we'll get you through probation."

After three weeks of heckling from Art, Rayleen knew she was up against a personality conflict loaded with hostility. Rather than take it any longer, she asked Art to meet her at a coffee shop after work. It was a strained evening, but Art finally relaxed. Much of the hostility disappeared, and the next day he was off Rayleen's back. Rayleen never knew for sure the real cause of the conflict. However, the crew seemed happier, and productivity was better.

Serious testing can be harassment

Chances are good that personal testing will never happen to you personally; but, occasionally, an employee will get on the receiving end of some nonorganizational or personal testing from a supervisor. Consider what happened to Heimar in his first job.

■ *Example: Serious Testing #2*

Heimar. Heimar graduated near the top of his class in nursing school. He took the first job he interviewed for as a vocational nurse in a community nursing home for elderly people. But Heimar quickly discovered that he was on the receiving end of some rather vicious testing from his supervisor.

Heimar was not surprised when he was assigned mostly unpleasant tasks his first few days on the job. He knew it was traditional, so he pleasantly went about giving baths to some of the most difficult patients. He had many disagreeable duties, all of which were assigned to him by the supervisor. His supervisor was a registered nurse who had been at the home for many years.

Heimar didn't complain; he didn't want any special favors. He took everything that came his way because he wanted to prove to himself that he could take it. But slowly he began to sense that something more than routine testing was involved. His supervisor seemed to dish out the ugly assignments with a strange, subtle bitterness. Not only that, but even after two new vocational nurses had joined the staff, Heimar was still doing all the really dirty jobs.

Although he was fearful of prejudice from the beginning, he tried to play it cool and hoped for a change. He said nothing. But soon his fellow workers, most of whom were his age and also vocational nurses, got the message. When they did, a confrontation took place that finally reached the desk of the nursing home owner. The pressure on Heimar was quickly removed. No one was sorry a week later when the registered nurse responsible for the problems resigned.

It is sometimes impossible to know the deep-seated motives behind some of the serious testing that takes place. Often the people responsible do not know themselves. Prejudice—whether it be associated with age, race, sex, jealousy, or other factors—is only one of the many causes. It is best not to judge others but to try to find ways to get through the awkwardness of the situation. Consider the case involving Mario.

Unknown motives may result in serious testing

■ *Example: Serious Testing #3*

Mario. Mario was really pleased about his new construction job. At last he would be able to put his apprenticeship training to work and make some good money. He anticipated all the teasing he got from the old-timers at the beginning, and he took it in stride without any big scenes. But his foreman's attitude was something else. No matter how hard he tried, Mario got the needle from his foreman at every turn. No matter how much work Mario turned out, the foreman was on his back. Mario took it for about a week; and then, in desperation, he asked the advice of one of the older crew members. Here is what the older man said: "Look, buddy, our beloved supervisor is an uptight conservative. Your long hair, your flashy sports car, and especially your free and easy lifestyle all get to him. Frankly, I think he has some trouble with his own sons, and you remind him of them. At any rate, he's all wrong. What you do to get him off your back, though, is your own problem. Good luck."

Mario gave it some serious thought and decided that he would face the foreman and see what happened. It was a tough decision to make because he didn't want to lose his job. He waited until they were alone, and then he put all his cards on the table. He said, "You've been on my back, and you know it. I think you should either tell me why or start treating me the way you treat the others." There were some tense and awkward moments. But when it was all over, the foreman managed a small smile. From then on, things were noticeably better for Mario.

These three examples represent only a few of the many different cases that could be presented.

ADDRESSING NEGATIVE TESTING

Sometimes testing can present a challenge for you in your new job. Sometimes supervisors are responsible; sometimes they are not. The question is, of course, what can you do if you come up against a serious testing situation? A few pointers that may help you follow.

Extreme Testing Usually Requires Serious Action. Accept the testing situation willingly until you have time to analyze it carefully. Take testing as part of the initiation period and conduct yourself in such a manner to not aggravate the situation. It may pass by itself; or someone else, without your knowledge, may come to your rescue. If time does not take care of it and you come to the point at which you sincerely feel that you are being pushed too far, approach the person who is doing the needling with a "let's lay all the cards on the table" attitude. In your own words, without hostility, say something like this: "If I have done anything to upset you, please tell me. Otherwise, I feel it is time we started to respect each other." Seek out an accountability solution. Confronting the negative situation will not be easy for you to do. But in cases of extreme testing, it is necessary to make the tester account for his (or her) actions. There is no other solution.

Focus on how to stop negative testing rather than on who is doing it

Respect Yourself to Gain Others' Respect. Unfortunately, some individuals will push you around indefinitely if you permit it. And if you permit it, they will never respect you. Chances are that you will not be subjected to excessive pushiness by your supervisor. But if you are, you must stand up to the situation and solve it yourself. It is important to you and to the company that you do so.

Address Negatives with Positives. Of course, you need to go about addressing negative testing in the right way. Try not to have a chip on your shoulder. Do not make accusations. Try not to say anything personal about the person needling you. Your goal is to open up the relationship, to find a foundation upon which you can build for the future. Your goal is to demolish the psychological barrier, not to find out who is responsible for it. You must make it easy for the other person to save face.

The EEOC May Be a Last Option. In most cases of testing (even when a healthy relationship has yet to be built), the principles and techniques found in other chapters of this book are applicable and it may be helpful for you to consider them. Unless the testing is extremely severe or prolonged, you may be better off not going to others either inside or outside your organization for help. However, if you can prove that discrimination or sexual harassment has occured, you should feel free to take your case to your company's affirmative action officer or to your local Equal Employment Opportunity Commission (EEOC).

You will be respected for taking care of the problem yourself. If, however, you have made every effort to clear up the problem over a reasonable length of time and you have had no success, you should go to your supervisor and discuss it honestly and freely. Situations of this kind should not be permitted to continue to the point at which departmental morale and productivity are impaired.

Summary

Your comfort level as a new employee may depend upon how quickly you adapt to your supervisor and coworkers—and they to you. No doubt, you'll find some adjustments are necessary on your part for you to become a productive contributor and effective team member in your new environment.

While some personal teasing and organizational testing may be inevitable as you assume your new job or assignment, you should not be subjected to questionable or long-term personal testing. Do not anticipate encountering negative and excessive testing and teasing in your new job. If you do anticipate it, however, you are sure to "find" what you are looking for and end up making more out of the situation than you would have if you had been more positive.

By keeping a positive outlook, you may never encounter the rare occasion when such a problem comes your way. You may even get through a rather negative situation without realizing it, mainly because you took a positive approach to handling it. Also keep in mind that all negative situations may not be able to be resolved without using some of the more direct and drastic actions presented in this chapter. If you are forced to take specific steps to diffuse a negative situation, it is still to your advantage to be as positive as you can. Your future interactions will depend on it.

So, for the most part, you will find that teasing and testing probably will be good-natured. You may even find that the teasing and testing you experience as a new employee are enjoyable. Lighthearted initiation rites can be fun and can help you become accepted by your team—if you have the right attitude.

Test Your Understanding

Respond to the following items to test your understanding of the chapter.

Part A: Circle the correct answer (T = True; F = False) for each of the following statements.

T F 1. Being on the receiving end of teasing and testing is the price a person pays for being the new person on the block.

T F   2. Personal teasing (not testing) is often based upon deep-seated prejudice.

T F   3. Using your assigned work space for stacking department materials would be a good example of organizational testing.

T F   4. An individual should just go along with teasing or testing, even though it destroys his (or her) human dignity.

T F   5. Hostility does not manifest itself in pure personal teasing.

Part B: Circle the letter of the correct answer for each of the following items.

6. If you are on the receiving end of some healthy personal teasing, you should (a) not take it personally, (b) challenge the person who is initiating the teasing, (c) go to your supervisor to get it stopped, (d) resign.

7. To address negative testing that has lasted longer than a reasonable length of time, it probably is best to (a) continue to ignore it, (b) make personal accusations, (c) confront the situation to settle the issue, (d) get the EEOC involved as quickly as possible.

Part C: Write a short response to demonstrate your understanding related to the following item.

8. Discuss the differences between teasing, personal testing, and organizational testing.

Turn to the back of the book to check your answers.

If you can turn a negative
situation into a positive one,
you have conquered
one of the most powerful
attributes known to man.

Think and Respond

Respond to the following items with two or three complete sentences.

1. Explain why it is important to gain acceptance in a new work environment.

2. What is teasing and why is it done?

3. What is the purpose of organizational testing?

4. What is personal testing and why is it done?

5. Explain how negative testing can and should be addressed.

Classifying Teasing and Testing

Listed in the following table are ten "situations." Read each one carefully and then select the proper column (classification) to write out briefly how you would handle it. Suggested answers are provided for the first two situations to help you get started. After you have finished the remaining eight, you may wish to compare your answers with the suggestions that follow the activity.

IMPROVEMENTS	PERSONAL TEASING	ORGANIZATIONAL TESTING	PERSONAL TESTING
1. A high-school student gets a job in a fast-food operation and is immediately assigned the job of cleaning the restrooms.	_____	*Say thanks and do a good job.*	_____
2. A new employee in a steel mill has her (or his) hard hat hidden the second day by a coworker.	_____	_____	*Go along with the gag.*
3. An employee is asked to serve on a credit union committee and is immediately assigned to take minutes of the meeting.	_____	_____	_____
4. An autocratic boss assigns a minority employee to a task that he (or she) is obviously not ready to perform successfully.	_____	_____	_____
5. A coworker gives an employee the silent treatment for six months.	_____	_____	_____
6. An employee is left on a starting job for what seems a long time.	_____	_____	_____
7. Someone keeps misplacing a new employee's time card.	_____	_____	_____
8. An employee complains to her (or his) supervisor about the behavior of a coworker.	_____	_____	_____
9. A supervisor keeps reprimanding a new employee in front of others.	_____	_____	_____
10. A new employee is told that overtime is illegal for the first month an employee works.	_____	_____	_____

Suggested Answers for Improvements

1. See suggested answer provided.

2. See suggested answer provided.

3. Organizational testing: Accept the assignment with a good attitude.

4. Personal testing (challenging): Go along with it until you have won support of coworkers; then ask for more training.

5. Personal testing (challenging): Ignore it with a smile, do not let it bother you, and keep trying to establish a relationship.

6. Organizational testing: Stay positive as you ask your supervisor what you can expect in the future.

7. Personal teasing: Make up a time card of your own. Do not let it bother you.

8. Personal testing (challenging): Confront the employee.

9. Personal testing (challenging): Confront the supervisor.

10. Personal teasing: Enjoy the comment and joke back.

CASE 15

Confrontation

"A person's attitude can stand just so much."

Jonas graduated from a state college as a consumer science major. He was ambitious, talented, and determined. In practically no time at all, he had found a good position with a highly reputable retail operation. His position involved working in a laboratory in which all consumer products purchased by the buyers were tested for safety, wearability, and other standards.

Jonas received many compliments on his work from his supervisor. In addition, he was able to build good relationships with all his coworkers except Ms. Robertson. Ms. Robertson was a longtime employee and very critical of Jonas. She constantly made unkind and seemingly uncalled for remarks about Jonas.

Jonas decided it was time to do something about the growing negative relationship with Ms. Robertson. By checking around, Jonas discovered that two previous employees had resigned because of Ms. Robertson. Feeling a little better that there probably was nothing personal about the trouble he was having, Jonas waited for the right opportunity to meet with Ms. Robertson. This is what Jonas said to her: "Ms. Robertson, I have been here for two months and I seem to be getting along with everyone but you. I like my job. I want to keep it. If I have done anything to offend you, please tell me and I'll certainly make a change. I want very much to win your respect, but I do not intend to put up with your unfair treatment of me any longer."

A. Discuss: Did Jonas do the right thing? Was he too forceful in his approach? What would you have done in his place? If you were the supervisor, how would you resolve the conflict?

B. Expand Your Understanding: Research the organizational practices of new employee orientation and initiation. Use human-relations textbooks/journals and talk with employers, employees, and human-relations managers. Determine if there are differences in teasing/testing practices over the decades. Then offer some suggestions to Jonas and Ms. Robertson. Suggest practices new employees should expect and how they should respond to various initiation situations.

CHAPTER 16

Absenteeism Can Damage Relationships

"What? Late again?"

> Thought for the Day: Even the very best intentions can never take the place of being dependable, punctual, reliable, and credible.

PERFORMANCE COMPETENCIES

- Understand that absenteeism and lateness are very problematic for management.

- Appreciate the accepted conditions for absenteeism that are included in most organizations' absenteeism policies.

- Recognize the challenges of absenteeism and lateness faced by employees in building relationships and a work career.

- Identify nine tips to help you avoid abusing your company's attendance requirements and to help you build good working relationships.

"Sorry I didn't show up for work yesterday, Rich. I had a little too much to drink at Harry's party, so I decided to stay in the sack and sleep it off."

"Khatir, I hope things weren't too hard on you last Friday. I had a case of the blahs, so I stayed home and got a few personal things taken care of."

"Tyrese, did you hear that snide crack from my supervisor? She surely gets uptight when I'm a little late now and then. You'd think that I'd committed a major crime."

"Don't breathe a word to the boss, Roz, but I'm going to make this a three-day weekend so I can go on a hiking trip. See you Tuesday."

"Hey Bob; I've got to sneak out and take care of something personal. Cover for me while I'm gone, will you?"

MANAGEMENT'S VIEW OF ABSENTEEISM

Why Is Absenteeism Increasing? Absenteeism is a phenomenon that management lives with on a daily basis. So are the problems of lateness and of employees leaving their workstations without authorization. Such practices are reflected in a worker's dependability, reliability, and ethical standards—or lack of these desirable work attributes.

Pride in good attendance is an admirable, valuable personal trait

Most experts agree that fewer and fewer people are taking pride in their attendance or on-time records. Why? Those close to the scene have come up with many answers regarding why work absenteeism and lateness are increasing. Frequently, the same reasons also are given to why worker dependability and ethical standards appear to be decreasing. The four main reasons follow.

- *Commitment to an employer is not what it used to be.* People no longer commit themselves to a career or company as much as they did in the past. Many employees feel that even if they show commitment to their employers, they receive little or no reciprocity. That is, some people feel that because many organizations do not appear to value and reward employee loyalty, loyalty of the employee to an organization does not need to be returned. Employees who believe or follow this rationale will not develop the good work ethics needed to build a career.

- *School habits are transferred to work.* Schools and educational institutions have become so relaxed that the adjustment to the discipline of a business setting is more difficult than it was even a few years ago. Many people also are taking a much more casual approach to their lifestyles. While a casual lifestyle is not a negative, this casualness frequently is reflected in the work environment by such things as relaxed dress codes, less formal workstations, increasingly informal communication (e-mail, memos versus letters, etc.), casual group and team meetings, fast-food working lunches, and so forth. Many businesses have created more casual working environments so employees are more comfortable and, thus, more productive. However, when casualness negatively affects an employee's work performance, problems arise. Employees who translate casualness into poor work habits also jeopardize their working relationships.

- *Organizational rules are not valued as much as they used to be.* Many people do not feel obligated to live up to attendance standards or rules imposed on them by organizations. Some people feel that many companies appear to be too rigid for today's fast-paced society. Some feel that management's focus on productivity and the bottom line has forced workers to follow unrealistic policies and procedures. As a result, some employees feel it is unnecessary to pay attention to company rules or, worse yet, that the rules don't apply to them. Work rules usually are established for the benefit of employees—for worker safety and for an understanding of management's view of the work environment. Employees who don't follow the rules put their jobs at risk.

- *People take their personal lives to work.* People allow personal problems to spill over into their work environment more than in the past. More and more employees are using their employers' time and resources to take care of their personal challenges. For example, consider today's technology access. While technology tools have helped to improve many work tasks, some people feel technology access at work can be used for personal communication needs. Some people feel that such access (including use of personal cell phones and other devices) gives them the right to communicate with family and friends while at work. Also, some people feel that because their coworkers take personal privileges at work, they, too, should be permitted to do so—they feel it is their right. However, employees who allow their personal lives to affect their work, who take their employers' time to solve their personal problems, or who are absent from work for personal reasons are not giving their employers an honest effort. Management wants satisfied workers, but cannot afford the luxury of doing so if the cost is too high.

The preceding discussion should have given you a fairly good idea about differences that exist between the views of management and workers—and why productivity, responsibility, ethics, and especially absenteeism are issues of concern to management. Employees who give reasons and rationale for not being dependable and reliable and for not practicing good ethics merely reinforce poor work behavior and bad habits. They misguide their thinking, and such thinking can lead to career disaster.

No doubt, the wise person will avoid finding justification for bad habits and practices at work. It is important to understand why management views your work contribution as it does and why management is so concerned about the phenomenon of absenteeism. If you understand these things you'll find the best advice you can possibly follow is to take pride in your work and value your employment; develop the attributes that will help you build strong and healthy relationships needed for career success.

ABSENTEEISM POLICIES

Acceptable Conditions for Absenteeism.
More than likely, there will be times you will be absent from work. There are acceptable and unacceptable reasons for work absences. Because absenteeism has become such a troublesome issue for management, most organizations have developed policies relating to work absences. What is the basic policy that most business and government organizations have toward absenteeism and reporting late to work? What is acceptable and what is not? What is management's attitude toward the problem? What action do most companies take with those who consistently violate their policies?

Most professional managers in business and government endorse and try to get their employees to live within the framework and spirit of a basic absenteeism policy. Such a policy usually spells out the conditions that employees should follow when determining whether or not they should be absent from work. There are three generally acceptable reasons why an employee should be absent from work. That is, an employee should not come to work if any of these conditions are applicable.

1. By coming to work, the employee may endanger his (or her) own health or that of workers who work with him.
2. The employee is in a psychological or emotional state that could hurt on-the-job productivity and possibly create an unsafe condition.
3. The employee has a serious personal or family emergency.

If none of the previously listed conditions exists, employees should be on the job and, except in special cases, they should be there on time. This basic absenteeism policy might sound harsh and autocratic, but organizations have had years of experience with the problem of absenteeism and lateness. They feel that unless they take a firm stand, they will be misinterpreted by some and taken advantage of by others.

Need for an Absenteeism Policy.
In order to make a profit and stay in business, most organizations must operate under tight production and service schedules. These schedules are built around employees. An assembly line from which a few workers are absent is no longer an

assembly line. When a customer wants to buy something in a retail store and there is no one available to help, a sale can be lost. If a customer goes to a restaurant and the waitperson is doing the work of two because another waitperson didn't show up, the customer may never return.

Management has learned that when an employee or supervisor doesn't show up for work as scheduled, immediate and costly adjustments are necessary if production is to continue and customers are to be kept happy. Sometimes, but not always, the other employees can pitch in and fill the gap. But most of the time, the company pays at least a small price in loss of efficiency, loss of sales, or loss of customer faith. In short, the absence of an employee usually costs the company money in one way or another. If the absence is necessary, no one complains. But if the absence is unnecessary, then management must become concerned and involved.

There is a direct, inverse relationship between absenteeism and profitability

Chronic lateness by an employee, although not usually as serious or expensive for the company as absenteeism, is still a problem. A late employee can delay the changing of shifts. An employee who is constantly late can upset a conscientious supervisor and make her (or him) more difficult for others to work with for the rest of the day. Most serious of all is the negative influence the consistently late employee has on the productivity of others. The supervisor who takes a soft approach to such an employee stands the chance of losing the respect of other, more reliable employees.

EMPLOYEE ABSENTEEISM CHALLENGES AND CONSEQUENCES

Employee Challenges Associated with Absenteeism.
Absenteeism, lateness, and unauthorized time away from work are not only management problems. They should also be viewed as problems and challenges to the employee. That is primarily what this chapter addresses. How should you look at these problems? How will they influence your future?

Supervisors and workers who fail to build a good record in these areas will almost always pay a very high price in terms of their relationships with others for reasons that follow.

- *Basic rule #1: A poor attendance record will keep you from building good horizontal working relationships with your coworkers.* Your coworkers may deeply resent having to pick up some of your responsibilities and work tasks when you are absent. Few kinds of behavior will destroy a relationship more quickly than being frequently absent and causing coworkers to "carry" your load in your own department.

- *Basic rule #2: A poor attendance record will strain the vertical working relationship with your supervisor.* Your absences will make more work for your supervisor personally, it will cause her (or his) department to be less efficient, and it will put her on the spot with other employees. Most experts agree that it is almost impossible for an employee who is guilty of chronic absenteeism to maintain a healthy relationship with an immediate supervisor.

In addition to the preceding two basic rules with reasons an employee should avoid absenteeism and lateness, the following four reasons should receive consideration.

1. *Excessive absenteeism and lateness will build a credibility gap between you and management.*   A credibility gap can seriously hurt your future because those who cannot be depended upon are seldom promoted. It should also be pointed out that, right or wrong, some management people feel there is a moral aspect to the problem. If an individual accepts employment, he (or she) agrees to abide by the rules, within reason. Absence without sufficient cause is interpreted by management as moral failure.

2. *Records that reflect heavy absenteeism and lateness are permanent.*   Attendance records can be forwarded upon request to other organizations. The record you are building now could help or hurt you should you decide to move elsewhere.

3. *If you have a poor attendance record, your integrity may be questioned.*   Demonstrating good attendance at work is a good way to show responsibility. When you can be depended on to be at work and on time, you build integrity and trust that shows you take your job seriously. As a result, when you need to request to be absent for personal and nonemergency reasons, your request probably will seem more acceptable.

4. *Job security is jeopardized by excessive absenteeism.*   A poor attendance record is good cause for your being passed over for promotions and is a consideration when the workforce needs to be reduced. That is, in case of layoffs, cutbacks, and reassignments, those people with poor attendance records are usually the first to be terminated or reassigned.

The attendance record you establish today will still be there tomorrow

Abusing Rules Has Consequences. Most organizations want to be understanding about employees' problems. They realize that there are exceptions to the rules, and they are willing to listen and make adjustments. Employees who consistently abuse the rules are usually counseled and given adequate warning. Those who play it straight with their companies usually receive fair and just treatment in return. To illustrate the causes and results of absenteeism and lateness among employees and supervisors, the following five examples are cited.

Dennis. Dennis was a productive worker. When he was on the job and feeling well, nobody could complain about him. He had plenty of skill and a great sense of humor and was always willing to pitch in and help others.

His only real problem was drinking. Every other week, he would really tie one on and call in sick.

About a year ago, Dennis and his supervisor had a series of heart-to-heart talks about Dennis's drinking. Three months later, Dennis and a counselor from the human resource department discussed the problem on three different occasions. Six months ago—half a year since his first talk with the supervisor—Dennis was referred to the company physician for professional help. Last week, with full documentation by the organization, Dennis was given his termination notice. His record showed that he had been absent more than thirty days during the previous year. The organization Dennis worked for had tried to help, but Dennis had refused to help himself.

Tamika. When she first came to work, Tamika showed great promise. She had all the skills necessary to become a top-flight employee, and she was great with people. Among some of the staff, she quickly became known as the "too" girl. She was too pretty, too vivacious, and too popular. She also received too many invitations to too many parties; and, as a result, she was absent too frequently.

It became clear to her supervisor that Tamika just didn't have the physical endurance to lead such an active social life and hold down a demanding full-time job at the same time. During the first six months of employment, she was absent eleven times, each time for one day, and her excuse was always illness. After repeated counseling, Tamika's supervisor finally asked that she be transferred to another department. Management made an attempt to transfer her, but when other supervisors checked on her absentee record, they refused to accept her. After additional unsuccessful counseling, management had to let her go.

Katherine. Katherine was highly ambitious, talented, energetic, and respected by both fellow employees and management. Everybody expected her to move a long way up the executive ladder. She seemed programmed for success. But Katherine's desire for quick recognition and more money caused her to hurt her reputation inside the company. Here is the story.

Katherine took a moonlighting job with a musical group that was good enough to get four or five bookings each week. The job paid good money, but it demanded a lot of energy. After a few months, Katherine not only looked beat, but her on-the-job productivity started to drop. Soon she started calling in sick from time to time. Within six months, she had seriously hurt her reputation.

Fortunately for Katherine, she had an understanding supervisor. After some counseling, Katherine quit her moonlighting and started to build back the fine reputation she had once enjoyed. It cost her at least one promotion, but Katherine did learn an important lesson: any outside activity that drains one's energy to the point at which frequent absences are necessary eventually spells trouble.

Vinnie. Vinnie was an excellent salesperson in a fashion department. He was so good, in fact, that he was being trained as a fashion coordinator and buyer. But Vinnie had one bad habit that he could not shake. He could not organize his day to the point at which he could get to work on time. His time card showed that he was five to fifteen minutes late two or three times each week.

Vinnie's supervisor and the store manager counseled him; Nobody wanted to lose him, but, in the final analysis, management had to weigh the influence of his lateness on the morale and productivity of others. Reluctantly, the decision to release Vinnie was made. He didn't have any trouble getting another job, but the new job didn't have the potential of the one he had lost and the new management was less tolerant of his problem.

Karli and Hugo. A national chain organization was forced to cut back its workforce because of lower sales. It was decided that they could get by with one instead of two employees in a particular department in one of their stores. One individual, either Karli or Hugo, would be transferred to a less-desirable job in another section.

A careful analysis was made to see which of the two employees should be moved. Both were highly respected, and they were equal in all but two respects. Karli had three years' seniority over Hugo, so normally she would stay. But Karli's absentee record was much poorer than Hugo's. Management decided that because Hugo had the better attendance record, he deserved to keep the better job. When Karli was notified and given the reason for the decision, she admitted she had no defense even though she had seniority.

These cases are just a few examples of how employees can hurt their long-range careers by frequent absenteeism or chronic lateness. Based on the five cases just presented, what can you do to avoid the mistakes these employees made? As you ponder your answers, consider three or four beliefs or feelings you have about punctuality, dependability, and similar attributes. Consider also your opinion about work (or school) absenteeism. Then complete the following exercise.

ACTIVITY

My Attitude about Work Absenteeism and Dependability

In this activity, you are asked to formalize your "value statements" about absenteeism and dependability. Record your opinions in the following table and determine how important they are to you. Rate your values by circling the number that best reflects how you feel about it: 1 = Critical in Importance; 2 = Very Important; 3 = Important; 4 = Somewhat Important; 5 = Not Very Important. If you rate any one item as 4 or 5, rewrite the statement—your goal is to identify values that are important to you.

Finally, summarize your value statements into one sentence—preferably a sentence that says something about your attitude.

Provide an opinion you hold about work (a) attendance, (b) absenteeism, (c) punctuality, and (d) dependability.	Rate the importance of the value.
a.	1 2 3 4 5
b.	1 2 3 4 5
c.	1 2 3 4 5
d.	1 2 3 4 5
Summary:	

Is your summary statement an affirmation that you are a motivated, highly dependable worker with a positive attitude and good human-relations skills? If so, great!

If not, read the tips that follow to help you to refocus or redirect your thoughts. Once you realize how important it is to be a worker who is valued by management and take the necessary action in that direction, you'll be on your way to ensuring your future success.

ATTENDANCE RECORD TIPS

Here are a few tips that will help you be a conscientious employee who does not abuse the company policy on absenteeism and lateness.

1. *There are three conditions to be absent from work.* You should stay home from work under the three following conditions: (a) when you are honestly sick and feel it would hurt your health or that of others if you reported to work, (b) when your emotional or mental condition is such that you know you could not contribute to the productivity of the department and may endanger the safety of others, and (c) when you have a family emergency and are urgently needed.

2. *Your employer should be notified as soon as you know you will be absent.* Notify the company at once of your decision to be away from work. Tell your supervisor in an honest and straightforward way why you can't make it. Talk to your supervisor, not to a coworker.

3. *Give a daily update if you are absent longer than a day.* If you stay at home for more than a single day because of illness, it is wise to provide a daily progress report on your condition. Also, you should suggest a time estimate of when you will be able to return.

4. *Save your authorized sick-leave time for real emergencies.* Sick leave provided by your employer should be viewed as a cushion that, if you ever need it, might come in handy. If you never use it, you should assume the attitude that you were lucky you didn't have to do so.

You are accountable for your responsibility—be dependable; be on time

5. *Always give yourself a little lead time when getting ready to report to work.* Do not put yourself in a position in which a small delay getting ready for work or on your way to work will make you late. It is better to be ten minutes early than one minute late. On those rare occasions when you are late, give management a real reason for it.

6. *Take your allotted breaks, but don't extend them.* Breaks should be taken, but don't be absent from your workstation longer than the appropriately specified time. People who always stretch their coffee breaks are not appreciated by their coworkers or supervisor. When emergencies do come up and you must forgo or delay a scheduled break, don't nurse the feeling that you have been cheated and that you need an extra-long break to make up for it.

7. *Be at your workstation when you are supposed to be.* Don't be absent from your workstation for long, unless you work it out in advance with your supervisor. Also, let your coworkers as well as your supervisor know where you will be when you are away. The best way to keep a supervisor from breathing down your neck is to earn your freedom by keeping him (or her) adequately informed.

8. *Insofar as possible, plan absences with your supervisor.* When you have a special reason for being absent from work, such as a family wedding, funeral, or court appearance, work it out with your supervisor as far in advance as possible.

9. *Work out longer periods of absence in advance.* In planning for a medical leave or seeking a leave of absence to act as a care provider for a family member, work out the details with your superior or the department of human resources as far in advance as possible. Make appropriate plans for a competent temporary replacement to be located and trained, so that productivity levels will not suffer during your absence.

Summary

Your attention to being punctual and dependable, as well as to following accepted policies and rules, goes a long way toward building strong relationships with friends, with family, and especially with coworkers and management. In this chapter, we have learned several important points:

1. Absenteeism is problematic for management. While there are many reasons that absenteeism is increasing, most are not acceptable if you want to build the relationships that are necessary for a successful career.

2. Most companies have absenteeism policies based on three general conditions for not going to work: (a) endangering the health of

yourself or others, (b) being so emotionally upset that you could be harmful to others, and (c) experiencing a serious personal or family emergency.

3. Your relationships—both horizontal and vertical relationships—are put in jeopardy by a poor attendance record. In addition, there are at least four other serious consequences of absenteeism that offer a challenge to many employees. Several examples are provided to illustrate some of the causes and results of absenteeism and lateness.

4. Nine tips related to being a conscientious employee are provided to point out why it is your responsibility to be conscientious about attendance, work time, and taking time off. These tips suggest the importance of being accountable for your own responsibility.

A good attendance record shows management that you are sensitive to the needs of others. It shows both management and coworkers that you are a motivated rather than a reluctant worker. It also shows them that you are ready for better opportunities.

Test Your Understanding

Respond to the following items to test your understanding of the chapter.

Part A: Circle the correct answer (T = True; F = False) for each of the following statements.

T F   1. Management people agree that more and more employees are taking pride in their attendance and on-time records.

T F   2. The absence of an employee usually costs a company money in one way or another.

T F   3. Supervisors who are lax about absenteeism and lateness usually are highly respected by both their employees and superiors.

T F   4. It is illegal to forward or discuss the absentee record of a former employee to or with another organization.

T F   5. It is foolish to save your authorized sick-leave time for real emergencies.

Part B: Circle the letter of the correct answer for each of the following items.

6. Absence without sufficient cause is interpreted by management as (a) forgetfulness, (b) moral failure, (c) inexperience, (d) acceptable.

7. A good attendance record includes (a) working out in advance, insofar as possible, planned absences; (b) counting on coworkers to cover for you; (c) taking time off when you believe you deserve it; (d) being secretive about your reasons for an absence.

Part C: Write a short response to demonstrate your understanding related to the following item.

8. Discuss some of the challenges related to absenteeism and lateness that are faced by both employees and management.

Turn to the back of the book to check your answers.

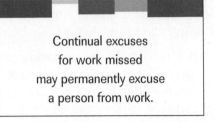

Continual excuses
for work missed
may permanently excuse
a person from work.

Think and Respond

Respond to the following items with two or three complete sentences.

1. Discuss two reasons work absenteeism is on the rise.

2. What are two of the three acceptable reasons for not going to work?

3. Why do most organizations have an absenteeism policy?

4. Explain two reasons—and the consequences—why absenteeism can hurt an employee.

5. Suggest two tips related to work attendance that can help you be a conscientious, valued employee.

SUMMARY ACTIVITY

Tolerance Level Exercise

The purpose of this activity is to provide some insight into your own tolerance level for certain behavioral characteristics. If your tolerance level is high, probably coworkers who are frequently absent or late may not significantly hurt their relationship with you. If your tolerance level is low, probably they will damage their relationship with you. You are to assume the roles of both *employee* and *supervisor* so that you can compare your tolerance levels in both positions.

Using the scale of 1 to 10, indicate your personal tolerance for each of the ten behavioral patterns listed. If your level is extremely high (it doesn't bother you much), you should write in the number 8, 9, or 10. If your level is extremely low (it really upsets you), write in the number 1, 2, or 3. If you have an average tolerance level, write in a 5.

BEHAVIORAL CHARACTERISTIC OF THE INDIVIDUAL	YOUR TOLERANCE SCORE AS A COWORKER	YOUR TOLERANCE SCORE AS A SUPERVISOR
1. Frequently late to work (less than ten minutes)	_____	_____
2. Frequently late to work (more than ten minutes)	_____	_____
3. Uses sick leave when not sick	_____	_____
4. Frequentl absent without plausible excuse	_____	_____
5. Frequent and extended personal telephone calls	_____	_____
6. Consistently overextends coffee break	_____	_____
7. Spends too much time socializing and discussing personal matters	_____	_____
8. Frequently late to staff meetings (more than five minutes)	_____	_____
9. Needs to be reminded to turn in reports on time	_____	_____
10. Frequently takes extended lunch hours	_____	_____

As you analyze your scores, remember that some of your coworkers or your supervisor may have a lower tolerance level than yours. Your present attitude toward being late and absent could be damaging your relationships with others more than you think.

CASE 16
Balance

"Nobody could balance my act."

Lorraine works in the Internal Documents unit of a large gas and oil firm. She is an assistant to Mr. Hodges, whose job is to write employee manuals relating to company policies and procedures. Lorraine assists Mr. Hodges in updating the company database and informing all the right people as soon as a manual is in effect and available to them.

It is easy to like Lorraine. She is highly efficient at her job, always willing to pitch in to help others, and often forgoes her break or stays late to catch up on her work. Lorraine, however, creates real concern for her supervisor and coworkers by her excessive absenteeism. Some of Lorraine's coworkers often bet on just which day she will fail to show up.

Lorraine has trouble balancing home and career. A highly protective single parent of a three-year-old daughter, Sissy, Lorraine sometimes stays home to catch up on home chores or when Sissy has the sniffles. When Lorraine calls in (she doesn't always phone), her excuse almost always relates to an illness—either her own or Sissy's.

Over the last three months, departmental productivity has dropped measurably because of adjustments made to compensate for Lorraine's absences. For example, Lorraine's coworkers are frequently pulled away from their work to do hers. Reassigned employees must be informed in a timely manner about mergers, ongoing sensitive acquisitions, employee transfers/layoffs, and other critical events that, if delayed, could create serious legal implications for the company. Mr. Hodges needs someone he can depend on to meet deadlines and who takes responsibility for job assignments. Lorraine's work is commendable, but Mr. Hodges never knows when he can count on her to get it done or when he has to follow up. All in all, Lorraine's relationships with Mr. Hodges and coworkers are paper thin.

A. Discuss: How far, in your opinion, should Lorraine's supervisor and company go to protect Lorraine's job?

B. Expand Your Understanding: Research the topic of absenteeism as it relates to work productivity and human relations. Vary your sources to include Internet research, company policy manuals, personal interviews, human-relations books, and so forth. Draw some conclusions about your findings that would be good advice for Lorraine, Mr. Hodges, you, and, for that matter, anyone.

CHAPTER 17

Avoiding Six Common Human-Relations Mistakes

"Mistakes? Don't look at me!"

Thought for the Day: It is totally unrealistic to expect a quality result without giving a quality effort.

PERFORMANCE COMPETENCIES

- Understand why a failure to listen, the first of six common human-relations mistakes that people make, can seriously damage your communication skills.

- Recognize that underestimating others, a second common human-relations mistake that people make, is an assumption that can be hurtful to you and others.

- Recognize that a failure to report and admit a mistake, a third common human-relations mistake that people make, can turn a minor problem into a big one.

- Appreciate why the failure to provide your own motivation, a fourth common human-relations mistake that people make, can affect your personal and career progress.

- Consider why permitting others to turn you into a victim, a fifth common human-relations mistake that people make, will negatively impact your positive attitude.

- Appreciate why falling prey to negative drift, a sixth common human-relations mistake that people make, can drag you down to where you lose focus on what is important to you.

Both new and experienced employees make human-relations mistakes that damage their personal progress. It is the purpose of this chapter to single out and explain the implications of six of the most common mistakes: (1) failure to listen, (2) underestimating others, (3) failure to report or admit mistakes to management, (4) failure to provide your own motivation, (5) permitting others to turn you into a victim, and (6) falling prey to negative drift.

Understanding the importance of avoiding these six common human-relations mistakes will go a long way in helping you to build strong, healthy relationships. While it will take work on your part to rise above these pitfalls, you are sure to reap the benefits that go with being in control of your motivation and positive attitude.

FAILURE TO LISTEN (HUMAN-RELATIONS MISTAKE #1)

Listening Is Critical to Relationships. The art of listening is a basic human-relations skill. Many excellent books on the subject can be found in your public library and local book stores. If you read just one, you will improve your competency in this area. Our discussion of the art of listening will be brief and to the point.

Concentration: A Learning Basic. Listening requires concentration. *Thus, the first step in learning how to listen is to learn how to concentrate.* Hearing is a selective process. Most people hear only what they want to hear. Your challenge, then, is to listen to what is important and push other sounds to the outer edge of your hearing. There are so many sounds around you that you may not be picking up the ones that are vital to your happiness and success.

Listening is critical to good communication

On the job, hearing is a matter of practical communication. When a supervisor or fellow worker wishes to transmit an idea, a warning, or a change in procedure to you, he (or she) frequently does it verbally. There may be other sounds he cannot eliminate. It may be the end of the day, and you may be tired. His words may mean one thing to him and another to you. Good, clear, accurate communication is never easy.

Let us assume, however, that the person initiating the message does the best job possible. Does this ensure that you will receive the message? Of course not! You are the receiver; if your mind is focused elsewhere when the message is transmitted, *you may hear the sounds but fail to get the message.*

Advertising executives and specialists have recognized for years how difficult it is to get a verbal message home. The difficulty is most apparent in television commercials. There, the name of the product is often repeated six or more times in thirty seconds. If you are really listening, you may feel that such repetition is an insult to your ability to receive. You would be justified in having this reaction. But the advertising people do not assume that you are a good listener. They assume that you are a typical (that is, poor) listener. Consequently, to be sure the product name makes an impression, they pound it home through repetition.

Your supervisor is not an advertising expert, nor does she (or he) have the time to pound her message home. She feels she should be able to say it once and have it understood. She assumes you are a good listener.

Why Listening Takes Effort. Sometimes it is very difficult just to sit back and listen. There are three basic reasons why listening is difficult:

1. *Some people get overly caught up in their own thoughts.* People are often so busy with their own thoughts and desires, related and nonrelated, they are 90 percent sender and only 10 percent receiver. When this happens, the communication system breaks down.

2. *Some people are extremely self-centered.* Some individuals are so self-centered that they think only in terms of themselves. That is, instead of listening to what is being said, they merely wait for the speaker to finish so they can talk. Getting their thoughts organized keeps them from being good listeners.

3. *Some people analyze others instead of listening to them.* Some people allow themselves to analyze the motives or personality traits of the person speaking and, again, fail to hear what is being said.

Listening Can Be a Dollar-and-Cents Matter. In business and industry, the ability to listen is often a matter of dollars and cents. A draftsman who doesn't hear an architect tell him to make a certain change in a blueprint can cause the loss of thousands of dollars when a bid is accepted on specifications that are not correct. A salesperson who fails to hear a message from a client and, as a result, does not comply with an important delivery date can lose not only the sale but also a valued customer.

Poor communication can be costly—in money and human relations

Communication problems can also cost money in factories. Consider, for example, Dan's failure to get the right message from his shop foreman and how costly it was to his company.

Dan. On his way to his regular morning coffee break—and somewhat preoccupied with his own thoughts, Dan was stopped by his foreman and was told to change the tolerance on a machine part he would be turning out for the rest of the day. After his coffee break, Dan returned to his machine, made an adjustment, and worked hard the rest of the day to complete all of the parts. The following day, he was called on the carpet for producing parts that were too small. What had happened? Dan had been told to increase the size of the part, but he had decreased it instead. His failure to receive—and retain—the right message was a serious mistake, and it cost his company money in terms of both time and materials.

You can think of many other examples. It can even be said that when safety precautions are the subject of the message, the ability to listen can be a matter of life and death.

Are You a Good Listener?

Let's look at your ability to listen from the viewpoint of your supervisor who is, after all, the primary sender of important messages to you. Here are some questions you can ask yourself to determine whether you are a good listener:

- Does your supervisor have to fight to get your attention?

- Do you find yourself thinking about something else the moment your supervisor starts talking?

- Does your supervisor insult you by repeating the message because she (or he) senses you are a poor listener? Or do you find you must go back and ask the supervisor to repeat it?

- Do you sometimes feel confused about instructions given to you when you start to do the requested job?

If you can say "no" to these questions, you may be a good listener. If not, you should concentrate on improving your listening skills.

Being a good listener is not easy. It will take a conscientious effort on your part. But one of the finest compliments you will ever receive from a superior will be something like this: "One thing I really like about Prabir is that if you tell him something once, you know he's got it. You never have to tell him twice."

In the following exercise, you will find several good listening tips—tips that can help you every single day to become a better communicator.

ACTIVITY

My Listening Skills

In the box provided for each of the following items, rate yourself on how well you listen. For example, 10 = Excellent . . . 1 = Poor. Then, for every item you rated as "8" or less, develop a strategy for improving that skill.

1. ☐ Always look at the person who is sending the message. Looking at the speaker will help you concentrate and close out unimportant noises. Your eye contact also will send a message to the speaker that you are listening.

Strategy: _____

2. ☐ If your supervisor has trouble sending out clear signals, you must make the extra effort to listen more carefully. Although it is primarily his (or her) responsibility to be a good sender, it is still to your advantage to receive the message as clearly as possible.

Strategy: _____

3. ☐ To remember the message, take some notes. Review the notes. Repeat the message in your mind a few times. Put any change ordered in the message into practice as soon as possible. When appropriate, repeat the message to your supervisor.

Strategy: _____

4. ☐ Refrain from coming up with an excuse when you receive criticism. You will improve more if you listen to what you are doing wrong rather than if you quickly come to your own defense.

Strategy: _____

5. ☐ Think, reply briefly if necessary, and then continue to listen so that you receive the complete message.

Strategy: _____

6. ☐ Always ask questions right away if you don't understand something. If you don't ask for clarification of a point, you may not fully get the message that follows.

Strategy: _____

7. ☐ If you find yourself in conversation with someone who is overly talkative, do not hesitate to interrupt after a polite period of time. If you do not interrupt, you may become so irritated you may not listen anyway.

Strategy: _____

UNDERESTIMATING OTHERS (HUMAN-RELATIONS MISTAKE #2)

Your Assumptions May Be Faulty. The second of the six big mistakes, according to human resources people, is that of underestimating others. A superior or coworker may not appear to be doing much from your limited perspective. You may, therefore, wrongly assume that he (or she) is coasting. Assuming could be a big mistake.

Do not confuse assumptions with facts

Here is a simple case to emphasize the point.

Horace. Once Horace completed the thirty-day training program of his new job with a major metropolitan department store, he was assigned to Ms. Smith, the manager of inexpensive women's apparel.

Horace soon discovered that he was part of a rather hectic operation. Merchandise moved in and out of the department quickly. Ms. Smith was not an impressive person to Horace. Her desk was disorderly. She seemed to move in many directions at the same time. She seemed to spend more time than necessary talking to the employees.

Horace decided that he had drawn an unfortunate first assignment.

It was his good luck to meet a young buyer at lunch one day. From this woman, he learned that Ms. Smith had the most profitable department in the store and an outstanding reputation with all top management people. Ms. Smith had trained more of the store's executives than any other person. It was then obvious that Horace had received one of the best assignments and had seriously underestimated Ms. Smith.

The new employee in this case learned an important lesson without getting hurt. He quickly changed his attitude toward his supervisor before the relationship was seriously damaged. He was fortunate.

Damage from Underestimating Others. When you fail to build a quality relationship with a supervisor or coworker because you underestimate her (or him), you may hurt yourself in the following ways.

- Your negative attitude may cause you to learn less from a supervisor or coworker than you otherwise would.

- Coworkers may sense the mistake you are making and see your attitude as a sign of immaturity.

- The individual you have misjudged may sense your attitude and resent it, causing a serious human-relations problem.

Avoid prejudging others

If you are a new employee or have recently accepted a new assignment, remind yourself that you are in the poorest position to estimate the power, influence, and contribution that others are making to the organization, *especially when these people are already in management positions.* You will be smart to avoid prejudging others. Different people make different contributions to the growth and profit of an organization. Top management can see the whole picture, but usually you cannot as a new employee.

If the temptation is too great and you must "at times question the effectiveness" of others, keep your impressions to yourself. You can easily trap yourself by being a "Monday morning quarterback." Underestimating the value of others can keep you from building relationships that are important to your personal progress.

FAILURE TO REPORT OR ADMIT MISTAKES TO MANAGEMENT (HUMAN-RELATIONS MISTAKE #3)

Admit Judgment Errors and Rule Violations. A third common human-relations mistake is failure to admit or report to management personal errors in judgment or violations of company procedures, rules, and regulations.

Everyone makes minor blunders from time to time. Even a good employee is not perfect. Precise and methodical people sometimes make mistakes in calculations. Logical thinkers who pride themselves on their scientific approach to decision making sometimes make an error in judgment. A conscientious person who is very loyal to the organization will, on occasion, violate a company rule or regulation before he (or she) knows it.

Major Damage Can Come from Little Mistakes. Making mistakes happens to the best of people; and, unless you are a most unusual person, they will happen to you. These little mistakes will not damage your career if you admit to them openly. They can, however, cause considerable damage if you try to cover them up and, in so doing, compound the original mistake. To illustrate, take Kari's incident.

Admitting mistakes is part of good human relations

Kari. One of Kari's numerous responsibilities working for a large bank was to deliver documents to various branch operations in the banking system. To make her deliveries, she checked out a company car from the transportation department.

On one such assignment, Kari dented the fender of a company car while backing out of a crowded parking lot. She knew that she should report the damage to the dispatcher, but the dent was so insignificant that she thought it would go unnoticed. Why make a federal case out of a little scratch? Why spoil a clean record with the company over something so unimportant?

Two days later, Kari was called into the private office of her department manager. It was an embarrassing twenty minutes. She had to admit that she was responsible for the damage and that she had broken a company rule by not reporting it. The incident was then closed.

The slight damage to the company car was a human error anyone could make. The big mistake Kari made was in not reporting it. Looking back on the incident, she admitted that the damage to the car was far less than the damage to her relationships with others.

Avoid Smoke Screens. Most little mistakes—and, sometimes, many big mistakes—are accepted and forgotten when they are openly and quickly reported. Throwing up a smoke screen to cover them is asking for trouble. The second mistake may be more damaging than the first.

FAILURE TO PROVIDE YOUR OWN MOTIVATION (HUMAN-RELATIONS MISTAKE #4)

Motivation Comes from Within. The modern approach by management to provide the best possible working environment—and then *give employees the freedom to motivate themselves in their own way*—often leaves a few individuals on the sidelines, unmotivated. It is a human-relations mistake to allow yourself to fall into this category simply because you failed to provide your own motivation to willingly contribute and get your job done to the best of your ability.

In all reality, your own motivation is up to you—you control it. You are the "keeper" of your motivation, just as you are the "keeper" of your attitude. Being in charge of your own motivation and attitude means that you do not have to depend on others for you to stay upbeat and positive. It means you do not have to rely on others to stimulate you or coerce you to get things done; and it means you control your life—in the way you want to control it—because you have found ways to be a positive, productive individual within your environment. You have found ways to move in positive directions and to take positive actions even when there may be negatives all around you.

Motivation is something only you can do for yourself

New employees are expected to possess sufficient self-confidence to engage in the normal work process without always having to be nudged by others. Experienced workers are expected to stay alert and productive without special counseling by their supervisors. Those who stand or sit around while coworkers are busily involved in productivity set themselves apart and, in so doing, injure their relationships with both supervisors and fellow employees.

In the workplace, everyone is expected to be a part of the team and contribute at acceptable levels. Those who wait around expecting or refusing to be motivated leave themselves on the sidelines, where learning opportunities and promotional possibilities are limited.

Positive Motivation Efforts Are Worth It. Of course, anyone can occasionally have an off day. But self-motivation is primarily an attitude of consistent willingness to do whatever it takes (within legal and ethical bounds) to get the job done while meeting established time lines and quality standards. Initially, it may take some extra effort to get your internal motivational generator going. Be willing to try harder and go the extra mile for your organization without constant prodding. More than likely, your managers will be more willing to reciprocate. And, no doubt, you'll be a happier person because you have expended your efforts in a positive direction. Refer to other chapters in this book for more insight into motivation.

PERMITTING OTHERS TO TURN YOU INTO A VICTIM (HUMAN-RELATIONS MISTAKE #5)

Victims Pay a Price. When people are unfortunate and become victims of automobile accidents or needless crimes, they often pay a high price. The consequences can be similarly serious when we permit others to influence us in negative ways; we become human-relations victims. Consider the following.

- Statistically, only a small percentage of people become direct victims of serious crime. Everyone eventually becomes a victim of a damaged relationship.

- Financial loss due to robbery, fraud, or physical injury can be high. So can the loss of a career opportunity that results from unrepaired relationships.

- The emotional and psychological damage of being a human-relations victim can sometimes be as traumatic as being a victim of crime. Becoming a victim of a damaged relationship can cause moodiness, loss of confidence, resentfulness, indignation, and mental distress.

Victimization Is Needless. There are three primary ways people needlessly victimize themselves. People can become victims when they

1. refuse to correct human-relations mistakes quickly,
2. do not make an effort to correct a no-fault situation, and/or
3. permit the emotionalism of a relationship conflict to churn them up inside.

Three States of Victimization. Many times, a conflict will emerge within a relationship and both parties will become increasingly involved in a process that accelerates to more damaging stages. The victimization process can be described in three progressively serious stages:

Stage 1: There is only surface damage and low "hurt" involvement. Restoration possibilities are excellent—no harm is done.

Stage 2: Emotional damage is usually more serious for one individual than for the other. Restoration is more difficult.

Stage 3: As a result of lack of communication, conflict becomes needlessly severe. Both parties become victims. Professional counseling may be needed.

The victimization process varies depending on the individuals and the nature of the conflict. Once started, however, it often becomes a continuous development, until both parties end up losers. Thus, the sooner any damage—no matter how slight—is repaired, the better. Just as both individuals can become victims, both can also become winners.

Suggestions for Avoiding Victimization. To help you avoid self-victimization, here are several suggestions.

- Refer to other chapters in this book to learn about ways to release your frustrations and aggressions harmlessly.

- Remember that the more meaningful a relationship is to you, the higher the risk of self-victimization should a conflict occur.

- A substitute phrase for *self-victimization* is "*holding a grudge.*"

- Let small irritations pass.

- Every time a relationship conflict occurs, ask yourself this question: *Who will become the ultimate victim?*

Let your positive attitude attack negative villains

Obviously as you become more competent at human relations, fewer conflicts surface and there is less of a chance that you become a victim; but, once a conflict develops, you become vulnerable and the steps you take to restore the relationship are critical. If you are not willing to take action (regardless of who may be at fault), you may nullify much of the human-relations progress you have made.

FALLING PREY TO NEGATIVE DRIFT (HUMAN-RELATIONS MISTAKE #6)

Negatives That Override Positives. Frequently, there is a subtle but consistent pressure that pushes us from positive to negative thinking. For lack of a better term, let's call this phenomenon *negative drift*. Similar to a pall of dark smoke that hides a sunny landscape, negative drift is a gloomy cloud that prevents us from seeing the more positive factors in our lives.

What are the causes of negative drift? Most people believe negative drift occurs because there are increasingly more and more negative factors to contend with in today's society. For example:

- Jobs are faster paced and more stressful.

- There is more crime, violence, traffic, litigation, and bureaucracy.

- The media provides an overdose of negative images.

The premise, then, is that we all must live in an environment with considerable negative stimuli and, if we are not cautious, we become more negative *without knowing that it is happening.*

Watch Out for Negative Creep. So how can we avoid becoming prey to negative drift? Most people agree that a strong counterforce is necessary. The problem intensifies when we recognize that an opposing force must be sufficiently powerful to hold back negative drift. Negative drift can creep up on us without our knowing it and, at the same time, cause us to lose focus on the positive factors in our jobs and personal lives. In other words, it is more of a challenge to stay positive in our society today than it was in the past.

Summary

Reflect for a moment and think of the most consistently positive person you know. Now ask yourself this question: Does this individual have to work at it each day to stay positive? Chances are that the answer is a resounding "yes." Even when people have few negatives in their lives, they must continue to "prop up" their attitudes on a daily basis to avoid common human-relations mistakes.

Recognizing some of the pitfalls you can fall into if you drift away from being positive should motivate you to hone the skills that contribute to good human relations. That is, employ whatever motivation you need to

1. Listen carefully to improve your communication.
2. Give people the benefit of the doubt.
3. Admit mistakes.
4. Provide your own motivation.
5. Ward off others who try to turn you into a victim.
6. Avoid letting negative drift take over.

Human-relations mistakes can be costly; they can injure relationships and even cripple careers. While it isn't easy to be positive all of the time, remember that *Your Attitude Is Showing!*

Test Your Understanding

Respond to the following items to test your understanding of the chapter.

Part A: Circle the correct answer (T = True; F = False) for each of the following statements.

T F   1. Most people are good listeners.

T F   2. You will do a better job of listening if you anticipate what people say before they say it.

T F   3. People seldom, if ever, know when you are underestimating them.

T F   4. A substitute phrase for self-victimization is "holding a grudge."

T F   5. Everyone eventually becomes the victim of a damaged relationship.

Part B: Circle the letter of the correct answer for each of the following items.

6. A conflict in a relationship that is more serious for one person than another is considered a "Stage 2" conflict that (a) will require professional counseling, (b) may be difficult to restore, (c) will not harm either person, (d) is merely surface damage.

7. When you make a mistake, it is best to (a) ignore it and go on as if nothing happened, (b) admit it openly, (c) cover it up, (d) blame it on someone else.

Part C: Write a short response to demonstrate your understanding related to the following item.

8. Discuss some of the ramifications should you fail to provide your own motivation (especially motivation to avoid human-relations mistakes).

Turn to the back of the book to check your answers.

If your attitude barometer
suggests the need
for a change in weather,
give it a positive upturn.

Think and Respond

Respond to the following items with two or three complete sentences.

1. Why is listening so important to good communication?

2. What do assumptions have to do with judging others?

3. Suggest two reasons that it is important to admit and report mistakes.

4. Why do you need to take responsibility for your own motivation?

5. How does permitting yourself to become victimized contribute to your becoming negative?

SUMMARY ACTIVITY

Listening Assessment
(Evaluatee Instructions)

To help you improve your listening skills, ask a friend, coworker, or even a family member to rate you on this exercise. Select an individual who knows you well, who will take the survey seriously, and who will give you fair and honest responses. Do not use the questionnaire to restore a relationship with an individual. Use it only with someone with whom you currently have a very healthy relationship.

   Before you start, however, you should be aware of the following:

(1) Most of us are not good listeners, so you may not rate as high as you expect.
(2) If you should discover that you are an average listener or below, do not take it as a personal affront; after all, the idea is to improve your skills from where you are, not from where you think you are.
(3) If you rate above average ("5" or higher on the scale), this is a compliment to your present listening skills. Once you have evaluated the results, make a serious contract with yourself to improve your listening skills.

(Have Evaluator Complete Form)

Now, reread the second paragraph of this exercise and review the responses of your evaluator. Start immediately to improve the areas on which you did not rate high. If you received some compliments, consider the following statement from an anonymous source:

> *"Nothing improves a person's hearing as much as praise."*

Listening Assessment
(Evaluator Form)

Dear Friend, Coworker, or Family Member:

Would you please complete the following form based upon the communications we have had in the past. First, through a comparison with others with whom you have frequent verbal contact, rate me on the following listening scale by circling the number you believe represents my listening skills.

Listening Scale		
Outstanding listener (best listener I know)	10 9 8 7 6 5 4 3 2 1	Extremely poor listener (worst listener I know)

Second,
place a check mark (✓) in the box next to any item you think is applicable to me and will help me improve my listening skills. Please add any suggestions for improvement not covered in the questionnaire.

Suggestions for Improvement

1. ❑ You might consider talking less.
2. ❑ Refrain from interrupting so much.
3. ❑ Be less defensive in communications.
4. ❑ Try to stop forming a reply before you hear me out.
5. ❑ Relax when you communicate.
6. ❑ Slow your mind down so that you won't anticipate what I say before I say it.
7. ❑ Be more attentive and send me signals through your eyes so I know you are listening.
8. ❑ Improve your concentration.
9. ❑ _____
10. ❑ _____

Additional suggestions (including compliments)

_____

_____

Thank you for your open and honest assessment.

CASE 17

Motivation

"Bjorn's okay—he just needs motivation."

Bjorn seemed to have everything going for him: He graduated with academic honors near the top of his class without putting in a lot of extra effort. He had acquired an excellent general knowledge and had mastered a wide range of technical skills well beyond the level of many of his classmates. Bjorn also had excellent human-relations skills, enjoyed sports, and was able to balance his many talents with exceptional ability.

With all of Bjorn's advantages, one would expect him to be highly successful in his first position as he started his work career. Not so. For some reason, Bjorn didn't even begin to live up to his potential. Could it be that as an only child he accepted too much emotional and financial support from his family? Is Bjorn lazy? Is everything too easy for him? Is he too easygoing?

After six months on the job, Bjorn's boss called him into his office for a discussion. Bjorn's boss put it to him this way: "Bjorn, you truly do have everything going for you, but for some reason, you expect others to motivate you. Your inability to be a self-starter is putting you out of step with your coworkers. Frankly, I don't have the time or patience to motivate you to try to help you reach your potential. Even if I did, I wouldn't know where to start. Unless you are willing to try motivating yourself, it won't happen around here, and you will be the loser."

A. Discuss: What, in your opinion, is wrong? What can Bjorn do to become a self-motivated professional?

B. Expand Your Understanding: Develop a thoughtful paper about motivation and the importance it has in everyone's life. Conduct research on the topic as well as on the role motivation has had in the lives of two or more persons you admire. As a result of your research, offer some recommendations to Bjorn. Then make some recommendations you can use in your life. Draw some conclusions about your research that can be used by anyone.

CHAPTER 18

Business Ethics, Rumors, and the Confidence Triangle

"You call that ethical?"

> Thought for the Day: Don't underestimate the power of the golden rule that translates to: "Treat others the way you want to be treated."

PERFORMANCE COMPETENCIES

- Understand that your ethical behavior is seen in your attitude and actions—that is, your ethics are reflected in the way you live your life.

- Evaluate the impact and influences of rumors, rumor mills, and the grapevine.

- Identify six factors that contribute to high ethical standards and good relationship building—factors that help management and you.

- Understand the implications and consequences associated with two types of rumors and confidence triangles.

A discussion of ethical behavior standards in today's workplace has become as common as providing an employee with general information to assist him (or her) in carrying out work duties and tasks. In fact, it has become a general practice for companies of all sizes to give their employees policy manuals, training sessions, and in-house publications related to acceptable personal and organizational ethical practices. Why has business ethics received much more attention in recent years than in the past? Does this mean that personal and company ethics are more important today than only a few years ago?

Ethical behavior should be just as important today as it was ten, twenty, fifty, or even a hundred or more years ago. However, we hear much more about unethical behavior today, possibly because of increased ethics abuse and possibly because both the media and technology give us greater access to know about unethical practices taking place in society. Certainly there is a prevalence of cases associated with unethical practices and fraudulent behavior. There is more than an abundance of questionable ethics issues—related to both companies and individuals—and many of these issues are being debated in our courts of law.

No one is immune to unethical practices and outcomes. That is why organizations must focus on ways to combat the erosion of ethical standards for conducting day-to-day business. Many schools also have found merit in providing more ethics education for students. Learning the importance of values and ethics is the first step to the development of good ethical practices in your life. Demonstrating ethical values and behavior is paramount in developing and building strong human relationships.

ETHICS AND YOUR BEHAVIOR

Dr. Albert Schweitzer once said, "In a general sense, ethics is the name we give to our concern for good behavior. We feel an obligation to consider not only our own well-being, but also that of others and human society as a whole."

Value your ethics in all your actions

Relationship Awareness. Business ethics involves being fully aware of what we are doing in the area of human relationships. Are we treating people the way they want to be treated? Are we complying with rules, such as the laws of the land, the customs and expectations of the community, the principles of morality, and the policies of the organization? Are we being true to ourselves?

Being Honest with Your Employer. Consider, for example, an honest employee who would never steal money from a cash box but who might use the company car to run personal errands while making sales rounds; or a high-producing, devoted employee who might work overtime in an emergency, but tell her (or his) boss he (or she) got caught in traffic upon arriving late the next day when, in fact, he overslept; or a sympathetic employee who knows a coworker is operating a small business on the side (often using company office equipment and supplies), but says nothing.

Attitudes to Be Adopted. Obviously, maintaining high ethical standards is not easy when coworkers may view the subject differently. Following are three attitudes that can help you throw off temptations and be true to yourself.

- *Respect company rules, procedures, and standards.* Remember, you can be unethical without breaking the law. Use common sense and assess the potential damage of an unethical act to your career. Violations are not worth it in the long run.

- *Be willing to test your ethical thinking frequently.* Ask yourself: "Is this the right thing to do? Is it fair? Is it honest? Am I creating a guilt feeling for nothing?"

- *Keep reminding yourself that relationships are built upon trust.* Unethical behavior can destroy relationships because it is difficult to respect an individual who flirts with accepted ethical standards.

ACTIVITY

Practicing Ethical Behavior

Human relations involves being true to yourself and treating people the way they want to be treated. Following are seven mistakes to avoid for maintaining high ethical standards. Read each statement. Then rate the statement according to the way you "practice" the statement: A = Always, F = Frequently, S = Sometimes, or N = Never. That is, circle the letter of the behavior that best describes your actions.

Do I	Rating
1. misrepresent the facts about my job activities or those of a coworker?	A F S N
2. divulge personal or confidential information to coworkers, customers, competitors, or the general public?	A F S N
3. permit, or fail to report, violations of any federal, state, or municipal laws or regulations?	A F S N
4. protect unethical coworkers from corrective discipline?	A F S N
5. condone or fail to report the theft or misuse of company property?	A F S N
6. cover up on-the-job accidents and fail to report health and safety hazards?	A F S N
7. pass on coworkers' ideas as my own?	A F S N

Review your answers. Any items you rate A, F, or S, will need your attention if you intend to build strong relationships.

RUMORS, RUMOR MILLS, AND GRAPEVINES

Rumors. If we consult Webster's *New World Dictionary*, we would find this definition of *rumor*: "General talk not based on definite knowledge; mere gossip; hearsay; an unconfirmed report, story, or statement in general circulation."

All organizations have information collectors—employees who set up and maintain informal networks that keep them informed about what is going on at all times. An informal communication network is generally a harmless activity, provided that it doesn't interfere with the employee's personal productivity and is not used to spread rumors and malicious gossip.

Unauthenticated reports, or rumors, seem to originate and circulate within every group of people, especially when a group's members have common interests and competitive goals. Rumors are common in small communities, social and service groups, schools, churches, and, of course, business organizations.

Rumors and their interpretations can be very dangerous

Why Rumors Circulate. Rumors are based on people's need to share their anxieties with others. Some rumors get started because of faulty communication or unintentional misinterpretation of the original message. Others consist of malicious gossip designed to hurt another person.

Rumor Mills. Two popular expressions have become associated with the circulation of rumors. One is *rumor mill*. This familiar expression implies that rumors, like grain being processed in a mill, are turned out regularly in large numbers, altered, and circulated within the confines of a certain group or organization. Workers who are information collectors are, all too frequently, the chief providers of grist for the rumor mills.

Grapevines. The second popular expression is *grapevine*, which is an unofficial, confidential, person-to-person chain of verbal communication. The grapevine can best be viewed as an underground network that operates within an organization. The rumor mill may get the message started, but the grapevine keeps it moving. The grapevine has the reputation of operating without official sanction; and, usually, the information transmitted has an aura of secrecy.

Not all information that gets into the rumor mill and travels along the grapevine is false. It can be the truth. But the person who introduces the information must have the facts right, and those facts must be transmitted without misinterpretation. These conditions are, of course, seldom present. Even when the original information is accurate, facts can become distorted as they move along the grapevine.

The Reliability of Rumor Mills and Grapevines. The important thing to realize is that information processed through the rumor mill and passed along the grapevine is not reliable. It may not be based upon the facts. It may be slanted to serve the interests of a second, third, or fourth party. It may even be malicious.

For these reasons, the rumor mill should be viewed with considerable caution and information coming through the grapevine should be discounted. You cannot depend on it.

Because rumors occur in all organizations, it is only natural to find them in business and industrial concerns. It follows that there may be a rumor mill in your organization. If there is, be forewarned. Accepting rumors as the truth can cause you to make serious human-relations mistakes. You may, for example, damage a good horizontal or vertical relationship you have built; or you may permit false information to get in the way of building a relationship that would contribute to higher productivity and, perhaps, enhance your own progress.

Be cautious about the significance of the grapevine

Management's Position. What is management's position in regard to rumor mills? This book, of course, cannot speak for your particular management. However, we can say this: The term *rumor mill* is not new to those in leadership positions, and management usually knows when a grapevine exists.

We do not mean that the people responsible for management condone the grapevine, but they know when it is in operation. We know this because they occasionally step in and squelch a false rumor before damage is done to either an individual or the company. They may also deliberately leak some positive information into the grapevine so that employees will get an accurate message in a hurry.

You should realize that keeping employees fully informed on company matters through regular channels is a huge task. Conferences, bulletins, company periodicals, and other media are often not fully effective. But even if they were, it is doubtful that rumors would be eliminated. Management knows this. So if you are on the receiving end of rumors in your job and you sense the existence of a rumor mill, do not let yourself believe that management is not concerned. It is!

Good two-way communication helps to dispel rumors

BEING ETHICALLY RESPONSIBLE

Management is aware that unfounded rumors can cause unnecessary anxiety among employees and that such anxiety hurts the morale of the organization. Management also knows that rumors can sometimes be malicious and that innocent employees can be hurt. Management will do what it can to prevent harm to employees.

Employee's Role. In order to be successful, management needs the help and support of every employee. What might you do to help management?

And, more importantly, what might you do to help yourself? Here are six suggestions:

1. *Admit that there is such a phenomenon as a rumor mill in your organization.* If you are blind to this situation, you may introduce and transmit harmful rumors to others without knowing it.

2. *All information received through the grapevine, especially if it has implications of intrigue, should be viewed with skepticism; and you should not permit grapevine information to disturb you personally.* If it is true, you will have time to adjust to it after you receive it from official sources. Be patient until you get the facts. Partial information is dangerous. Give management time to give you all the facts. Do not take any action or make decisions until you know all the facts.

3. *Do not be guilty yourself of introducing rumors into the grapevine.* You may, by accident, overhear something of a confidential nature and pass it on to someone as the truth, only to discover at a later date that you heard only part of the story. Or you may see something a little unusual and draw the wrong conclusion, as in the case of Rebecca.

   Rebecca. When Rebecca noticed that her supervisor, a young married man, took her coworker, Florence, who was divorced, home two nights in succession, Rebecca decided something was going on between them. Without any malicious intent, Rebecca introduced the matter into the local grapevine; and, as so often happens, the rumor got out of hand. A number of people, including Rebecca herself, ended up hurt. The supervisor was transferred and his replacement was less effective. What was the truth? Florence had put her car in the repair shop for two days, and the supervisor had volunteered to take her home so that she would not have to walk the dark streets alone. Nothing more was involved.

Don't start rumors—your assumptions may be wrong

4. *Refuse to pass on unsubstantiated information you receive secondhand.* If you don't pass on questionable secondhand information, you may break the circuit in the grapevine and perhaps keep others from being disturbed unnecessarily. For instance, sometimes during coffee-break talks, it may be possible to steer conversation away from rumors and onto harmless tracks, such as to sports or television shows.

5. *If you must complain about company matters or company people, do so in the proper manner to your immediate supervisor or blow off steam at home or with a trusted person—but not with your fellow workers.* Avoid complaining at work to eliminate the possibility of having your personal gripes misinterpreted and introduced into the rumor mill. It will also keep anyone from using your complaints to hurt your relationship with your superiors.

6. *Try not to let a nonpersonal rumor that may involve your future with the company upset you until you get the facts.* If you do, there may be a noticeable drop in your personal productivity that will needlessly hurt your future. Make every effort to ignore a rumor until you receive official information. If you find you cannot keep from getting upset, consult your supervisor or someone else in management for the facts before you draw unwarranted conclusions. Many employees have injured their future by premature action based upon a false rumor. Don't fall into this trap.

RUMORS AND CONFIDENCE TRIANGLES

Types of Rumors. We could fill pages with examples and descriptions of the various kinds of rumors that travel along the grapevine. It will serve our purpose best, however, to place them all into two broad classifications: personal and nonpersonal rumors.

Personal Rumors. Many on-the-job rumors involve people's personal lives and are not related to job situations. Some of these fall into the back-fence category. Some are little more than coffee-break gossip. Although there is considerable intrigue in such rumors, the new employee would be wise to keep working relationships strictly that—intrigue— and stay a safe distance from such rumors.

Organizational or Nonpersonal Rumors. Rumors of the second kind concern the organization. They pertain to things that may or may not happen to the company. Although they influence employees, they are not personal. For example, there may have been rumors about layoffs with no factual foundation; rumors that departments were to be eliminated when, in fact, they were to be enlarged; rumors of resignations when, in fact, none were ever contemplated; and rumors of terminations that turned out to be transfers.

Organizational rumors have an enormous influence on the productivity of employees and the general progress of the company. Management, by keeping the official channels of communication open, tries to eliminate them. Rumors continue to exist in most companies, however. Unless employees develop a way to insulate themselves against rumors, they can become constantly insecure about their jobs and their future. Their personal productivity will go up and down based upon the latest rumor. And all for nothing!

Organizational rumors can affect productivity and employee morale

Confidence Triangle. Have you ever heard the expression *confidence triangle*? A confidence triangle is the way a confidential comment can be transmitted to a third party. The following description and diagram will help explain the idea.

We will assume that you are Mr. A. You have a strong, healthy relationship with Mr. B. Occasionally, you talk things over with him in confidence. One day at lunch, you mention that Mr. C has been of great help to you in completing a certain project and that you have considerable respect for his ability and perception.

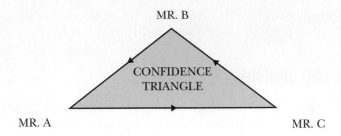

You do not realize that Mr. C has a strong, healthy relationship with Mr. B and that your comments will be transmitted from Mr. B to Mr. C. Of course, this will not hurt your relationship with Mr. C. In fact, it will improve it, because the favorable comments have been made in confidence and transmitted by a person Mr. C respects.

Positive and Negatives of Confidence Triangles. So far, the confidence triangle has worked in a positive manner. But what if your comments had been negative? Instead of improving your relationships with Mr. B and Mr. C, you would have damaged them. The confidence triangle works both ways. The truth is, then, that you can strengthen or weaken relationships with some people through others. When you say something positive about a third person to an individual with whom you have good rapport, relationships can improve. When you say something negative, the opposite can happen.

Nobody likes to accept advice. Even when advice comes at the right time from the right person in the right way, it is difficult to accept. Yet, sometimes accepting advice is the smart thing to do.

Let us assume that at this very moment the conditions are ideal and you are willing to accept advice. What might be the best human-relations advice you could receive? In all probability, it would be this:

Silence can be golden

If you can't say something good about a person, don't say anything at all.

Like most advice that comes in such simple terms, this precept is far easier to state in print than to put into practice. Yet the degree to which you observe this simple rule on your new job will have considerable influence on your success.

Summary

Adhering to acceptable ethical standards starts with a commitment or obligation to be honest and true to yourself. You select the standards that are important to you, and you reflect your standards through your attitude and behavior. Whatever path you choose to follow, your ethics show in everything you do. That is, your ethical behavior is critical to the respect of others, to all your endeavors, and to the building of strong positive relationships.

Understanding the nature of rumors, the power of the rumor mill, and the scope of the grapevine should teach you that your human relations and productivity can be easily damaged as a result of circulating talk that may or may not be fact. People have need for sharing their concerns and ideas with others; we do it every day. However, if communication is misinterpreted or, even worse, is malicious gossip, relationships can be damaged. Management as well as employees suffer; thus, the price that is paid can be rather high.

Being ethically responsible takes a conscious effort on your part. The chapter provides six suggestions to help you keep your ethics intact. The suggestions also help management because nonfactual information that may be passed around can have damaging effects on both individuals and an organization.

Rumors usually are of two types: personal and nonpersonal. Both have consequences and can have significant implications, especially when a confidence triangle is involved. The impact of the confidence triangle can be positive or negative—all the more important for you to be very careful about what you say to others.

It has been said that many human-relations problems are self-created. There is truth in this statement.

Test Your Understanding

Respond to the following items to test your understanding of the chapter.

Part A: Circle the correct answer (T = True; F = False) for each of the following statements.

T F   1. Business ethics involves being true to yourself and treating others the way they want to be treated.

T F   2. A good way to improve the relationship between you and the person with whom you are talking is to badmouth others.

T F   3. Chances are you will not find a rumor mill where you work.

T F   4. You should not permit information received via the grapevine to disturb you personally because it could hurt your productivity and, eventually, your career.

T F   5. Most human-relations problems are self-created.

Part B: Circle the letter of the correct answer for each of the following items.

6. Unethical behavior can easily destroy a relationship because most relationships are built on (a) trust, (b) keeping secrets, (c) talking about others, (d) rumors.

7. Information received through the grapevine should be considered (a) true, (b) false, (c) factual, (d) with skepticism.

Part C: Write a short response to demonstrate your understanding related to the following item.

8. Explain what is meant by the "confidence triangle."

Turn to the back of the book to check your answers.

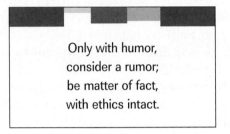

Only with humor,
consider a rumor;
be matter of fact,
with ethics intact.

Think and Respond

Respond to the following items with two or three complete sentences.

1. Discuss two attitudes of ethical behavior that can help you "be true to yourself."

2. Explain the differences (and similarities of outcomes) between rumors, rumor mills, and grapevines.

3. Describe two suggestions for being ethically responsible in your work environment.

4. Explain the difference between personal and nonpersonal rumors and their effect in the workplace.

5. What does "not saying anything at all" have to do with the confidence triangle?

The Confidence Triangle Exercise

One of the messages of Chapter 18 is that if you can't say something good about another person, don't say anything at all. In short, bad-mouthing others is dangerous. This activity presents five situations and then lists various possible outcomes. Place a check mark (✓) in the blank for those possible outcomes you feel might actually happen. You may provide more than one response to each situation. The purpose of the activity is to make you more aware of the dangers of casual conversations in which confidence is implied.

1. Nathalie is having lunch with Sue. Sue says "Just between you and me, I think that our supervisor is being unfair to you." Nathalie replies. "Don't worry about it. I am going to get her job if it's the last thing I ever *do*."

   _____ a. Sue might carry Nathalie's threat back to the supervisor.

   _____ b. Nathalie might lose Sue's friendship.

   _____ c. Nathalie might be motivated into unethical behavior to get the supervisor's job which could backfire.

   _____ d. Sue might be trying to stir up some tension in the department.

   _____ e. Sue might offer to pay for the lunch.

2. Felipe's supervisor calls him into his office and says. "I know that you are having trouble with your assistant, but don't worry about it because he is on his way out." Felipe, returning to to his department, comments to a coworker, "Relax, my assistant is being given the shaft by the boss."

   _____ a. The supervisor might lose his (or her) job instead of the assistant.

   _____ b. The coworker might carry the word to the assistant and get Felipe in trouble.

   _____ c. Felipe will have more respect for the supervisor.

   _____ d. The coworker will like Felipe better. Felipe will get a raise.

   _____ e. The assistant may be leaving, but not because he is being fired.

3. Esther is having coffee with her close friend, Lionel, who is a supervisor in another department. Esther says, "Lionel, my supervisor is a stinker. If he isn't making a play for me, it is one of the other women."

   _____ a. Lionel may tell Esther's supervisor that Esther is jealous of the attention he is paying to others.

   _____ b. Lionel may tell Esther's supervisor to cool it.

   _____ c. Lionel may report Esther's supervisor to upper management.

   _____ d. Lionel may think less of Esther.

   _____ e. Lionel may say nothing.

4. Mia and Marge are having lunch in the company cafeteria. Mia says, "Tell me, how are you getting along with that new employee, Sylvia? Frankly, I think she is the best new worker we have had around here in years." Marge replies, "I couldn't agree more."

_____ a. Marge may pay Sylvia a compliment by communicating Mia's comments.

_____ b. Mia may pay Sylvia a compliment by communicating Marge's comments.

_____ c. Mia and Marge may get along better in the future.

_____ d. If Sylvia hears about the compliment, she may try even harder to win acceptance of others.

_____ e. Marge may want Mia's approval so much that she'll agree with anything Mia says.

5. Luis is a supervisor competing with Dolores for a midmanagement job. While having coffee with Randy from another department, Luis says, "I guess I will have to wait longer for my promotion than I thought. I know Dolores is going to get the promotion because she is the right sex and comes from a minority culture. I'm going to polish up my resumé and scramble to another company."

_____ a. Randy may feel Luis is bigoted and fight against his progress in the future.

_____ b. Luis's comments might kill his chance for this promotion.

_____ c. Randy might spread the word that Luis is so unhappy that he has found another job.

_____ d. Randy could feel sorry for Luis and do more to help him.

_____ e. Randy may relate the conversation to Dolores, who in turn will intensify her efforts to win the promotion.

_____ f. Dolores, upon hearing that Randy is leaving, may slow down her efforts to get the promotion, thus letting Luis get the edge.

_____ g. Dolores may decide to "get" Luis.

_____ h. Luis may live to regret his comments.

Note: While all responses for each of the five situations would appear at least somewhat feasible, only 1e, 2d, and 4c would appear to be the most unlikely outcomes because they appear to have very little bearing on the situations.

> "The only thing to do with good advice is to pass it on. It is never of any use to oneself."
>
> Oscar Wilde

CASE 18

Dilemma

"Me? Fall for a rumor?"

When Keejo began her new job as a human-relations specialist, she was very optimistic about her future. After all, she was young, serious-minded, well educated, and capable. More than anything else, she wanted a management role with her company.

Keejo worked extremely hard for three years, and she did an excellent job in human relations. Her personal productivity was never questioned. Ms. Eichberg, her supervisor, encouraged her to prepare to take over her job. She helped Keejo considerably in this respect, but, of course, she could make no promises.

One day, Coleen, a close friend of Keejo's who worked in another department of the company, shared some rather disturbing news with her. Coleen had heard that Mr. Young, an employee from another department, was being trained to take Ms. Eichberg's place as department head.

Although she said nothing and did not show it on the outside, Keejo was very distressed by the news. It was hard to believe that management could make such a decision so long before announcing a promotion for Ms. Eichberg. Keejo fretted about the news constantly and could not keep her mind on her work. As a result, she made more and more mistakes, and several important reports were turned in late. Over the next six months, the excellent relationship she had with her supervisor slowly deteriorated.

Then, just as Coleen had said, top management made an official announcement that Ms. Eichberg was promoted and Mr. Young was made department head. Keejo was deeply hurt and disappointed.

A. Discuss: What mistakes did Keejo make that might have contributed to her ultimate disappointment?

B. Expand Your Understanding: Research the topics of rumors, assumptions, and facts. Find Internet and other sources to define each topic as well as to explain the significance of each in the workplace. Provide a list of "dos and don'ts" for each topic—a list that would be helpful to Keejo as well as to any other person. Draw some conclusions about your findings.

PART V

Success at Expanding Your Assets

CHAPTER 19

Goal Setting and Your Attitude

"Must I have a goal?"

Thought for the Day: With enthusiasm and energy, ignite your fire to reach the goals that are important to you.

PERFORMANCE COMPETENCIES

- Understand why it is important to set realistic goals and how they contribute to your positiveness and expectations.

- Recognize that meaningful rewards provided at various intervals will boost your attitude and help you make progress toward your goals.

- Appreciate the significance of developing a "goal pattern" or having a balance of goals to achieve a lifestyle that is satisfying and rewarding.

- Realize that without goals and rewards that motivate you, you will lose a critical connection between your goals and a positive attitude.

- Recognize why, for both career and lifestyle success, it is wise to have a time-management "goal."

What do you really want out of life? Do you have certain ambitions that you intend to reach? Have you considered what it will take to satisfy your wants and needs a week, month, year, or ten to twenty years from now? Have you taken time to assess the options that may be open to you—options and opportunities that point to taking a specific pathway for personal and career success? In other words, what are the things that you believe will give you happiness and satisfaction?

The answers to these and similar questions are good reasons that many people set goals for themselves. Goals represent the values that are important to you. Goals are those reachable "things" and milestones that make your life worthwhile. Goals provide motivation that can help you achieve and move you toward something that is satisfying and rewarding. And, in most cases, goals are positive aspirations that *you* determine—goals set by you to help you to be a better person.

SETTING REALISTIC GOALS

Realistic Goals Can Give You a More Positive Outlook.
If you were to survey your friends, you would probably discover that those with the most positive attitudes have important goals they want to reach. Why does having goals make them more positive? One reason is that goal-oriented people are so involved in reaching their goals that they don't have the time or inclination to focus on negatives.

Goal-oriented people are apt to have positive attitudes

Following are three examples of people who became more positive when they set new goals for themselves.

Hector. Hector, a government employee, was dragging along with little self-motivation and a negative outlook when he and his wife took a vacation at a nearby mountain resort. When it was over, they had a motivating goal: They wanted to earn and save money for a mountain cabin for getaway weekends. From that moment on, Hector had a more positive attitude.

Cheryl. An office employee with a large corporation, Cheryl showed excellent potential but little interest in improving her career. Then, after taking a seminar on empowerment, she decided it was foolish to waste her potential. She decided she wanted to become a manager. Within days, Cheryl's coworkers noticed an improvement in her attitude.

Darryl. After ten years in a career that bored him, Darryl decided that a change was needed. His first step was to return to college for a higher degree. Once involved, he became so motivated that he started to look at his present job in a different light. Result? He lost his boredom and received a promotion before he earned his degree.

Obviously, there is a connection between goals and having a more positive outlook. What about you? Are you as goal-oriented as you should be?

Would giving yourself one or two new goals improve your attitude, lead you to greater career success, and eventually result in more personal fulfillment?

Goals Can Give You Direction and Expectations. We have defined *attitude* as the way you mentally look at things. Without goals, you are not heading anywhere. There is little or no expectation! With no direction and no expectations, it would be easier for you to talk in a negative way, think negative thoughts, and become a negative person.

Adelle. Making excellent progress in becoming a high-school science teacher, Adelle is handling her most difficult courses with relative ease. Adelle is an outgoing person yet somewhat self-conscious because she is about forty pounds overweight. When two of her friends convinced her to join them in an on-campus exercise and weight-loss program, Adelle gave herself a new goal. Along with earning her degree, she would lose the forty pounds and give herself a new image. What happened? Because of her new goal, she not only lost weight but improved her grades. Without knowing it, she needed a new, more challenging goal to improve her attitude.

REWARD YOURSELF

Rewards for Reaching Goals Are Attitude-Booster Pumps. Goals that are meaningful to you usually are those that have rewards attached to them. If a goal provides you with the motivation you need to move toward accomplishing a goal, you are more apt to reach it. Some goals, of course, are easier to reach than others. That is, some goals may be small and easily attainable just because they aren't complicated. Some small goals also may be integral parts of larger goals. Some may not take very long to reach just because of the access to the necessary elements to get you where you are going quickly. Still others may not require much effort to accomplish. Whatever the goal, big or small, reaching it can be a real boost to your attitude. And, if you have had to encounter considerable challenges and roadblocks to successfully reach a goal, your attitude boost may give you a reward that lasts for a considerable period of time.

Rewards reinforce goals

Many people, in establishing goals, underestimate the value of giving themselves rewards for making progress. Goals that do not provide rewards along the way are often forgotten. But when daily, weekly, and long-term rewards are attached, goals can have a major influence on attitudes. Consider this story about Drake.

Drake. With three years of experience on a police force, Drake decided to become a lawyer. Encouraged by his chief, he was given daytime schedules so he could take night classes. Drake figured it would take him five years before he would be in a position to take the bar exam. Thinking only about his long-term goal, which seemed merely an impossible dream, Drake became so discouraged the first year that he almost gave up. It was then that he realized he needed a weekly goal to keep him motivated. Drake remembered how he enjoyed the volleyball team while attending college. When he discovered there was a Sunday volleyball game at the YMCA near where he lived, he knew he had found what he needed. In the future, he would do a professional job as a police officer during the day, attend classes and study at night and on Saturday, and designate Sunday as reward day. How did it work out? Drake passed the bar examination in four years instead of five.

Interim Rewards for Your Goals. Planning rewards at various intervals along the path to reach a goal is an excellent idea. Most people need periodic rewards, especially if the goals require considerable time to reach. It is also a wise idea to plan your rewards at the time you set a goal. If you wait to establish rewards until you need them, it may be too late. Most people who give up on a goal give up not because the goal is too big but because they haven't planned rewards to reach the milestones needed to achieve the goal.

Motivation Is Key to Rewards. So what kinds of rewards are needed to achieve a goal? Different people require different rewards at different times, the same way people differ about what goals are important to them. It is nearly impossible for someone else to tell you when a reward is needed and the type of reward that will give you satisfaction. It is up to you to identify appropriate rewards—rewards that are based on what motivates you.

Because your motivation is up to you (similar to the way your attitude belongs to you and not to someone else), you may need to take some time to determine the type of motivation and the motivators that will work for you. Additional discussion on motivation in other chapters of this book may be useful to you as you establish your goals and identify rewards that will motivate you to continue pursuing your goals.

BALANCING YOUR GOALS

Finding an appropriate balance in your life is a goal in itself

The Right Balance of Goals Works Best for Most People. Each individual needs to design a "goal pattern" for himself (or herself) that produces the best results and attitude over the long term. A "goal pattern" can be best described as a balanced life that contributes to your positive attitude.

To discover more about a balanced goal pattern, goal setting, and your attitude toward goals, complete the following activity.

ACTIVITY

Rate Yourself as a Goal-Oriented Person

The following activity is designed to help you "review your attitude" toward the advantages of setting goals for yourself. Read each question and place a check mark (✓) in the appropriate box that best describes your attitude about that question.

	Yes	No	Undecided
1. Do you feel you are more positive when you are reaching for a goal?	❏	❏	❏
2. Does a day go better for you when you wake up with a goal to achieve?	❏	❏	❏
3. Do you think it is a good idea to write out daily and weekly goals?	❏	❏	❏
4. Do you believe each goal should have a reward attached to it?	❏	❏	❏
5. Do you feel better at the end of the day when you have accomplished something you set out to do?	❏	❏	❏
6. Do you feel goals are beneficial whether they are reached or not?	❏	❏	❏
7. Would your friends recognize you as a goal-oriented person?	❏	❏	❏
8. Are you convinced that goal-oriented people are more positive?	❏	❏	❏
9. More than anything else, do goals help you live up to your potential?	❏	❏	❏
10. Are goals worth having, even if they might cause frustration and disappointment if not reached on time?	❏	❏	❏
Total Points ❏			

Each "Yes" answer is worth three points. Each "Undecided" answer is worth one point. Each "No" answer is worth zero points. If you scored 20 points or higher, you are enthusiastic about setting goals and feel they contribute to your positive attitude. If you scored between 10 and 20 points, you recognize the importance of goals in keeping an upbeat attitude. If you scored below 10 points, it would appear that you prefer to live with few, if any, goals and may be able to stay positive in other ways.

However, a low score may also indicate that you are in need of goals to be more positive. Continue reading to gain more information about goals and their importance. You may find that if you set just one goal that is important to you and identify some rewards and motivators for reaching that goal, you will be on your way to a more positive life. Once you have made some progress toward that goal, revisit this exercise. Your new score may reflect that goals are more important to you than you once thought!

Cameron provides us with an excellent example of a goal-oriented person and how a balance of goals work for him.

Cameron. Now thirty-two years of age and in a middle-management position with a large utility firm, Cameron was asked to state the most important thing he had learned in college. His reply: "This may sound strange, but looking back, it was learning how to organize myself. I had many goals. First, of course, was earning a good GPA. I had some tough courses, so I had to concentrate. Then I needed some work goals because I had to pay my own way, and I wanted to establish myself as a responsible worker so that I could qualify for the best opportunity upon graduation. I also had exercise and diet goals. I worked out in the gym three or four times each week. To reach all of these goals took organization. I had a study schedule with specific goals for each course. Each Sunday, I would write out my goals for the following week.

"But I was a senior before I learned about my need for the most important goals of all. With so much study, work, and exercising, I forgot that I also needed fun time to balance things out. Result? I set aside every Saturday for pure pleasure purposes. I would play some basketball during the day and go dancing at night. Frankly, it was my weekly pleasure goals that pulled me through.

"Today I try to maintain a balance between career, family, and pleasure goals. You ask if there is a relationship between keeping an upbeat attitude and having goals. My answer is an emphatic yes."

GOALS THAT MOTIVATE ME

From Short- to Long-Term Goals. People need to get to know themselves well enough to discover which goals are motivating and how many are required to maintain their upbeat attitudes.

Discover the goals that motivate you to be positive

As part of the motivation process, they also need to discover whether they respond best to goals that are short term, long term, or something in between and in what combination.

Short-term goals usually are of a short duration—possibly as short as a day, week, or month or as long as a year or two. Short-term goals frequently are rather specific, are less complicated than longer-term goals, and usually have fewer elements or factors that can influence long-term goals.

Long-terms goals, partially because they take longer to achieve, also tend to be more general in nature than short-term goals. Goals that are considered to be long term usually are those that may be projected for at least five, ten, twenty, or more years. Lifetime goals obviously fit into this category. Frequently, long-term goals need to be "general" because there may be many elements that influence how they will be achieved. For example, you know that long-term career and life goals may change many times due to a variety of factors. They may be complicated by twists and turns and unforeseen challenges along the way. Because a long-term career goal cannot be completed in a day, a week, or even a year, the approach you take to achieve such a goal has many options. In fact, there are so many ways to approach and achieve long-term goals, a person probably will need a series of short- and intermediate-term goals to accomplish them.

The purpose of this discussion is not to determine exactly how to classify goals into categories that might be described as short, intermediate, or long term. Rather, the reader is directed to identify the goals and rewards that will be motivators to achieve what is important to her (or him). Consider how the following descriptions of four types of goals may serve this purpose.

- *Daily goals.* Creating and maintaining a daily checklist of tasks works well for those who want a feeling of accomplishment each day. For many, the feeling is all the reward needed. Others reward themselves with simple pleasures such as watching television, playing computer games, taking a walk, or enjoying a special dinner or dessert.

- *Weekly goals.* Many people create weekly goals for themselves (usually on Sunday) and then reward themselves the following Saturday with some type of leisure activity. Leisure activities such as a game of golf, watching a sports competition, going to a movie, or taking a short trip can be both goals and rewards. Most people find that leisure goals as rewards work best to keep them motivated and upbeat on the job during the week.

- *Yearly goals.* Annual goals, such as going on a holiday, are motivating for a lot of people. Usually, however, people who have such goals need to establish smaller goals to motivate them throughout the year. The smaller steps help them to reach the more distant vacation goal. Longer-term goals that are realistic and meaningful and that are supplemented with shorter ones can be very satisfying and rewarding.

- *Life goals.* Career and life goals usually are long-term goals that often are general and vague. If such goals are not planned with short-term and intermediate-term goals and rewards, these long-term goals can be nonmotivating. However, most people who have long-term career goals are admired because they pay attention to the smaller but critical incremental goals that help them reach important milestones. Many are so determined to achieve their goals that their drive to do so also helps them achieve at a higher level on a daily basis. It is easy to defend the premise that those fortunate enough to have such goals live more positive lives.

Lifestyles that meet the needs of individuals and produce happiness and fulfillment usually are built around a combination of highly individualized goals. People with spouses or partners have the challenge of working out goals that satisfy both individuals while giving each other the freedom to build a few of his (or her) own.

Consider family needs in setting your own goals

Janette. Because Janette and her husband did not succeed in designing a lifestyle that contained goals suitable to both of them, Janette found herself a single parent. For the first two years after their separation, Janette's three goals were to raise her daughter in the best way she knew how, make progress toward her career, and accomplish housekeeping chores so she and her daughter could do some fun things together. Everyone was surprised by her upbeat attitude—at least for awhile. But, as time went on, Janette became more and more negative. What was missing?

Through the help of a close friend, Janette finally realized that she needed time for a leisure goal. By working out an arrangement with her parents, Janette was able to leave her daughter with them on Sundays so she could have some free time for herself or to share with friends away from all responsibilities. The new arrangement provided the right combination of goals; and, within weeks, Janette regained her positive attitude.

People of all ages sometimes are blind to their need to have some quality time for themselves. They become so involved in career, family, and household goals that they forget to establish a leisure goal that provides the balance required for a positive attitude. Good advice to anyone is: *Being able to develop a balance of realistic goals with rewards that are motivating is a goal in itself—a goal that should not be overlooked.*

A TIME-MANAGEMENT "GOAL"

Goal setting and time management go hand in hand

Individuals who become effective goal setters and achievers usually get a head start by becoming excellent personal-time planners at some time in their life, frequently while still in school. Consider the time management of Eduardo, a successful forty-three-year-old executive.

Eduardo. Eduardo explains his planning strategy in these words: "College taught me a lot of things but nothing more valuable to my career than personal-time management. I had to juggle six balls at the same time—attend a full load of classes, schedule study hours, allocate twenty hours per week for my part-time job, arrange time for physical exercise and personal tasks such as doing laundry, get enough sleep, and save some time for leisure or fun. To balance everything was no easy challenge. I've been a good planner ever since!"

Whether in or out of school, in your first job, or well established in your career, good time management involves at least six important elements:

1. List and prioritize your weekly goals.
2. Make and use a daily "to-do" list.
3. Establish some long-term goals that give you excitement to achieve.
4. Identify and use your motivators to keep you on track.
5. Concentrate on what you are doing at the time.
6. Save some time for pure leisure activities.

An additional factor of consideration associated with goal setting and planning can be summed up in a single sentence: *The absence of effective goal setting and personal-time management can result in confusion and cause an individual to lose her (or his) positive attitude.*

Summary

It is up to you to decide the direction that is best for you. That is, if you wish to become a more confident, positive, and successful person in your own individual style, giving more attention to setting goals for yourself may be your best approach. Taking such an approach involves the following:

1. Set realistic goals that give you both direction and expectations. Realistic goals and a positive attitude have a good connection.

2. Establish a reward system along with your goals. Rewards should reinforce goals and boost your attitude.

3. A good balance of goals—between work, career, family, and pleasure—cannot be overemphasized. The right balance will head you in a positive direction toward success.

4. Most people need both short- and long-term goals that are powered by motivation and rewards. Goals that are not motivating and don't offer rewards to reinforce your progress may not be realized.

5. Good time management is a "goal" in itself. Managing your time and setting effective goals will lead to a more positive attitude and a more productive, enjoyable life.

Keep in mind that all goals that produce results come from within the individual. People seldom succeed in imposing goals on others. Because it is up to you to take the needed action, establish and work toward the goals that are meaningful to you and your career. Also, because it is up to you to motivate and reward yourself, choose your goals wisely as you travel the road of life. And, because it is up to you if you want to be a happy and satisfied person, project a positive outlook every single day. Yes, *Your Attitude Is Showing* and you know that your success depends on it!

Test Your Understanding

Respond to the following items to test your understanding of the chapter.

Part A: Circle the correct answer (T = True; F = False) for each of the following statements.

T F   1. Your positive attitude usually is boosted by having realistic goals.

T F   2. Management experts claim it is a good idea to write down daily and weekly work goals.

T F   3. Most people are blind to their need to set a leisure goal to have some quality time for themselves.

T F   4. When you are expecting to reach a goal, you bias your chances to successfully reach it.

T F   5. The only goals worth having are those that are self-motivating.

Part B: Circle the letter of the correct answer for each of the following items.

6. Realistic long-term goals can be best achieved if you (a) get someone to help you reach them, (b) use rewards only at the completion of a goal, (c) supplement the goals with shorter-term goals, (d) ignore everyone around you until the goal is reached.

7. Poor time management usually results from (a) saving some time for leisure activities, (b) making "to-do" lists, (c) not concentrating on what you are doing at the time, (d) taking time to work on your positive attitude.

Part C: Write a short response to demonstrate your understanding related to the following item.

8. Discuss some of the ways goal setting contributes to a more positive outlook.

Turn to the back of the book to check your answers.

The journey through life
is most successful
when driven by goals.

Think and Respond

Respond to the following items with two or three complete sentences.

1. What is a "goal pattern" and why should you have one?

2. Suggest two things that usually result from setting realistic goals and attaching rewards to them.

3. Describe what is meant by having a good balance of goals and give an example to support your answer.

4. Explain the differences between short-term goals and long-term goals, especially in terms of their motivational value.

5. Give two good reasons why it is wise to establish goals for yourself.

Designing a Master Goal Pattern

Using the following outline, identify your current goals and the rewards you have attached to them. Keep in mind that you are identifying (a) career, (b) lifestyle, (c) family, and (d) pleasure goals. Try to identify goals for at least three of the four types of goals in each category.

	GOALS	REWARDS
Daily Goals		
a. Career	_____	_____
b. Lifestyle	_____	_____
c. Family	_____	_____
d. Pleasure	_____	_____
Weekly Goals		
a. Career	_____	_____
b. Lifestyle	_____	_____
c. Family	_____	_____
d. Pleasure	_____	_____
Monthly Goals		
a. Career	_____	_____
b. Lifestyle	_____	_____
c. Family	_____	_____
d. Pleasure	_____	_____
Annual Goals		
a. Career	_____	_____
b. Lifestyle	_____	_____
c. Family	_____	_____
d. Pleasure	_____	_____
Life Goals		
a. Career	_____	_____
b. Lifestyle	_____	_____
c. Family	_____	_____
d. Pleasure	_____	_____

Keep in mind that a variety of goals, from short- to long-term goals, are critical for most people to maintain a positive attitude. Personal goals versus work goals also contribute to good balance in your life. Because goals can help motivate you beyond their specific boundaries, capitalize on the fact that a personal or work goal can help you do better in a nonrelated area.

Also, don't ignore the need for "fun"; include some leisure goals. Most people need a balance between career, family, and leisure goals. Thus, how successful you are at identifying your goals may be dependent upon how well your "goal pattern" moves you in a positive direction to achieve high levels of accomplishment and satisfaction.

CASE 19 ———————————————————————

Conflict

"I need to find myself."

Deric and RayLyn will graduate from their university in a few months. They have been romantically involved for almost two years. Deric is capable and popular and shows great promise of succeeding in any career he selects (his major is sociology); but, so far, he is not heading in any direction. When it comes to the future, he often appears confused and listless. RayLyn, however, is highly goal-oriented. She knows she is going to be a civil engineer, she wants children (one or two) by the time she is twenty-eight, and she is anxious to work out a lifestyle with the right partner. Hopefully, it will be Deric.

Last night, in what started out as a casual discussion, RayLyn lost her patience with Deric. Why? Because he got on his old theme of taking a one- or two-year moratorium upon graduation so he could "find himself" before making any career or relationship commitments. RayLyn responded, "I know myself. I need to be headed somewhere. It's not ambition or money or anything else—it's just the way I stay positive. I have to have reachable goals ahead of me. I wouldn't be comfortable or happy trying to build a life with a person who avoids specific goals."

"Fine," replied Deric. "When it comes to goals, I may feel as you do in a few years, but I'm not sure. I don't, at this time of my life, want a goal-oriented existence. So far, I've pretty much done what my parents and society expect. It's time for me to live a life of pure freedom. You go your way; I'll go mine. Perhaps in a few years we can get back together and create a lifestyle that would bring fulfillment to both of us."

A. Discuss: What chance do Deric and RayLyn have of restoring their relationship? Should they try? Will Deric eventually come to view goals differently?

B. Expand Your Understanding: Interview several people you highly respect (supervisors, coworkers, friends, family, or others) to identify the importance they place on goal setting. Research the topic of goals—types of goals, establishing goals, and so on. (You may need to include the topic of "objectives" in your research as some authors do not distinguish between goals as the larger picture and objectives as the smaller, more specific tasks and means to accomplish goals. Similarly, you may also want to include the topic of "mission" in your research as most authors view a mission as a larger, more encompassing term than goals, but one that has significant meaning to goals.) Draw some conclusions from your interviews and research. Suggest some of the advantages of having goals and engaging in goal setting throughout life. Finally, include a statement or two about how you can have goals and still enjoy the flexibility you need and want for life to happen.

CHAPTER 20

Strategies for Advancing Your Career

"I hate decision making."

Thought for the Day: A positive attitude can make a "world of difference" in making decisions and achieving success.

PERFORMANCE COMPETENCIES

- Evaluate the advantages and disadvantages of staying with one organization as a career-building strategy.

- Evaluate the advantages and disadvantages of taking a zigzag approach by moving from one organization to another in building a career.

- Identify seven important career-planning suggestions—suggestions relating to human-relations factors that should be considered in career planning.

- Consider the value of research that includes evaluating the working environment of a prospective employer.

- Understand how developing a Plan B and a personal business plan can significantly contribute to a positive attitude and career success.

Building a successful career probably will involve making a wide range of choices over your working lifetime. That's why goal setting is so important (refer to another chapter in this book for a discussion about goals). Because your career will be based on more than work-related decisions, preparation, and knowledge, you will need to keep your options open to consider the opportunities that come your way. You may have a goal of self-employment; yet, you may find along the way that a more rewarding career can be built by exercising your leadership as a valuable team member in a comfortable, productive work unit. You may also find that your career takes several lateral moves across different departments where you can be creative. Additionally, you may have opportunities to move up the ladder to a management position as good managers are needed in all types of organizations. Whatever lies ahead, more than likely, you can expect several career moves during your working lifetime.

PROMOTION FROM WITHIN

Stabilizers and PFW. If you believe management is your "cup of tea," it is important to understand the two basic paths to a top management position. One is to join and stay with an organization, climbing the ladder of success rung by rung. The other is to move from one company to another, improving your position with each move. Those who prefer to make a lateral move from one department to another or to move up within the same organization are *stabilizers*. Those who prefer the zigzag route from one organization to another are *scramblers* (more is said about scramblers and the zigzag approach in the next major section of this chapter).

Your comfort zone as a stabilizer or scrambler can help you reach career success

If you go about it in the right way, you can usually build a rich and rewarding career as a stabilizer. The practice that makes this possibility attractive is called *promotion from within*, or *PFW*.

PFW: Tradition Still Reigns. Promotion from within (PFW) is an old practice in many companies. That is, there really is nothing new about PFW. It has always been the custom to move those who demonstrate that they are capable and responsible into higher positions when vacancies occur. If effective people are available, management usually wants to promote from within the company's own ranks. A PFW policy encourages loyalty, provides some security, and has other advantages. It should be remembered, however, that even companies that have such a policy may make exceptions on their own or can be forced into adjustments because of layoffs and reorganizations.

In order to understand the implications of the PFW idea in a given corporation, it's wise to study the organizational structure. Each company grows to maturity in a different way; each firm develops a different "culture." Every company has its own interpretation and application of a PFW policy.

Because of the wide disparity in business organizations and practices, generalizations are dangerous. You, the reader, must interpret the following pages in light of the policies and practices of your own company. It is important, however, to give the new worker a perspective on the employee's career possibilities. The following triangle will get us started.

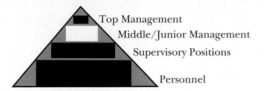

The preceding diagram could represent a business or an industrial or governmental organization. Size is not important. It could be a company with 200,000 employees or one with 200 or even 15. Management—those people who are responsible for the leadership and direction of the company—is, of course, at the apex of the triangle. Some organizations divide management into three classifications: top management, middle/junior management, and supervisory positions. In recent years, many organizations have eliminated middle/junior management positions primarily to remain competitive and profitable.

As organizations have become flatter, frontline supervisors have had to assume more responsibilities. The elimination of many managerial positions also has pushed decision making to lower levels.

Decision making is not just for upper management

Top-management executives with large firms are usually the president, chief executive officer, chief financial officer, chief information officer, and vice presidents—frequently, the people who have highly critical decision-making responsibilities. Middle-management people are usually division heads, branch and plant managers, and management assistants. Supervisors are next in line.

Leadership Is Needed at All Levels. Below the management level are many kinds of personnel, depending on the type of organization. In a manufacturing business, for example, we find different levels of technical people: engineers, technicians, skilled craftsmen, semiskilled workers, and helpers. In other kinds of organizations, there are many different patterns and many varied backgrounds that exist. Of critical importance, regardless of the level of employment, is that every employee needs to give her (or his) best effort to the overall function of a business. That means you are expected to contribute your positive attitude, human-relations skills, technical knowledge, and other competencies, as well as whatever leadership ability you have. While more is said later about leadership, it is appropriate to mention here that exercising leadership is *not* only reserved for upper management. Every person needs to take some leadership responsibility for work performance at whatever level he (or she) works.

Supervisory positions, as illustrated here, usually outnumber higher-management positions. A supervisor for every twelve employees in an organization is quite common; however, it is not uncommon to have a lower or higher employee-supervisor ratio, such as a supervisor for five to thirty-plus employees, depending on the type of business. The supervisory position is extremely important to the new worker for, in most cases, this is the first position leading to upper management.

Now that we have seen the top of the triangle, let us look at the other levels. All organizations employ the majority of new workers at lower-level entry positions.

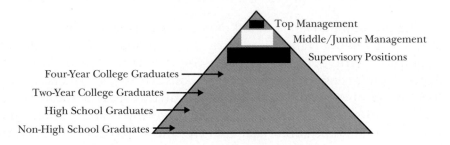

Not all companies have four entry levels. Some have only one, two, or three. For example, some organizations may hire only four-year college graduates with specialized degrees. Other companies may seek employees who have experience or special skills. The important thing is that all employees have an opportunity to grow. Each employee, regardless of where she (or he) starts, can and should seek a rewarding position in the organization. Moving up the career ladder or moving into a more responsible position in an organization is the meaning of PFW.

Pros and Cons of PFW. There are both advantages and disadvantages to building a lifetime career as a stabilizer in a single organization. Those who join companies with PFW intentions usually compete with those inside the company for better positions. They need not worry so much about outsiders who might be hired to fill positions to which they aspire. Theoretically, everyone has a chance to compete, despite differences in education and experience. When someone at the top retires, a chain reaction can open up many positions all the way down the organizational ladder. Several position openings, of course, are possible only if reorganization does not take place or certain positions are not eliminated.

Every employee has an opportunity for job growth

Organizations with PFW policies usually provide good training for their employees so that they are ready to assume more responsibility when opportunities arise. Because on-the-job time is spent on training of all kinds, it also usually means that such companies will encourage their employees to continue their formal education and will often pay for tuition. As a result, employees are less likely to be ignored or lost in the shuffle.

Just as there are many advantages, there are also disadvantages to working for a company that likes to promote from within. Many highly ambitious people claim that promotions come too slowly. People are trained too far ahead of time. There is too much waiting. These are usually the same people who claim that the best way to reach the top is to move from company to company instead of staying with one organization. They point out that it is also possible that while waiting for an opening, a reorganization can take place, thus eliminating the position you were preparing to occupy. Moreover, the human-relations role is more critical because management and nonmanagement people seldom forget anything. *In short, a person who makes a serious human-relations mistake in a PFW company must live with it longer because the people affected will be around to remember.*

In the rapidly changing technological and global economic climate, organizations realize that they must be more flexible if they are to remain profitable. In some cases, restructuring and massive layoffs have been necessary. As a result, the emphasis on PFW is much reduced; in some organizations, it has been discarded.

ZIGZAG APPROACH

Scramblers and the Zigzag Approach. Many people feel the PFW approach to building their careers is less attractive than if they use the zigzag approach. The zigzag approach, or scrambling, involves an entirely different approach to career planning. Scramblers feel that, in order to enhance their careers, they must move from one organization to another. The zigzag approach is illustrated as follows.

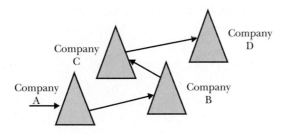

Pros and Cons of the Zigzag Approach. Just as there are advantages and disadvantages of a PFW approach for building your career, there also are pros and cons to a zigzag approach.

One of the advantages of the zigzag or scrambling approach may be for a person to be promoted quickly. That is, for those who are willing to move about geographically and who are sufficiently aggressive to make the effort to seek out profitable transfers, the route to the top can be faster. Sometimes an individual can achieve a wider and more valuable learning background by moving from one company to another.

In other words, she (or he) can learn something new in each company and take it to the next one. Increasing one's expertise by moving from one company to another is especially true in high-technology fields.

Another advantage to the scrambling approach is that it is easier to leave serious human-relations mistakes behind. Getting a fresh start in a new company may include leaving behind unresolved human conflicts or personality differences.

Serious human-relations mistakes may force you to be a scrambler

There are also disadvantages to the zigzag route. Most people agree that it takes more energy to build an industrywide reputation to ensure that profitable transfers come your way. There is also a degree of risk involved. You could discover, for example, that your most recent move was a mistake. Scramblers are not always successful.

Zigzagging Requires Accepting Change. Transferring often means uprooting the entire family and making profound personal and social, as well as professional, changes in your life. Certain benefits, like profit sharing, cannot always be transferred from one company to another without loss or adjustment. Also, during periods of recession, when layoffs occur in many organizations, scrambling becomes more difficult and risky. Thus, with the zigzag approach to career building, it is a good idea to do extra research and exercise more caution than you might do with a more conservative approach.

ACTIVITY

Evaluating Career-Building Strategies

Based on what you have learned about the PFW (promotion from within) and the zigzag approaches to career building, provide a reason that you believe each of the approaches would or would not work for you. Write your responses in the spaces provided.

The PFW approach to career building

a. would work for me because

b. would not work for me because

The zigzag approach to career building

a. would work for me because

b. would not work for me because

Some people use a combination of the two approaches to build their careers. The best way to determine which approach is "right for you" as a career-building strategy is to learn as much as you can about the organization where you work and about the prospective department or organization where you want to work. Conduct as much research as you can *before* you make your move. Then carefully evaluate your findings. Even with extensive research, you probably will still find that, after your move, there will be plenty of unanticipated factors associated with your new job.

CAREER-PLANNING SUGGESTIONS

Seven Human-Relations Factors. As you plan your career, take the following seven career-planning suggestions into consideration. Note that all of the suggestions include important human-relations factors.

1. *Identify opportunities.* The longer you stay with a growing company, the more opportunities you will have, provided that you continue to learn and maintain good horizontal and vertical relationships. Look for challenges. Be willing to change. Demonstrate a positive attitude in all that you do.

2. *Consider cross training.* Moving horizontally into every possible department in an organization is a good idea, even if the move does not give you an immediate pay increase. Not only will you improve your knowledge base about other areas of an organization (cross training) but you will also be in a position to build new relationships that can help your career progress.

3. *Study promotion practices.* Discover and study the various channels of promotion in your company. Attempt to move laterally across units or move up through the channel that best suits your ability. Set the stage for promotion through your human-relations skills.

4. *Be assertive.* Within bounds, do not fear being aggressive and assertive. Submit ideas that have been well researched. Communicate upward. Let management know you would like to consider leadership beyond what you demonstrate in your current position. Show your human-relations skills at every opportunity.

5. *Pursue options.* When a position becomes vacant, let management know in the right way that you are interested. Do not assume that your supervisors know you are interested in a career move. It doesn't hurt your relationships with others to ask about options that may be open to you.

6. *Establish networks.* Cultivate and maintain relationships outside your organization. Networking with people in professional or trade organizations definitely provides career advantages. If it

becomes obvious that your organization cannot provide you with the growth opportunities you desire, the individuals you have in your network of contacts can help you scramble.

7. *Continue learning.* Keep in mind that the training you receive as an employee (whether as a stabilizer or a scrambler) may be preparing you to enter a new career in an emerging field or to open a business of your own. For example, entrepreneurship is continuing to increase and is experiencing rapid growth in most parts of the world. E-commerce, service occupations, health care, and improving communication technologies also are creating exciting opportunities for all types of people, especially entrepreneurs.

EVALUATING WORK ENVIRONMENTS

Research Your Potential Career Move. It is good advice to the job seeker to do some homework about a prospective employer before joining a new company. Your research may reveal some aspects of a company you feel will greatly benefit or hinder your career aspirations. Also, your research may help you formulate some strong feelings you have about the type of environment in which you want to work. Once you have landed a job, it still may take a few weeks before you, as a new employee, are in a position to analyze the organization's working environment and be able to answer the following questions: Does this working environment (culture) fit my long-term needs? Is it within my personal comfort zone? Can I see myself moving up or into more responsible positions?

Although the more investigation that takes place in advance the better, many new employees discover that the working environment they anticipated is not suitable for them. As a result, they may develop a new career plan that will eventually take them into their comfort zone.

ACTIVITY

My Working-Environment Preferences

In evaluating a working environment, the following six issues/factors need to be taken into consideration. Read each issue and then formulate an opinion about how important that factor is to you. Write your opinion about each issue in the space provided after that factor. As you contemplate the type of environment in which you believe you would enjoy working, there may be other issues you would want to consider. Start a file of your working-environment preferences to help you identify the factors that are important to you. Keep a positive attitude as you develop your list and be realistic about your preferences.

1. Is there a profit-sharing or stock-option plan that causes employees to stay longer and be more protective of their respective roles and of the firm as a whole?

   _____

2. How stable is the organization? Is the firm strong enough to withstand a takeover attempt by an outside firm? Is management sufficiently flexible to adjust to the economic winds of change?

   _____

3. Is there a career-class system within the organization? For example, hospitals have their medical doctors at one level, nurses at another, and nonprofessionals at another. Would you be comfortable in a similar environment?

   _____

4. Would it bother you to work for an organization (e.g., a restaurant) in which the steady turnover of employees makes it difficult to build long-term relationships?

   _____

5. How do you feel about off-hours, shift, or overtime work? Hospitals, restaurants, and many factories have shift work that can have a major impact on one's lifestyle. Working for an airline, a hotel, or a travel agency also can mean longer-than-usual hours (paid or nonpaid) than a regular business-hours position would require.

   _____

6. Would working in a highly creative, ever-changing environment be within your comfort zone? Some industries and retail organizations (e.g., high-fashion, music, art) create a "haute couture" environment that some enjoy but others do not.

   _____

DEVELOPING A "PLAN B" AND A PERSONAL BUSINESS PLAN

Plan B. The professional scrambler always has an alternative plan, or a Plan B, that he (or she) can put into operation when needed.

Having a Plan B is similar to a company that has a business plan. The company has a vision and mission for its future. It has strategies to achieve its goals. Its business plan describes what the company does, where it plans to go, and how it will get there.

Develop a personal business plan to help bias your attitude and career future in a positive way

Personal Business Plan. Just as a company develops a business plan, you can benefit from doing the same thing. By developing your "personal" business plan, you identify your career (and personal) goals and the viable routes you may take to reach your mission. The best Plan B, as part of a personal business plan, includes a well-thought-out strategy (including an up-to-the-minute resumé, outside contacts, and constantly updated skills) that will permit the scrambler to locate a better position with another firm in the shortest possible time.

For the most part, in years past, stabilizers did not feel the need to have a Plan B. There are two reasons why a single career plan is no longer viable. First, stabilizers have discovered that scramblers have often substantially improved their career positions by having and using an alternative plan. Second, organizational changes (mergers, buyouts, restructuring, etc.) have frequently left stabilizers holding the bag. The result? More and more stabilizers are going back to school to upgrade their skills and develop a formal Plan B as part of their personal business plan.

Benefits of a Plan. Both scramblers and stabilizers can benefit from developing a Plan B and a personal business plan, basically for two reasons:

1. If the winds of change eliminate your position, you are prepared to move on to something better because you have your goals identified in your personal business plan.
2. Having a Plan B ready makes it easier for you to maintain a positive attitude where you are presently working.

Many workers become either discouraged with their progress or fearful that their jobs will be eliminated without doing anything about it. When they develop a personal business plan (which includes several alternative routes, such as a Plan B or C, to reach career goals), they not only eliminate some of the fear that goes along with losing a job but also feel better about their current positions. As a direct result, their attitudes improve, they become more productive, and they receive promotions. With so many positive factors in their favor, there really is no need to scramble.

Summary

Building a career that is both goal-oriented and flexible is a wise approach because you can evaluate and take advantage of opportunities along your career path. Whether or not you are interested in moving laterally across departments or moving up into management, this chapter has provided you with a discussion about two basic ways you can build your career. One strategy for building your career is to join and aim to stay with one organization (being a stabilizer using the promotion-from-within approach). The other strategy is to move from one organization to another (being a scrambler using the zigzag approach). While you may prefer one route over the other, there are advantages and disadvantages associated with each career-building strategy. Weighing the pros and cons of each strategy will help you formulate what is important to you in pursuing the most appropriate career path.

Seven career-planning suggestions that reflect human-relations factors are offered in this chapter. These suggestions provide good advice to guide the actions you will take to reach your career goals. In addition, it is a good idea to conduct some research on your prospective work environment before you make a move. Evaluating a career move *before* you move will give you a much better picture of whether or not your new working environment will be satisfying. To help you conduct your evaluation, several questions are provided for your consideration.

Because your career should not be taken lightly, it is highly recommended that you formalize your career-path strategy by developing a Plan B as part of a personal business plan. Your personal business plan, with personal and career goals, will help you understand several human-relations factors that are important to your career. A well-developed plan also will help to bias the odds in your favor primarily because, as you follow your plan, you will give considerable thought to keeping a positive attitude in your quest for career success.

Test Your Understanding

Respond to the following items to test your understanding of the chapter.

Part A: Circle the correct answer (T = True; F = False) for each of the following statements.

T F   1. Economic conditions (mergers, reorganizations, etc.) have forced many organizations to abandon their PFW policies.

T F   2. The more competitive and aggressive you are, the more you probably should consider building a career by moving from one organization to another whenever there is an advantage to do so.

T F   3. The zigzag approach provides more security and probably less moving from one geographic area to another.

T F   4. A Plan B usually means switching to a different career area.

T F   5. A Plan B often helps an employee do a better job with his (or her) initial personal business plan.

Part B: Circle the letter of the correct answer for each of the following items.

6. A person who makes a serious human-relations mistake may be better off to consider the career route referred to as a (a) PFW approach, (b) zigzag approach, (c) stabilizer approach, (d) conservative approach.

7. People who develop a well-thought-out strategy that includes career and personal goals (a) have defined their personal business plan, (b) are scramblers, (c) have become insecure, (d) may be quite likely to find change extremely difficult.

Part C: Write a short response to demonstrate your understanding related to the following item.

8. Compare and contrast some of the advantages and disadvantages associated with the two basic career routes.

Turn to the back of the book to check your answers.

Having a career alternative
could help stabilize
the wind beneath your wings
should you be forced from your perch.

Think and Respond

Respond to the following items with two or three complete sentences.

1. Discuss how career building can be rewarding whether or not you seek or end up in a top-management position.

2. Explain what is meant by PFW and give two reasons it is considered a viable option for building a career.

3. Explain what is meant by a zigzag approach to career building and provide two positive aspects of the approach.

4. Describe two of the career-planning factors and how they can influence your choice of working environment.

5. What is a personal business plan and how does a Plan B fit into it?

Scrambler versus Stabilizer Scale

Chapter 20 discusses the advantages and disadvantages of building a career with one organization (promotion from within) versus taking the zigzag route (moving from one firm to another). This exercise may give you some additional insight into your behavioral characteristics which, in turn, can lead you to a better decision.

Read both statements associated with each item that follows. Then, circle the number that indicates where you fall in the scale from 10 to 1 on each of the factors.

1. I need a lot of freedom. Rules and regulations annoy me.   10 9 8 7 6 5 4 3 2 1   I can easily adhere to rules and regulations without becoming hostile.

2. I like to take risks, even if I get into confrontations with management.   10 9 8 7 6 5 4 3 2 1   I hate risks, and I want to avoid any confrontations with management.

3. Two or three years is long enough to stay with any organization.   10 9 8 7 6 5 4 3 2 1   I like the idea of spending my entire career with the same organization.

4. I do not have enough patience to succeed inside a large organization.   10 9 8 7 6 5 4 3 2 1   I have all the patience necessary to be successful in a large organization.

5. If I cannot have both, I would rather have a high salary and smaller benefits.   10 9 8 7 6 5 4 3 2 1   I would rather have a lower salary and a much better benefit package.

6. I have plateau periods and will fight to overcome them.   10 9 8 7 6 5 4 3 2 1   I can learn to live gracefully through long plateau periods.

7. I love to beat the system.   10 9 8 7 6 5 4 3 2 1   I never try to beat the system.

8. I have always considered myself to be something of a rebel.   10 9 8 7 6 5 4 3 2 1   My characteristic is to adjust rather than fight.

9. I will move anywhere to get a better job at a higher salary.   10 9 8 7 6 5 4 3 2 1   I would turn down a better job at a much higher salary to stay where I am.

10. I get tense when people try to box me in or stifle my creativity.   10 9 8 7 6 5 4 3 2 1   I can remain calm when bureaucratic restrictions are imposed.

Total Score _____

Total your scores for the ten items. If you rated yourself 60 or above, you may be receiving a signal that you should be a scrambler. If you rated yourself above 80, the signal is much stronger. Perhaps you would be uncomfortable in an organization with a highly structured environment. You might find yourself fighting the restrictions and hurting your career progress, that is, the zigzag route to the top could make more sense for you than joining and staying with a single, promotion-from-within organization for your entire career.

If you rated yourself under 40, you may be getting a signal that you should be a stabilizer. A slower, more secure career pattern may be better for you. This means that you may be able to handle problems and progress faster inside a conservative firm.

If you rated yourself between 40 and 60, you are not receiving a clear signal either way. You may find it difficult to handle a high-risk, fast moving firm; on the other hand, a very conservative firm may cause you to be impatient. The signal may mean that you should stay clear of both a highly aggressive company and a highly conservative company—something in the middle could be the best working environment for you.

A growing number of ambitious people opt for or are forced by the winds of change to take the zigzag route to career success. The movement of employees from one company to another is on the increase—especially at upper levels—because more and more large organizations are going through reorganizations. Thus, whether they want to or not, stabilizers tend to become scramblers. There are no guarantees; but with a positive attitude and hard work, your career success will be biased in the right direction. Go for it!

CASE 20

Preference

"I'm a stabilizer."

Angelo, an experienced wireless-equipment technician, had been promoted to manage a technical division in his organization because of his demonstrated technical and human-relations skills. However, due to a major restructuring at his company when it entered the e-commerce arena, his position was eliminated and he was forced into the labor market. Angelo was interviewed the same week by Company A and Company B, two high-profile e-businesses. It took nearly three weeks for both of the firms to "check out" Angelo's background. The result was that both companies offered him a job, but both were lower-paying positions than Angelo had had in his previous position.

Company A is a dynamic high-technology corporation that makes little effort to develop its own people. In fact, it takes great delight in hiring top people away from its competitors. Company A is interested in Angelo primarily because of his technical skills and the fact that he would become productive immediately.

Company B, however, is a technical organization that offers a lot of security to employees because of its rather firm PFW policy. They like Angelo not just because of his technical abilities but especially because of his long-range potential for management.

Although the starting salary with Company A is substantially higher, the training program with Company B is superior. *All other significant factors are similar.*

A. Discuss: In which company do you think Angelo should accept a position? What factors should he consider in making his decision?

B. Expand Your Understanding: Because Angelo probably could benefit from developing a Plan B, identify the elements he should include in his personal plan. Research the topic on how to develop a good business plan. Then adapt what you learned to help Angelo develop a "Personal Business Plan." Start by describing each of the business-plan elements that are critical to a good personal plan. You may want to include a recommended plan format that Angelo and others could follow in developing their own plans.

CHAPTER 21

Keeping a Positive Attitude through Plateau Periods and Reorganizations

"It's hard enough during regular times."

Thought for the Day: Appreciate the rules of the road—caution, stop, and go—as you keep a watchful eye on the important targets in life.

PERFORMANCE COMPETENCIES

- Understand why you will need to wear a "patience suit" during a plateau or waiting period in your career.

- Recognize that plateau periods and reorganizations are normal in all organizations.

- Contemplate six questions and answers that can help shorten plateaus or convert them into learning and preparation periods.

- Appreciate why a positive attitude is critical to the three plateau-related actions steps that can help shorten or make it easier to cope with plateau periods.

The waiting period of a plateau can be significant

Keeping a positive attitude takes on a new dimension when an ambitious employee reaches a plateau period in her (or his) climb up the corporate ladder. (A *plateau* is a long waiting period in which the role and the responsibility of the employee remain static.) Small automatic or cost-of-living pay increases may occur, but significant jumps do not. Frequently, a plateau period is due to the reorganization of an organization. Sometimes plateau periods and reorganizations can last for years.

WEARING A "PATIENCE SUIT"

Why are plateaus so difficult to live through?

A Dichotomy of Ambition and Patience. In the first place, business and industry seem to intensify the problem because they seek out and hire highly ambitious people. They want and need dynamic men and women; they want and need people with energy; and they often imply, but give no assurances, that personal progress will be swift and regular. Consequently, after hiring these ambitious people, it is often necessary to turn around and ask them to be patient.

"It takes time in any organization, Laura. Your day will come. Just sit tight and *wait*. You'll see."

"You are doing great, Joe. Just *wait* for the right opportunity, and you'll be off and running."

"Continue to prepare, Henry. Learn all you can in your present job. You are in a plateau period, but you will get your chance. Just *wait* and see."

Sometimes the "patience suit" that management suggests other employees wear during plateau periods and reorganizations becomes too tight, too confining, and too uncomfortable. When this happens, even confirmed stabilizers may consider scrambling to another firm.

Promotions May Take Patience. Patience isn't something one learns in school or college. Indeed, the pattern of almost automatic promotions in school is the direct opposite of the pattern found in the world of work. Through our school systems, people become accustomed to promotions according to age. They start at the first grade and move up to the twelfth and beyond like clockwork—each year a step up, until regular promotions are expected without waiting. Small wonder that some people begin to think that life is one progressive step after another, whether the step has been truly earned or not.

Our society contributes in other ways to the "make it in a hurry" attitude. For example, both economic and social upward mobility have been the pattern for most Americans in the past few generations.

Patience is a virtue in our "hurry-up" society

As a result, most young people whose parents have "made it" have been raised in an affluent environment. Why should they wait for thirty years to get to the same point? Why should they wait until they're ready to retire to reach the higher rungs of the ladder, when they might do it by the time they're thirty?

Yet, when they get their first job, many young people must start at the bottom. Many start with a relatively low income and no fixed promotion schedule upon which to depend. Small wonder that many become impatient and seek shortcuts to better positions and higher incomes.

COPING WITH PLATEAUS

Plateaus Happen for Most People. There are many reasons for plateau periods. The following quotations from three ambitious individuals are examples.

Stella. "I work for a fine company, but we have been undergoing unavoidable retrenchment for over three years. There has been a freeze on new hires and promotions. I think things will open up soon, but, believe me, it has not been easy to readjust my personal goals and keep my attitude from showing."

Jhatni. "In our organization, everyone must sweat out a long plateau between management levels. I have had three frontline supervisory roles over the past few years, each with more responsibility. My next jump will be into middle management. But there are many people waiting ahead of me. If I could make a move to a competing company, I might save myself a few years of waiting."

Kae. "I was all set to move into a role I had spent three years preparing for when my organization went through a consolidation period. The position I wanted was transferred to another city. Not wishing to move there, I had to readjust my goals. So here I am, in another plateau period."

Even if things could be normal in business organizations, which is seldom the case, promotions are not automatic. Plateaus still exist. So how is one to cope?

What You Should Know about Plateaus. First, the ambitious employee should learn as much as possible about plateaus so that he (or she) can see the value of staying positive during such periods. Second, the employee should study ways in which such periods can be shortened.

Business and industrial leaders believe in promotion by merit. They know that the opportunity to succeed in open competition with others provides the vitality their organizations must have. Seniority, experience, minority status, and age are not always enough to warrant a promotion. Capability must also be demonstrated. But even the most capable employees reach plateaus. The opportunities to move up still exist, of course, but they sometimes come only after long periods of waiting.

Periods of waiting for promotions are critical, can destroy confidence, and can create problems. But far more important than all other factors is what happens to the attitude of the employee during such periods of waiting. Here is what frequently happens.

When employees who are living through a plateau period permit their attitudes to turn negative, they defeat themselves. At the very point when management is watching and they should be working up to their potential, they let things fall apart. When things unravel, the plateau is often extended, and others, who have better control of their attitude, are given the promotional opportunities that exist. Another way of saying this is that an ambitious employee cannot afford the "luxury of being bored."

It is not easy to ask an aggressive person to remain positive and wait, but often there is no alternative. Opportunities can and do open up in organizations overnight, but it is almost impossible to produce a steady flow of opportunities to fit the time schedules of individuals.

Confidence and a positive attitude will get you through a plateau period

Frustration Is Normal. Management cannot eliminate all the pressure points that are faced by an employee stuck on a plateau. Management people can, however, understand the frustration that comes when a promising career gets temporarily bogged down. They know because they have usually been there themselves. They know it is a difficult period. They know it is a time when some people begin to seriously question their goals. They know it is a time when personal values are challenged. They know it is a time when some start to think about other careers or returning to college for more formal education. (Refer to other chapters in this book for a discussion on frustration.)

Being ambitious and capable has never been easy in our society. When employees are in their twenties, a year may seem more like five years. And yet many employees are past thirty before they are given an opportunity to fully demonstrate their true ability.

True, a few people do find success early. The entertainment field, professional sports, sales, and promotional activities, for example, may give an early break to the young person who has talent, ability, and desire. Also, starting a business of one's own may offer the success an ambitious person may need.

Rome Wasn't Built in a Day. While at first it may appear that professional people also achieve their goals early in life, it is easy to forget that those who build careers in medicine, engineering, law, and many other professions must invest considerable time in their formal education. Many physicians are often thirty years of age or older when they start their practices. The same is true for lawyers, engineers, and numerous other professionals.

REDUCING PLATEAU PERIODS

Understanding plateau periods may help an ambitious employee do a better job of coping, but aren't there ways to shorten them?

Six Questions to Ask Yourself. Should you be faced with a plateau period in the future, ask yourself these questions:

Use plateau periods to "ready" yourself for your career advancement

1. *Am I using my present role to improve my future, whether or not I stay with the organization?* Some people have the capacity to turn boring jobs into self-improvement periods. A good example is the ambitious supervisor of a shipping operation who wants to know more about data processing. On company time, she (or he) may start investigating the possibilities for her own department, thereby benefiting both her department and herself.

2. *Am I taking advantage of all the training opportunities available to me now?* Such opportunities could exist both inside and outside the company. Community involvement of any kind can help one live through or even shorten a plateau period. Many employees have found moonlighting both therapeutic and financially rewarding.

3. *Is it time to revise my career goals? Is it time to scramble?* When organizations change internally, employees must adjust. Instead of resisting changes, they must turn them into opportunities. For example, you might consider changing your channel of promotion by asking for a transfer to a growing, instead of a declining, department. Or even better, reassess your personal business plan, and, if needed, revise and put your Plan B to work. (Refer to other chapters in this book for a discussion on personal business plans and a Plan B.)

4. *Have I applied for a promotion?* Upward communication to let management know you feel you are ready for more responsibility is often worthwhile, even if nothing happens. It may not eliminate a plateau, but it could shorten it.

5. *Are there some company-sponsored activities in which I could become involved?* Often there are sports activities, study groups, and cultural programs that can give you additional employee and management contacts as well as pleasure. Such activities may not shorten plateau periods, but they may make them seem shorter.

6. *What about doing something spectacular?* Can you volunteer for a very tough assignment that nobody else has been willing to

tackle? A new assignment for which you volunteered could provide you with a personal challenge. It could also communicate a message to upper management about your potential and readiness to accept more responsibility.

ACTIVITY

Keeping a Positive Attitude through Plateau Periods and Reorganizations

In the first column provided below, suggest at least six ways for keeping a positive attitude during a plateau period or a company reorganization. You may include things to avoid, things to do, and alternatives to combat poor advice. Add enough explanation to your suggestions to help you take appropriate action. In the second column, suggest how often you should consider or implement your suggestions and ideas—daily, weekly, as long as the plateau period or reorganization lasts, at the beginning or end of the plateau period, and so forth.

Ways to Keep My Attitude Positive	When to Take Action
1.	
2.	
3.	
4.	
5.	
6.	

Now review your ideas and determine how many of them also are good for keeping your attitude positive at other times than just during a plateau period or a company reorganization. If several of your suggestions can help you keep your attitude positive at *all* times, not just during plateau periods, you may have found some excellent ways to motivate yourself to work on improving your attitude every single day!

PLATEAU-RELATED ACTION STEPS

Be cautious as you consider plateau-related action steps

Staying Positive While Considering Action. There are many other action steps people can take to shorten plateau periods, or at least to make them less difficult. There are also situations, such as company reorganizations, in which the employee should adopt the zigzag route to the top and initiate a move to another organization. In contemplating such action, keep the following three points in mind. They will help you remain positive.

1. *The first years with an organization should be viewed as an appren-ticeship.*   The training and experience must be considered the plus factors during this learning period. The employee is serving an internship similar to that in the medical profession.

2. *Many employees have received promotions before they were ready, and their careers have been permanently damaged.*   Will you be sufficiently trained for a good opportunity when it does come? Will you be ready for the responsibility? Will you be sufficiently mature to handle it? "Too much too soon" could be a real threat to your long-range goal.

3. *Although few people question the fact that personal advancement is often slow during their starting years, they seldom point out that the tempo of personal progress can increase greatly in later years.* Thus, don't set up a rigid personal timetable for yourself. Progress may be slow at the start of your career but very fast later. Yes, set a goal for yourself, but do not expect that goal to arrive exactly according to your time schedule. It may not fit that of your organization.

If you do set your own time schedule and management is unable to meet it, you may end up losing your positive attitude. Reducing or losing your positive attitude will hurt you as well as the company. The future of any company cannot be charted in detail many years in advance.

Your positive attitude will result from the positive actions you take. One of those positive actions should point to why you need to have a personal business plan and a Plan B to help you understand and cope with plateau periods. Developing a personal business plan will be a good step in the right direction. No doubt, it will contribute to your self-confidence and positive attitude—both of which will increase your propensity for success.

Summary

Today, more than any other previous period in time, organizations are going through massive, serious restructuring. Sometimes such changes create waiting periods, cause reassignments, and even result in layoffs. At other times, reorganizations create opportunities for those alert enough to perceive them. Not all changes are predictable. Not all changes can be converted into career opportunities. But some can. And it is your job to be ready when they occur—ready and waiting.

Patience is not a popular concept in our society. Yet, sooner or later, most people find they need to wear a "patience suit" when it comes to promotions and plateau periods. You should not let your ambition and impatience get you so caught up in the "fast track" for success that you "lose track" of a common fact: plateau periods are normal. Everyone has them. If you study and learn as much as you can about plateaus, you will not only reduce some of your frustration caused by them, but you probably will find ways to reduce the plateau periods themselves. In this chapter, six questions and answers are provided to help you decide what to do to reduce and cope with plateau periods.

Additionally, the chapter offers three action steps to help you shorten or live through plateau periods. The steps, along with a practical activity for you to complete, focus on the importance of keeping your attitude positive so as not to cause damage to your future.

More and more professionals are developing personal business plans and a Plan B to guide them in charting their future and to help them stay positive while implementing their plans. All in all, staying positive as you live through plateaus or reorganizations can be the greatest human-relations challenge you face.

Test Your Understanding

Respond to the following items to test your understanding of the chapter.

Part A: Circle the correct answer (T = True; F = False) for each of the following statements.

T F   1. The pattern of making nearly lock-step progress through each grade in school is very similar to progress that is experienced in the business world.

T F   2. Knowing more about plateau periods can help you live through them and reorganizations gracefully.

T F   3. The most dangerous possibility that can occur while experiencing a plateau period is that your attitude might turn negative, causing management to promote someone else.

T F   4. Assertive people usually have more success in shortening or eliminating plateau periods.

T F   5. When you find yourself on a plateau in an organization, the only thing to do is to be patient and wait it out.

Part B: Circle the letter of the correct answer for each of the following items.

6. In general, the first years with an organization should be viewed by an employee as (a) a time to scramble from department to department, (b) the fast track for seeking promotions, (c) the best time to wait for management to discover you, (d) an apprenticeship or learning period.

7. A plateau period is a time when your greatest human-relations challenge may be (a) to keep a positive attitude, (b) to impress your boss, (c) to make friends with coworkers, (d) to show how much you deserve a promotion.

Part C: Write a short response to demonstrate your understanding related to the following item.

8. Discuss some of the reasons for plateau periods and effective ways to cope with them.

Turn to the back of the book to check your answers.

A positive attitude
will provide solid footing
if a pause on the career ladder
becomes longer than expected.

Think and Respond

Respond to the following items with two or three complete sentences.

1. What is a "plateau" (related to your career) and why is patience important during such a period?

2. Explain two causes or reasons for plateau periods.

3. Discuss two ways to effectively cope with plateau periods.

4. Pose two questions you should ask if you are faced with a plateau and provide answers or solutions to your questions.

5. Discuss the importance of a positive attitude as it relates to some of the plateau-related actions you might take.

Things to Do to Shorten a Lengthy Plateau Period

Most ambitious employees eventually find themselves on a plateau where they must put on their "patience suits" until something breaks in their favor. The purpose of this activity is to help you select appropriate steps to shorten these periods or at least prevent them from hurting your attitude.

Following are twenty action steps you *could* take in a plateau period. If you have never been employed, this exercise can still be of value to you. You are asked to select *only* those steps that are appropriate to your style and personality—steps you would actually take. Place a check mark (✓) in the appropriate column for each possible step.

ACTION STEPS	APPROPRIATE FOR ME	NOT APPROPRIATE FOR ME
1. Become more assertive.	_____	_____
2. Start looking for another job, and let your organization know you are doing so.	_____	_____
3. Let the word out that you are looking for another job, but do not bother to do it.	_____	_____
4. Play some politics like the others, and do not worry about ethics.	_____	_____
5. Work harder. Become more motivated. Live closer to your potential. Do not give up.	_____	_____
6. Spend more time creating and maintaining good human relations at all levels. Improve skills in this area.	_____	_____
7. Keep your motivation up by taking a night course appropriate to your career goals.	_____	_____
8. Submit a well-researched suggestion to management to gain recognition.	_____	_____
9. Remain patient and effective; let others become aggressive and overplay their hands.	_____	_____
10. Talk to people who have lived through such periods, and follow their advice.	_____	_____
11. Ask someone in personnel to help you update your resumé.	_____	_____
12. Get a job moonlighting to earn more money so that some of the pressure on you will be dissipated.	_____	_____
13. Take your supervisor to lunch.	_____	_____

14. Start doing irregular things (not your normal behavior) that defy traditional protocol so that you can gain more attention.   _____   _____

15. Create some modest waves by doing a few things that need to be done without asking permission to do them.   _____   _____

16. Ask for a raise in pay.   _____   _____

17. Capitalize on the situation by deliberately projecting a "patient" image, but do everything possible to push yourself.   _____   _____

18. Ask for a transfer.   _____   _____

19. Talk to your supervisor's superior.   _____   _____

20. Resign.   _____   _____

Total   [_____]   [_____]

Now total your responses in each column. If you responded to eight or more items by checking the "appropriate for me" column, chances are you could shorten any plateau period. Of course, it would depend to some extent on the skill used in taking the steps. If you checked five or fewer, your chance of success would be less.

It should be obvious that taking some of the preceding steps could do more harm than good. But without some action on your part, management could ignore you or promote someone ahead of you—certainly you don't want management to believe you are a "nice patient person" who will not resign no matter what happens.

CASE 21

Change

"I hate change."

In a company-sponsored seminar on how to handle and adjust to change, Ingrid made this statement to the group: "When it comes to the future and the changes it may bring, I believe that hard work and good ethics plus sound human-relations techniques will see me through. If my present superiors do not recognize and reward me, then someone else will."

The following response came from Darla, a coworker and good friend of Ingrid's: "I think it is commendable for Ingrid to have so much faith in hard work and human-relations skills, but I think that adapting to change requires a more aggressive and creative approach. Ingrid, with her somewhat naive attitude, may be left behind. It has been my practice to try to turn change into opportunity through action. When a change occurs, I sit back for a day or so and figure out how I can use the change to my advantage and enhance my career. At such a critical juncture, I cannot rely on past performance and routine human relations. I must shift gears and look out for number one, even if it means temporarily stepping on the feelings of others. When change comes, it is not business as usual. I cannot prevent or control change, but if I am clever, I can turn it to my advantage."

A. Discuss: Who, in your opinion, is better prepared to handle the dramatic changes most experts claim will occur in the future, Ingrid or Darla? Is there a better strategy?

B. Expand Your Understanding: Interview two or more supervisors (or employees who have been working several years) to determine their views about how they have dealt with plateau periods. Then research the topic of career plateaus and offer several ideas for both Ingrid and Darla to "expand" their thinking about the approaches they are taking for career success. Include in your list of ideas such factors as ways to keep up with change and the role of education and training.

CHAPTER 22

When You Are Tempted to Scramble

"I'm ready for a fresh start."

Thought for the Day: Keep your house in order for you never know when your attitude and human-relations skills will influence your future.

PERFORMANCE COMPETENCIES

- Understand that free people have considerable flexibility in how they approach career building, but there still are risks when making a career move.

- Recognize that while no general rule exists, you should resign when you have been unhappy and unproductive for a considerable period of time.

- Appreciate that because personality conflicts and human problems cause most resignations, it is wise to heed eight suggestions for resigning gracefully.

- Realize that moving on for the right reasons can be rewarding if you accept change and learn from your mistakes and past experiences.

- Identify four ways to protect your positive attitude when facing a layoff or other situation associated with a career change.

Freedom to accept or resign a job, seek employment in a certain career field, or join the organization of one's choice is an important right. It should be appreciated by all free people. What does this freedom mean to you, a member of the workforce?

FREEDOM OF WORK CHOICE

In general, many people in most countries around the world have freedom to choose where they want to work. This freedom means you can be a stabilizer and, provided that you select the right firm, you can build your entire career within a single organization. It means you can leave a position with a large or small organization and go into business for yourself. It means you can leave your present occupation and go back to school to prepare for a new career. It also means you may choose to become a scrambler and follow the zigzag route to build your career by making a move to another organization every time you can substantially improve your situation. It means you can keep switching jobs until you find the occupation or company that's right for you.

Understand the ramifications associated with resigning

The Decision to Scramble. The decision to resign from a job, even in the best of circumstances, is a big decision. In "less-than-ideal" conditions, resigning can be an even bigger decision—probably even a very risky decision. That is, usually the temptation to scramble is reduced during periods of economic slowdown. There are two reasons for this phenomenon: First, many qualified people are unemployed and already in the marketplace, trying to capture the few available positions. Second, a person is less tempted to make a geographical move in uncertain times when it may be more difficult to relocate let alone sell an existing home. Even so, intense scrambling continues as creative opportunities open up in smaller companies.

Some resignations are positive actions; they benefit both the organization and the individual. Some make sense because reorganizations increase the possibility of future layoffs. Some resignations, for a variety of personal reasons, are unavoidable. Others, however, seem to stem from poor judgment and turn out to be mistakes.

There are dangers to any resignation. You could wind up with a job that is not as good as the one you left. You might even wind up temporarily stranded. Thousands of people leave organizations every year, only to regret it later. The pastures in another occupational area or company may, from a distance, look greener than they really are. Resigning a position, whether you have a door open elsewhere or not, is a serious step. Careful research is recommended.

WHY RESIGN?

When should you resign a position? As a general rule, you should: *resign when you have been unhappy and unproductive for a considerable length of time.* Under such conditions, your career with the company already has been seriously damaged. A new start in a new environment would most likely be to your advantage.

People who are ambitious should look elsewhere for employment when they discover they have not been working close to their potential for a long time. They should seek opportunities elsewhere when their productivity has been down for months and they can't seem to improve it. They should consider other options when their attitude has been negative for a long time and they do not seem to be able to do anything about it.

Surveys and statistics show, however, that most resignations are not due to the preceding reasons.

Human Relations Is the "# 1" Resignation Reason. You have learned that most people are hired, promoted, and fired because of their human relations skills (or lack thereof). Unfortunately, it is true. *Most resignations are based primarily upon personality conflicts and human-relations problems.*

Rather than leaving for a better position, people are getting away from the frustrations of their present job. Because such problems can frequently be solved, or at least made less traumatic, it would appear that many people resign their positions for the wrong reasons. In other words, leaving a job because it is not the right one for you is one thing. Leaving a job because of human-relations incompetencies is something else.

Be sure you have the right reasons for resigning

Resignation Questions to Consider. To help you avoid these and other mistakes, here are some questions to ask yourself when considering a resignation.

- *Are you resigning under emotional stress?* We are all tempted to chuck a job when everything seems to be going wrong or when we are frustrated and upset. It is a natural reaction. A resignation, however, should be a rational decision based upon many facts, and should be made only after long, careful analysis and planning.

  It is difficult to think clearly and logically when you are emotionally upset about a human-relations problem that cannot be quickly solved. During these periods, back away from such a serious decision. Sleep on it. Talk to another person. Give it time. Make another, more serious attempt to solve it. A resignation should not be an impulsive decision. In the majority of cases, it is irrevocable.

- *Are you resigning because of a personality conflict?* Resigning because of a single personality conflict can seriously hamper a promising career. This is not to say that such conflicts do not occur. They do. But they can usually be resolved with time and effort. Give someone in authority a chance to help. Give time a chance to help. Most of all, be honest with yourself and ask whether you can afford to let one person destroy a promising career—especially when it is yours.

■ *Are you resigning because you feel your job may be eliminated?* Almost all organizations make adjustments during lean economic times. Rumors of staff reductions circulate from time to time. During such periods, smart employees dig in to make themselves more valuable so that they will be less vulnerable to layoffs. They also improve their skills and set in motion a Plan B should the rumors prove to be true. To resign from a job during organizational adjustment periods can be a major mistake. Due to early retirement inducements, more responsible positions may become available for those who sit tight and continue to produce.

■ *Are you marking time?* Frequently, highly capable employees sense that they are not going anywhere in their present jobs, yet they do nothing to find a better opportunity. Such individuals often drag along for years, doing a disservice to both themselves and their organizations. Later you hear them say: "I should have made a change years ago!" Facing such a negative career situation head on may be justified to avoid the penalties and regrets of lack of progress later.

■ *Have you talked your situation over with your supervisor or the person who hired you?* Many employees are fearful about talking over a possible resignation with a management person. Some believe that it will be held against them if they voice their dissatisfaction. They feel that their chances of finding a better job elsewhere will be weakened. Some feel it would be an act of disloyalty. Others feel it to be a waste of time.

Open communication is the best way to resolve problems

Whatever your reason, you would be wise not to resign until you have discussed the problem with your supervisor or someone in personnel or upper management. A twenty-minute discussion with the right person has stopped many foolish resignations. Many problems can be resolved through free and open communication with management.

Give those in charge a chance to help you resolve your problem before you take final action. You have nothing to lose. You could even discover that the position you are thinking of leaving has more potential than any other positions you could find elsewhere.

■ *Are you resigning to save face?* Everyone makes mistakes. Sometimes you may overcommit yourself or take a stand on an issue from which you feel you cannot back away. Resigning on this basis can be a mistake, especially if you have exaggerated the difficulty of the adjustment. It may be better to admit such a mistake than to pay a price that is all out of proportion. Such a resignation might be harmful to both your future and the company.

■ *Have you exhausted all opportunities to learn more where you are?* A key factor in any decision to resign should be whether you can continue to grow in your present job. If you are completely boxed in, with no opportunity to improve yourself, then you should certainly consider a change. If, however, you can continue to learn while waiting for a break, your situation is not as bad as it could be.

- *Are you working close to your potential?* Your future depends on your having a position in a company where you can work close to your potential. If the gap between what you are capable of doing and your current level of productivity is too wide, your career progress may be stalled. You must be able to use your ability, aptitude, and talent to a reasonable extent. You must be productive to succeed. You must find a way to contribute.

Project Your Best Attitude. If you find that your position doesn't bring out the best in you, then it isn't fair to either you or the company for you to remain. You should find something more suitable. Employees who are not productive are doing themselves and the company more harm than good. *Your company is entitled to the best in you.*

Always give your best efforts to your employer

RESIGNING WITH DIGNITY

If, after serious consideration of all of the preceding questions, you decide to resign in the best interests of all concerned, how should you go about it? A wise person will resign with dignity and will display good human relations and a positive attitude. Consider the following eight suggestions for resigning gracefully.

1. *Resign on a face-to-face basis.* It is good human relations to go to the person who hired you, as well as to your supervisor, and resign face-to-face. A letter of resignation or a telephone resignation alone may leave a bad impression that could hurt you later. You will gain the respect of management when you resign in person. You will feel better, too.

2. *Convey the reasons for resigning.* It may be difficult for you to reveal the actual causes for your leaving, but you should do so anyway. Tell management the real reasons for your resignation. Reliable information of this kind can lead to changes that will benefit those you leave behind. Honesty is always the best human-relations policy.

3. *Give ample notice.* Be sure that you give at least the traditional two weeks' notice. If your company has a policy for tendering a resignation, follow it if at all possible. By following the policy, you could avoid damaging your present relationship with the company. Consider the company's position—a certain amount of time may be necessary for the company to recruit and train a replacement.

4. *Continue to be productive.*   Don't take advantage of the fact that you are leaving. You will gain respect from others, as well as personal satisfaction, by working hard up to the very last hour. Continuing your productivity is one way to leave a clean record behind you.

5. *Turn in all equipment.*   All company equipment, down to the most minuté item, should be officially turned in through regular channels and be in the best condition you can leave it.

6. *Transfer all responsibilities.*   Give the person taking over your job a break. Give your replacement all possible help and assistance by gracefully transferring all of your responsibilities to her (or him). Try not to leave your replacement with any problems you can take care of before leaving. Also transfer to her, insofar as possible, any good relationships you have developed.

7. *Swallow any negative comments.*   There is a temptation for some people to become negative and pour out their hostilities before they have turned in their resignations. Resist any vindictive instincts you may have. Don't be tempted to make any last-minute negative comments—you probably will regret later any remarks that didn't need to be said.

8. *Leave on the right basis.*   That is, always resign a position in such a manner that you will feel free to seek reemployment there at a later date. You are the sum total of all your experiences. When you leave a job, you do not leave empty-handed. You take your experience and training with you. And you take the knowledge you've gained from all your human-relations experiences. Such knowledge is never without value. Make that known.

With these suggestions to guide you, complete the activity that follows.

ACTIVITY

Questions to Ponder When Resigning

In the space provided below, formulate six questions that should be addressed when an employee makes the decision to resign from a job. You may wish to refer to the items listed in the section, "Resigning with Dignity" and rework the statements into questions. For example, the first item, "Resign on a face-to-face basis," could be restated as follows: "Why should I give my resignation face-to-face rather than in writing?"

Now, add answers to your questions. Save both the questions and answers in a file labeled "Resignation Tips" to consider (a) when you develop your personal business plan, which includes a Plan B, and (b) when and if you make a decision to resign from a job.

Finally, note the good advice offered in the second part of this exercise about protecting your positive attitude. Add at least two reasons why your positive attitude is a prized possession and should be protected, especially throughout a resignation process. You may wish to complete the reading of this chapter before you formulate your answer.

1. _____

2. _____

3. _____

4. _____

5. _____

6. _____

My positive attitude is a priceless personal possession. Two reasons I will strive to protect it are:

1. _____

2. _____

MOVING ON FOR THE RIGHT REASONS

Those who move on for the right reasons—opportunity to use new knowledge, gain broader experience, improve career status and financial benefits—avoid the consequences of repeating human-relationship mistakes and communicating instability on their job applications. However, as some would caution: the grass is not always greener on the

Be willing to accept change, but also be prepared to expect turmoil

other side of the fence. Consider the following statement made by Kendall, a shopping center manager:

Kendall. One of the most important things I learned in college was to anticipate and be willing to accept change. I expected I would walk into a dynamic, changing world; I was not prepared for the turmoil that really exists. Many outstanding people are left unemployed through no fault of their own.

Change Is Inevitable. Because change is everywhere and there is no escape from it, you must be ready to accept the challenges it brings. Easier said than done? Of course! But you can meet change head on if you keep a positive attitude, develop the best relationships you possibly can. Keep an open mind. Continue to learn. And, in general, be receptive to change. If you do, you will be much better prepared for the challenges than if you just let life happen.

Learn from the Past. As you plan for career success, and it does take a conscious effort, learn from your mistakes. Also learn from your successes and the collective experiences you have had. For example, your planning efforts should include being honest about an accurate assessment of your previous, present, and insofar as possible, future working environments. It is not difficult to tell when a working environment is comfortable, efficient, and productive. It can be observed from the attitudes workers display. There is more laughter. Employees are more tolerant of each other. Work is viewed more as a rewarding team effort than as a series of boring tasks.

But make no mistake! A single negative attitude can start turning a harmonious atmosphere sour. Don't you be the one to fall into a negative trap; and don't you be the one to run away from the many challenges that can become opportunities if you contribute to a positive environment.

PROTECT YOUR POSITIVE ATTITUDE

Like other things in life, organizations grow, decline, go through management shake-ups, and sometimes change ownership. The fear of a possible layoff, relocation, or adjustment to a new work environment and superior can turn an upbeat, productive employee into a negative one.

How would you protect your positive attitude under the preceding circumstances? Here are four important tips to help you stay positive as you contemplate a career change:

1. *Your positive attitude belongs to you, not to your company.*   Your positive attitude is a priceless personal possession, so protect it for your own happiness. Keep in mind that a rumor about an organizational change is still a rumor until it has been verified and a definite change in your status has been made. Contrary to popular belief, the majority of ownership changes do not result in layoffs and significant adjustments among lower-level managers and employees.

2. *To help you remain positive, start a Plan B.* Whether a forced change is coming or not, it is always a sound idea to explore other options through a Plan B. (Refer to other chapters in this book for a discussion on this topic.) Upgrade your skills where you are. Be a winner no matter what happens.

3. *Don't take organizational restructuring personally.* A company sale or change of ownership may appear to be a cold, calculated business decision, but it is transacted within the same free-enterprise system in which the company was created and nurtured in the first place. It is unfortunate when job losses occur, but neither you nor anyone else is to blame. Focus on the fact that if you keep your positive attitude, a prospective employer will likely see you as a lucky find. Sometimes unwelcome change leads an individual with the right attitude to a superior career role.

4. *Your reputation is not damaged by corporate restructuring.* It does not hurt your reputation to be caught in a situation in which an organizational change forces you into a career move. It is discouraging enough to go through any adjustment caused by a change in ownership. If you lose your positive attitude along with it, you are a double loser.

Summary

When you are tempted to scramble, you many seriously consider several resignation suggestions and tips that this chapter has provided:

1. Most people in the free world have work choices. If a person decides that scrambling is the best approach, he (or she) needs to know there are pros and cons to such action.

2. There are several critical questions that need serious, honest contemplation when a person considers resigning.

3. Resigning gracefully, with dignity, is to a person's advantage. Eight resignation suggestions are provided to help you protect your positive attitude and relationships.

4. If you do resign, move on for the right reasons. Learn from the past and make the most of your experience to advance your career. Always expect change.

5. When a career change is needed, especially when it is not your choice to make a change, protect your positive attitude. Remember, it is your most prized possession.

In a time of career change, particularly when the choice is not entirely yours, it is important to stay objective and professional while protecting your positive attitude. If it is to your advantage, go out and find yourself a more rewarding position!

Test Your Understanding

Respond to the following items to test your understanding of the chapter.

Part A: Circle the correct answer (T = True; F = False) for each of the following statements.

T F   1. Most resignations are based primarily on personality conflicts and human-relations problems.

T F   2. You would be wise not to discuss the problem with your supervisor or someone in the human resource department before resigning.

T F   3. The organization where you work is entitled to the best of you.

T F   4. Always resign a position in such a manner that you feel free to seek reemployment with the same organization at a later date.

T F   5. Having a Plan B helps one remain positive during periods of dramatic organizational change.

Part B: Circle the letter of the correct answer for each of the following items.

6. Resigning with dignity implies that you should (a) take advantage of the fact you are leaving, (b) keep your resignation a secret until the day before you leave, (c) resign by letter or memo, (d) turn in all equipment, down to the smallest item.

7. Because your positive attitude is so important to you—your priceless personal possession—you should (a) act on a rumor about organizational change and resign quickly, (b) resign and protect your good name by blaming the organization for your action, (c) resign and take the organizational restructuring personally, (d) be a winner no matter what happens.

Part C: Write a short response to demonstrate your understanding related to the following item.

8. Suggest some of the resignation questions you should ask, ponder, and answer before you actually resign.

Turn to the back of the book to check your answers.

To move mountains
of uncertainty and change,
you need to have
the right attitude.

Think and Respond

Respond to the following items with two or three complete sentences.

1. Explain why some resignations are positive while others can be negative.
2. Discuss two "good" reasons for resigning.
3. What are two suggestions for resigning gracefully?
4. Explain some of the "lessons to be learned" when moving on after a resignation.
5. Suggest two tips for keeping a positive attitude when making a career change.

Plan B Activity

A Plan B is a carefully researched and designed strategy to pursue a new job immediately should your present one disappear or lose its luster (Plan B is discussed in another chapter). A Plan B should be considered as a reserve plan that will match or be superior to your present job or career plan. The following exercise is designed to help you decide whether or not you should initiate a Plan B. Read both statements carefully, then circle the number for each of the ten items that is most appropriate in your case. A "10" indicates you have an extremely high desire to have a Plan B. A "1" indicates you have no interest.

1. I want to prepare now for possible "winds of change."

    10 9 8 7 6 5 4 3 2 1

    I'll face change when it happens.

2. I view a Plan B as a very important insurance policy.

    10 9 8 7 6 5 4 3 2 1

    I view a Plan B as a waste of time.

3. Having a Plan B will help me feel better about my personal business plan.

    10 9 8 7 6 5 4 3 2 1

    Nothing can make me feel better about my present career plan.

4. I agree a Plan B will help me get a new job if needed.

    10 9 8 7 6 5 4 3 2 1

    I intend waiting until the last minute to decide how to get a new job.

5. I understand a Plan B may require upgrading my skills.

    10 9 8 7 6 5 4 3 2 1

    I'm sticking with my skills as they exist.

6. A Plan B can help me get a promotion with my present firm.

    10 9 8 7 6 5 4 3 2 1

    Preparing a Plan B can get me fired.

7. Both scramblers and stabilizers need to develop a Plan B.

    10 9 8 7 6 5 4 3 2 1

    Advance planning leads to severe disappointment.

8. I agree a Plan B should be a written strategy including an updated resumé.

    10 9 8 7 6 5 4 3 2 1

    The only Plan B worth the effort is an idea in my mind.

9. I see the need for a Plan B and will start one as soon as I have landed a good job.

    10 9 8 7 6 5 4 3 2 1

    Sorry, I just don't see the need for a back-up plan.

10. A Plan B is designed to help me remain professional in my specialty.

    10 9 8 7 6 5 4 3 2 1

    I'm not worried about being a professional. All I want is a good job.

Total Score _____

Now, total your scores for the ten items. If you rated yourself 80 or above, you have an excellent attitude about the importance of a formal Plan B. A score between 60 and 80 indicates enough interest to start one. A score under 60 is a signal that even though you appear not to be interested, at this point, in having a backup plan, you should strongly consider how beneficial a Plan B, as well as a personal business plan (based on identified goals), can be for your career success (review other chapters relating to goals, a Plan B, and a personal business plan). Without a doubt, being prepared with alternative ways to approach your career can make a big difference in achieving both work success and life happiness.

CASE 22

Interview

"Attitude makes the difference."

Mark was quite discouraged when his job was eliminated. He was even more discouraged when, after seven job interviews in three months, he had no job offers.

Mark had tried extremely hard to get a job—he followed sound job-seeking practices, did research on all the organizations before the interviews, was meticulous in his grooming, was careful in completing the application form, and always submitted a resumé.

What was wrong? Were economic conditions bad?

When Mark asked the opinion of a very perceptive placement director about his dilemma, together they came to the conclusion that Mark was not communicating well or transmitting his best attitude during the interview. While Mark had more than the minimum qualifications for all the positions for which he applied, he was losing out to other applicants.

Because Mark is a good friend of yours, you decide to help him out in developing answers (and a strategy to ensure he is not too low key, too strong, too brief, nervous, phony, etc.) to the following four main questions he has been encountering in his interviews: (1) What made you decide that you would like to work for our company? (2) What do you feel you will be able to contribute to our organization? (3) What human-relations skills will you bring with you? and (4) What are some of your weaknesses?

A. Discuss: How would you answer each of the four questions? Are there other considerations of which Mark should be aware? Role-play or write out, word for word, the way you would reply to each of the questions.

B. Expand Your Understanding: Research the topics of "job resignation" and "job search." Once you have sufficient information on both topics, develop some recommendations that could have been more helpful to Mark (or to anyone else in the same situation) when his job was eliminated. Also, develop some recommendations on how Mark should proceed now if he is to be successful in his job search. Be sure to include some good advice relating to keeping a positive attitude (and back up your advice with several sources on the importance of a positive attitude).

CHAPTER 23

Attitude Renewal

"Something needs adjusting."

Thought for the Day: If you give your positive attitude away by praising others and taking positive action, you'll reward yourself and everyone around you.

PERFORMANCE COMPETENCIES

- Recognize that, especially due to stress everyone needs some type of attitude renewal from time to time.

- Appreciate the significance of humor in employing the "flip-side" technique to avoid attitudinal ruts (attitude-adjustment technique #1).

- Understand how rewards of thinking and talking about positive things capitalize on the technique of "playing your winners" (attitude-adjustment technique #2).

- Recognize why "giving your positive attitude away" is a very powerful technique (attitude-adjustment technique #3).

- Understand the importance of improving your image as a technique for "looking better to yourself" (attitude-adjustment technique #4).

- Appreciate why the technique of "accepting the physical connection" is critical to your attitude (attitude-adjustment technique #5).

Renewal means to restore or refresh. Employees at all levels occasionally need to renew their positive view toward their careers, rejuvenate their approach to the type of work they perform, or reestablish their positive focus toward their organizations. Everyone, even the most optimistic individual, should, from time to time, go through some form of attitude renewal. To some, maintaining a positive focus is a full-time job.

ATTITUDINAL REJUVENATION

Attitude and Stress. Job stress is self-imposed when workers set too many difficult goals for themselves and, as a result, move in an unorganized manner in too many directions at the same time. Most stress, however, is caused by the job itself. Some jobs—such as those of television news personnel, air traffic controllers, and police officers—are recognized as stressful.

Excessive stress can cause job burnout, which results in impairment of work productivity. Warning signals include feelings of frustration (see discussion in other chapters of this book), emotional outbursts, and withdrawal. Human relationships usually deteriorate.

Two important questions about stress and attitude are:

1. *Do those who maintain positive attitudes handle stress better than others?* Generally speaking, yes. When you focus on the positive elements of a work environment, you are more apt to envision yourself as a winner. The result is that you laugh more and find it easier to relax. With these behavioral patterns, less stress affects the individual, and the stress that does occur is dissipated with less damage.

   In contrast, those with behavioral patterns connected with negative attitudes appear to open the door to additional stress and hold the pressure created within themselves longer.

   The more stress that can be removed from any job (fewer deadlines, unreasonable demands, human conflicts), the better. However, all jobs generate some stress. Whatever the stress level may be, those who concentrate on maintaining good coworker relationships seem to handle it with less harm to themselves.

2. *Can returning to a positive attitude from a negative attitude be considered an antidote to excessive stress and possible burnout (long-term exhaustion with diminished interest)?* To a limited extent, yes. When excessive stress eventually gets to workers, they often focus more on the negative factors present. After an attitude-renewal program takes place (vacation, counseling, self-help), these same people see the more positive factors present. In this sense, returning to their positive attitude constitutes an antidote.

A positive attitude can help you to handle stress

Daily Attitude Renewal.
Attitude renewal, at the first level, is often a daily process. For a few, moments of early morning meditation are helpful. Others, who may get off to a bad start, call a friend in midmorning for a "boost" and then start the day anew. Other forms of adjustment (regaining a positive focus) can take place at other points throughout a given day.

At a more serious level, attitude renewal can be a weekend project. You hear both employees and managers make statements such as:

"I need a strong dose of weekend rest and recreation to get my attitude ready for Monday morning."

"Without the quiet time I enjoy during weekends, I would be a basket case Monday morning."

Without periodic time off or weekend attitude-adjustment periods, most people could not remain positive and productive in their work environments.

Attitude renewal contributes to productivity

Beware of Attitudinal "Ruts."
There are times, however, when even weekend renewals are not sufficient. A major overhaul may be necessary. A major attitude overhaul may be needed because now and then most individuals fall into an "attitudinal rut."

An attitudinal rut usually occurs when someone slips unknowingly into a pattern of negative behavior that, unfortunately, can continue over a long period of time. Although some days are better than others, the individual's focus is permanently skewed to the negative side of his (or her) perception. Obviously, remaining in an attitudinal rut can inflict severe damage on one's career.

Nevertheless, it is possible to fall into such a rut without knowing it. When you become physically ill, for example, your body sends you a signal—you get a headache, a fever, or pain—and you do something about it. When you slip into an attitudinal rut, your mind may be unable to send you a clear signal of distress because it does not inflict physical pain. Your coworkers or close friends may want to send you a signal, but it is such a sensitive area that they back away. As a consequence, some people stay in their attitudinal ruts for long periods.

Norm. Over two years ago, when he was passed over for a promotion he thought he deserved, Norm pushed himself into a negative rut. He is in the same trough today. Even if there were some easy way to tell Norm that he is negative, he would deny it because he has been in this entrenched rut so long that he thinks his behavior is normal. As a result, he cannot see that he is his own worst enemy.

The Attitude-Adjustment Rating activity that follows is designed to help you assess the current condition of your own attitude. View it in the same manner you would one of those electronic instruments used to determine if your car engine needs a tune-up. The results might send you a signal that, with a few adjustments, you could be a more positive, successful, and happy person.

ACTIVITY

My Attitude-Adjustment Rating

This activity is provided as a self-assessment for you to rate your current attitude. Read each statement and circle the number where you feel you belong. If you circle a "10," you are saying your attitude could not be better in this area; if you circle a "1," you are saying it could not be worse.

	High (Positive) ___ Low (Negative)
1. I'm not going to ask, but my honest guess is that my boss would now rate my general attitude as a . . .	10 9 8 7 6 5 4 3 2 1
2. Given a chance, coworkers and family would rate my attitude as a . . .	10 9 8 7 6 5 4 3 2 1
3. I would rate my attitude as a . . .	10 9 8 7 6 5 4 3 2 1
4. In dealing with others, I believe my current effectiveness rates a . . .	10 9 8 7 6 5 4 3 2 1
5. My current creativity level rates a . . .	10 9 8 7 6 5 4 3 2 1
6. If there were a meter to gauge my sense of humor at this stage, I believe it would read close to a . . .	10 9 8 7 6 5 4 3 2 1
7. My recent disposition—the patience and sensitivity I show to others—deserves a rating of . . .	10 9 8 7 6 5 4 3 2 1
8. For not letting little things bother me recently, I deserve a . . .	10 9 8 7 6 5 4 3 2 1
9. Based on the number of compliments I've received lately, I deserve a . . .	10 9 8 7 6 5 4 3 2 1
10. I would rate my enthusiasm toward my job and life, in general, during the past few weeks as a . . .	10 9 8 7 6 5 4 3 2 1
Total	

Now, total your scores on the ten statements. A score of 90 or higher is a signal that your attitude is "in tune" and no adjustments are necessary. A score between 70 and 90 is a signal that minor attitude adjustments may help. A score between 50 and 70 should alert you to take immediate action to improve your attitude. A score under 50 indicates that a complete attitude overhaul may be required.

Regardless of how you rated yourself on the scale, the attitude-adjustment techniques that follow can help you become a more positive and effective individual.

THE "FLIP-SIDE" (ATTITUDE-ADJUSTMENT TECHNIQUE #1)

Humor and Your Attitude. The pivotal factor between being positive or negative is often a sense of humor. Attitude and humor have a symbiotic relationship. The more you develop your sense of humor, the more positive you will become. The more positive you become, the better your sense of humor will be. It's a happy arrangement.

Some people successfully use the "flip-side" technique to maintain and enhance their sense of humor. When a "negative" enters their lives, they immediately flip the problem over (as you would a pancake) and look for whatever humor may exist on the other side. When they succeed, these clever individuals are able to minimize the negative impact the problem has on their positive attitude.

Jim. When Jim walked into his apartment last night, he was devastated. Everything was in shambles, and he quickly discovered that some valuable possessions were missing. After assessing the situation, Jim called Marcy and said, "I think I have figured out a way for us to take that vacation trip to Mexico. I've just been robbed, but my homeowners insurance is paid up. Why not come over and help me clean up while we finalize our plans?"

Humor in any form resists negative forces. It can restore your positive attitude and help you maintain a more balanced perspective on life. How do you define a sense of humor?

Humor Defined. A sense of humor is an attitudinal quality (mental focus) that encourages an individual to discover humor others may not see in the same situation. It is a philosophy that says: "If you take life too seriously, it will pull you down. Force yourself to pull back and laugh at the human predicament."

Humor is the enemy of a negative attitude

Countless incidents that you could improve with a humorous twist occur in your life each day. They will pass you by, however, unless you educate your attitude to see them. To find humor in a situation, it might be helpful for you to give this mental set a special name, such as *funny focus*. It may sound frivolous, but finding a funny focus describes what some wise people are actually able to do.

"Shandra always adjusts more quickly because she directs that creative mind of hers to the funny side."

"Semi is good company because he has the unique capacity to find humor in any situation."

Those who receive such compliments nurture a funny focus that permits them to create a more positive perspective. A humorous focus is their antidote to negative situations.

Humor Is a Funny Focus. How can you improve your attitude through a greater sense of humor? How can you develop a funny focus that will fall within your comfort zone? Recognizing the following elements should help.

- *Humor is an inside job.* Humor is not something that is natural for one person and unnatural for another. One individual is not blessed with a reservoir of humor waiting to be released while another is left to cry. A sense of humor is created. With practice, anyone can do it.

- *Laughter is therapeutic.* Negative emotions such as tension, anger, or stress can produce ulcers, headaches, and high blood pressure. Positive emotions can relax nerves, improve digestion and circulation, and otherwise contribute to physical and emotional wellness. Of course, you cannot laugh away all serious problems, but you can laugh your way into a more positive focus to help you cope with the problem. Laughter is soul music to attitude. It is a way of adjusting to a funny focus.

- *A funny focus can get you out of the problem and into the solution.* Finding the humor in a situation usually won't solve a problem, but it can lead you in the right direction. Laughing can help transfer your focus from the problem to the solution. Using the flip-side technique starts the process.

PLAY YOUR WINNERS
(ATTITUDE-ADJUSTMENT TECHNIQUE #2)

Winners Are Positive. When retailers discover that a certain item is selling faster than others, they pour additional promotional money into that product. Their motto is, "Play the winners; don't go broke trying to promote the losers."

The same approach can help you adjust and maintain a positive attitude. You have special winners in your life. The more you focus on them, the better.

Jason. At this point in his life, Jason has more losers than winners. Having spent ten years in the workforce, he is currently adjusting to a divorce, is deeply in debt, and has a car that is giving him fits. The only two positive factors are his job (Jason is making progress in the hotel management field he loves) and running. By pouring his energies into his career and running a minimum of six miles each day, Jason is able to maintain a positive attitude. He is playing his winners.

Each of us, at any stage in our lives, is confronted with both positive factors (winners) and negative factors (losers). If you are not constantly alert, losers can take over and push your winners out of your mental focus. When winners get shoved to the sidelines, you spend mind time dwelling on your losers. If continued over a period of time, your attitude will become negative and your disposition will turn sour. Your challenge is to find ways to push the losers to the perimeter of your thinking, where you can live with them, perhaps permanently, in a graceful manner.

How can you do this?

Three Ways to Play Your Winners. Here are three simple suggestions for playing your winners:

1. *Think more about your winners.* The more you concentrate on the winning elements in your life, the less time you will have to devote to the negatives. Thinking about winners means that your negative factors will receive less attention; and, as a result, many may resolve themselves.

2. *Talk only about your winners.* As long as you do not overdo it (or repeat yourself with the same person), the more you verbalize the happy, exciting factors in your life, the more important they become to you. Those who talk incessantly about the negative aspects of their lives do their friends a disservice and perpetuate their own negative attitude.

3. *Reward yourself by enjoying your winners.* If you enjoy nature, play this winner by taking a nature walk. If music is a positive influence, listen to your favorite artist. If religion is a powerful force in your life, play your winner by praying.

You play your winners every time you think or talk or pray about them. But obviously, the best thing you can do is enjoy them. If you are a golfer, playing eighteen holes will do more for your attitude than thinking or talking about doing it.

GIVE YOUR POSITIVE ATTITUDE TO OTHERS (ATTITUDE-ADJUSTMENT TECHNIQUE #3)

Sharing Your Attitude. When you get fed up with the behavior of others, you may be tempted to tell them off and give them "a piece of your mind." Telling someone off is understandably human. It is a better policy, however, to give others "a piece of your positive attitude." When you react positively, you permit others to help you adjust your attitude.

Shannon. Because she needed a psychological lift, Shannon asked Casey to meet her for lunch. Casey didn't feel much like it, but she accepted and made a special effort to be upbeat. When the luncheon was over, Casey had not only given Shannon a boost, but also felt better herself. Both women came out ahead.

When you give part of your positive attitude to others, you create a symbiotic relationship. The recipient feels better, but so do you. In a somewhat upside-down twist, *you keep your positive attitude by giving it away.*

Everyone has opportunities to give their positive attitudes to others. Taxi drivers who make their passengers laugh increase their tips. Employees who give coworkers deserved compliments increase their popularity. Home owners who send positive signals to their neighbors eliminate problems with them when they see them. And, vacationers can enhance their fun by making new friends simply by being pleasant to fellow travelers. Opportunities abound. The results are best, however, when the giving is toughest.

Enid. It was a difficult Friday for Enid. Due to an emergency staff meeting in the morning, she was behind in her work. Just as she was starting to catch up, the computer went down. Then her boss asked her to finish an unexpected project before leaving for the weekend. When she finally left work, all Enid could think of was getting into her hot tub and forgetting it all. But she had promised herself to visit her friend Wanda, who was hospitalized. The temptation to drive straight home was strong, but she resisted and paid Wanda a visit. An hour later, Enid arrived home refreshed and positive. She didn't need the hot tub.

Each individual winds up a winner by giving his (or her) positive attitude away in a manner suited to his own personal style.

LOOK BETTER TO YOURSELF (ATTITUDE-ADJUSTMENT TECHNIQUE #4)

Promoting Your Self-Image. You are constantly bombarded through media advertising to improve your image. Most messages state that only with a "new look" can you find acceptance and meet new friends.

"Discover the new you. Join our health club and expand your circle of friends."

"Let cosmetic surgery help you find a new partner."

Self-improvement of any kind should be applauded. However, the overriding reason for a "new image" is to look better, not for others, but for yourself. When you improve your appearance, you give your positive attitude a boost. It is not what happens outside that counts, but how your mind sees yourself.

While the term *inferiority complex* is not in popular use today, the old textbook definition is a good one: *An inferiority complex is said to occur when you look better to others than you do to yourself.* In other words, when you have a negative self-image, you make yourself feel psychologically inferior when you probably are not.

The truth is that you often do look better to others than you do to yourself. There may be periods when you feel unfashionable, unattractive, and dowdy—but this does not mean you look that way to your friends. The problem is that you are communicating a negative attitude because you don't look good to yourself.

When you have a poor self-image, it is as though you are looking through a glass darkly. You feel you don't look good, so nothing else looks good to you. Getting down on yourself occurs because your negative image psychologically distorts your attitude (e.g., the way you look at things mentally).

You see yourself first, your environment second. You can't remove yourself from the perceptual process.

Zahi. When he was a teenager, Zahi gave up on ever having a good self-image. All through college he was considered a reclusive grind. Approaching graduation, Zahi enrolled in a non-credit course designed to prepare students for a professional job search. Part of the program included doing a mock employment interview on videotape that would be critiqued by the instructor and fellow students. To prepare for this unwanted ordeal, Zahi purchased a new suit, had his hair restyled, and bought new, more fashionable eyeglass frames. He practiced his mock interview over and over at home. When his day arrived, Zahi did so well that he received compliments from all who viewed the tape. The recognition and support had a wonderful impact on Zahi. For the first time, he looked good to himself. Zahi's negative image was no longer a barrier to a good future.

Marry Your Attitude and Self-Image. The connection between a good self-image and a positive attitude cannot be ignored. In keeping a better image, it will help if you take this advice.

Appreciate the strength of a good self-image and a positive attitude

- Admit that, at times, you may look better to others than you look to yourself

- Play up your winning features—hair, smile, eyes, and so forth.

- Make improvements in grooming and dressing—when improvement is possible.

ACCEPT THE PHYSICAL CONNECTION (ATTITUDE-ADJUSTMENT TECHNIQUE #5)

The Connection Between Well-Being and Attitude. Apparently no one has been able to prove conclusively that there is a direct relationship between physical well-being and attitude. Most, however, including the most cynical researchers in the area, concede that there is a connection.

More than any previous generation, today's young adults are aware of physical fitness. A surprising number incorporate daily workouts into their schedules. Their commitment to the "attitude connection" is expressed in these typical comments:

"My workout does as much for my attitude as it does for my body."

"Exercise tones up my body and tunes up my outlook."

"I never underestimate what working out does for me psychologically."

Many fitness enthusiasts depend upon exercise to keep them out of attitudinal ruts:

"I've renamed my health club 'The Attitude-Adjustment Factory'."

"I take a long walk to push negative thoughts out of my system."

"An unusually tough workout will often get me out of a mental rut."

The Competitive Edge. No single group in our society gives such full attention to the psychological aspects of attitude as professional athletes. Increasingly, athletes engage year round in sophisticated physical conditioning programs. They realize they must stay in shape to remain competitive.

"Our same football team finished in the cellar last year. We made the playoffs this year because we have a new team attitude."

"I owe my success this season to my wife. She helped me adjust my attitude."

"My success this year is 90 percent due to a better attitude."

They must be trying to tell us something.

Summary

No one is immune from needing an "attitude repair" at some time or another. Frustration, stress, and other factors that can lead to negativism are part of life. When frustration and stress seem to be turning your attitude downward, you should recognize that attitude renewal is needed immediately. If you renew your attitude when it needs only minor repair, you can avoid long-term damage that comes from getting into an attitudinal rut.

Attitude renewal starts with self-appraisal. Once you have a good assessment of where you are, activate the attitude rejuvenation process to get your attitude into positive territory as quickly as possible. That is, use the results from the attitude-adjustment rating exercise as a self-assessment of your attitude. Then practice the five basic attitude-adjustment techniques to move you on your way to being a more positive you. The attitude-adjustment techniques include: the "flip-side", playing your winners, giving your positive attitude to others, looking better to yourself, and accepting the physical connection.

Assess and renew your attitude frequently. Always try hard to get hold of everyday stress before it gets out of hand. Also, try to avoid a prolonged negative attitude because you know the damaging ruts it can cause. However, if a "major overhaul" of your attitude is needed, do it without delay.

Your renewed attitude undoubtedly will lead you to greater productivity and will give you a boost to be a more positive, successful, and happy person.

Test Your Understanding

Respond to the following items to test your understanding of the chapter.

Part A: Circle the correct answer (T = True; F = False) for each of the following statements.

T F   1. Never accept the fact that some job stress is self-imposed.

T F   2. Humor in any form resists negative forces.

T F   3. It is better to give a coworker a piece of your positive attitude than a piece of your mind.

T F   4. An inferiority complex is when you look better to yourself than you do to others.

T F   5. More than ever before, many people believe good physical fitness contributes to their psychological attitude connection.

Part B: Circle the letter of the correct answer for each of the following items.

6. Warning signals of excessive stress do *not* include (a) a positive attitude, (b) feelings of frustration, (c) emotional outbursts, (d) withdrawal.

7. A good way to "play your winners" is to (a) stay alert so "winners" are not pushed out of the way, (b) promote the losers, (c) think about winners, but don't talk about them, (d) limit your winner rewards.

Part C: Write a short response to demonstrate your understanding related to the following item.

8. Discuss some ways you can improve your self-image and suggest how they contribute to a positive attitude.

Turn to the back of the book to check your answers.

Frequent attitude renewal
can turn ruts and roadblocks
into unforeseen opportunities.

Think and Respond

Respond to the following items with two or three complete sentences.

1. Explain why most people need an attitude renewal from time to time.

2. What is the "flip-side" attitude adjustment technique and how can it be effective?

3. Give two suggestions for using the attitude-adjustment technique of "playing your winners."

4. How is "looking better to yourself" an attitude-adjustment technique?

5. Explain what is meant by the "physical connection" attitude-adjustment technique.

SUMMARY ACTIVITY

Attitude-Adjustment Exercise

It is one thing to *learn*—it is another thing to *apply your learning.* That is, when you actually *use* a technique, you not only will remember it longer, but the chances are better that you will continue to use it in other situations. With this in mind, write out how you intend to use the following techniques to improve your attitude. When possible, tackle a current problem you may be facing.

Adjustment 1: The "Flip-Side." (Do you have a current problem you can turn around so you can laugh at it a little?)

_____

_____

_____

Adjustment 2: Play Your Winners. (How about rewarding yourself with one of your "Winners" tonight so that your attitude will be more positive tomorrow?)

_____

_____

_____

Adjustment 3: Give Your Positive Attitude to Others. (Why not be extra nice to somebody today whom you normally ignore?)

_____

_____

_____

Adjustment 4: Look Better to Yourself. (How about making a change in your hairstyle?)

_____

_____

_____

Adjustment 5: Accept the Physical Connection. (Could you benefit from a special workout today?)

_____

_____

_____

CASE 23

Focus

"I'll adjust later."

Up until about a year ago, Cathy made monthly deposits to her savings account. When shortly thereafter she took a higher-paying job, Cathy was sure she could get back to saving again. But, instead, she has continued to "dip" into her savings and is now using these funds to pay for her maxed-out credit cards. She is facing serious debt. Just last week, her boss told her that her positive attitude has slipped, her interaction with fellow employees is deteriorating, and she seems disinterested in her work. Furthermore, her tardiness (as a result of her "quick" shopping trips to the nearby mall) is chronic. If she doesn't get back on track, she may lose her job. Shopping is what gives Cathy a boost—isn't it? At least she thought it did until she really stopped to analyze it. Has she lost focus?

Lupe is suffering from the "campus blahs." With finals only a few weeks away, Lupe has lost her motivation to excel. Everything is a drag. Could it be excessive study time? A demanding part-time job? Home problems? Whatever the reason, she is even discouraged about her personal image. Why must life be so out of focus?

Arnold appears to be approaching career burnout. A very hardworking, highly successful professional sales representative, Arnold senses that he has lost touch with customers. For the first time, they are reacting negatively to his approach. Despite his need for more money to cover new personal financial commitments, his commission check last month was lower than in previous months. Even his daily jogging is not helping him maintain a positive attitude. Why are things so out of focus?

A. Discuss: Would you recommend the five adjustment techniques to Cathy, Lupe, and Arnold? Which do you think would help Cathy the most? Lupe? Arnold? Why?

B. Expand Your Understanding: Select two of the attitude-adjustment techniques to research. From your research, identify additional elements of both techniques—elements that will help you and others to better understand and apply the two techniques. Contrast and compare the techniques. List and explain several additional ideas for applying the techniques. Finally, formulate some recommendations and conclusions about the techniques, paying particular attention to the commonalities shared by both techniques.

CHAPTER 24

Leadership/ Management: Your Career on the Move

"Being a supervisor can be a big headache."

Thought for the Day: Because living is the pursuit of learning over a lifetime, always strive to become the best you can be.

PERFORMANCE COMPETENCIES

- Recognize that the value of dual competency (good human-relations and technical skills) for employees is even more valuable for leadership/ management roles.

- Consider some of the factors that may be problematic for you if you pursue management.

- Understand that there are many managerial and leadership essentials that are critical for success in a leadership/management position.

- Appreciate that you can be more successful in a management/leadership position if you continue to learn and grow.

By improving your human-relations skills and achieving greater insight into your positive attitude, you possess the foundation upon which you can build a more promising career. When you demonstrate the self-confidence that practicing good human relations produces, new career doors automatically open. You may or may not choose to enter such doors, but it will be personally rewarding to know they are open.

DUAL COMPETENCY

If your career path leads you into business management or a leadership role in a different career area of your choice, two things are certain:

- The more you practice sound human relations as an employee, the better you will be at performing many managerial tasks and the more likely it is that your superiors will promote you into management.

- Everything you learn and practice about attitude and good human relations now will contribute to your leadership skills and later, if you aspire to do so, will help you achieve a more responsible or higher-level leadership position.

Your human-relations sensitivity will lead to career opportunities

The Value of Double Competency. Wherever you may be employed now or in the future, your superiors will probably be sensitive to the fact that you are building and maintaining better relationships with people than your coworkers are and that you know how to operate effectively in a group—that is, you have a double competency. You are skillful technically. You are also skillful with people. Observing this double competency, your superiors will naturally assume that if you are good at human relations at the employee level, you will also be good at the management level. It is a wise assumption. Let us look at what happened to Cleo.

Cleo. A highly competent computer technician, Cleo concentrated on her personal productivity, but she did not neglect her human-relations skills. She would frequently stop her own work to help someone with a problem. She would sometimes pitch in at the end of the day to help others get out an urgent report. Her efforts to help her coworkers did not go unrecognized.

Cleo was invited to attend a supervisory course on company time. Two weeks after the course was over, she became a supervisor. She was elated, not only because she had very little seniority, but also because she was the youngest person in her department. Her quick promotion made her respect her human-relations skills more than ever.

Your Sensitivity. Your transition into a supervisory role should be smooth because all the human-relations competencies you practice as an employee can be transferred to your new role. In fact, some skills will make more sense to you as a supervisor. For example, having tried, perhaps unsuccessfully, to build a relationship with a difficult supervisor, you will be more sensitive to the problem once you are there yourself. Knowing how a conflict between two coworkers can injure the productivity of all, you will pick up on such situations faster and intervene sooner. Knowing the rewards your supervisor could have given you but didn't, you will be more sensitive to your employees' need for recognition.

This is what happened to Geraldine.

Geraldine. Disturbed by the behavior and insensitivity of her supervisor, Geraldine swore she would never become one herself. Then, because of a dramatic change in her personal life, she had second thoughts. Her rationale was as follows: Because the managers in my field are so ineffective, the opportunities should be limitless for someone like me who is willing to learn how to be a good supervisor.

What did Geraldine do? She took a basic course in human-relations skills and another course in management. As she studied, she made mental notes of the skills she would employ that her present manager did not. Her management opportunity came sooner than she anticipated; and because of her basic preparation, the transition was smooth. Geraldine has since received two additional promotions. What she learned as an employee provided her with a ticket to career success.

Self-Confidence Booster. The best thing about becoming more human-relations competent is that it makes one more self-confident. It happens every time. In short, the more you practice the human-relations skills discussed in this book, the more self-confidence you will build. Learning to establish strong working relationships with those who are older and more experienced than you builds confidence.

Self-confidence is enhanced by practicing good human-relations skills

Being able to restore a damaged relationship also builds confidence. The more you can prove to yourself that you are good at people skills, the less likely it is that you will be intimidated by others. Soon you will discover that you can work effectively with sophisticated, experienced superiors at all levels. You also will feel sufficiently confident to step out in front and be a leader. Jerry is a good case in point.

Jerry. A sensitive and quiet young man, Jerry completed a self-study course in human relations because he wanted to develop more meaningful relationships with people both on and off the job. It was a personal goal of Jerry's. He had no thoughts of ever becoming a leader. Such a role, he thought, was beyond his capacity. Yet, within two years, Jerry was so good at building relationships with coworkers that his personal confidence had increased significantly. To both management and fellow workers, he became a different person. When he was asked to become a supervisor, the only one surprised was Jerry himself.

TO PURSUE OR NOT TO PURSUE MANAGEMENT— THAT IS THE QUESTION

Should you pursue a management role? If you are already in a supervisory role, should you strike out for something in middle or upper management? The decision, of course, deserves careful consideration.

Considerations for Management. When you consider a management role, you will have a new relationship with people mainly because you no longer are a coworker. No matter how good your human-relations skills are as an employee, you will need to focus on honing those skills even more in a management position. Why? Because in management, you will make higher-level decisions and may need to discipline people in your unit. In general, you have more responsibility. Because of these and other factors, most people in management roles are more vunerable. Here are some thoughts you may wish to ponder in considering a move into management.

Managers must balance relationship building and discipline issues

- *If you are intrigued with human relations, it is probably a sign that you will also like management.* Although there are many facets to a management job, most involve considerable interaction with people. A management job involves counseling, leadership development, and building a competent staff. Some corporate presidents devote over 80 percent of their time to people problems. It is true that an executive manages resources and capital, but the first priority is working with people. The need to work with people will not change.

- *The discipline factor may not be for you.* Those who are not in supervisory roles have the luxury of building rewarding relationships without having to assume the responsibility of correcting the behavior of others. Human relations at the worker level does not involve discipline. Some individuals who are outstanding at human relations are so sensitive to the needs of others and so compassionate in their association with others that they cannot correct or discipline those who get out of line. These people are uncomfortable in most leadership roles. They should, therefore, remain subordinates and make their contribution at that level. Not only will they be unhappy with the constant responsibility to discipline, but they probably will not do it well.

- *Could you make hard decisions?* Supervisors must make many decisions each day. The farther up the executive ladder a supervisor goes, the more critical the decisions become. Most decisions are people decisions; and, frequently, people decisions are very difficult ones to make. And even those that are primarily productivity or financial decisions affect people.

The fact that you are good at human relations does not necessarily mean that you will be good at decision making. Indeed, the opposite may be true. For example, a manager may have to make a decision to give a layoff notice to a loyal and competent employee—perhaps even one with whom the manager has an outstanding relationship. There is some indication that the better you are at human relations, the more traumatic such a decision can be. No doubt, you will want to weigh the decision-making factor carefully before deciding to become a supervisor or manager.

- *Management people are more vulnerable.* If you are a highly sensitive person (one reason you may be good at building positive relationships with others), you may find it difficult to accept the criticism that goes along with a management role. Few, if any, managers are without detractors. In fact, whether or not a leader remains a leader often depends upon keeping detractors at a minimum or spotting them soon enough to bring them into the fold.

   Do not misunderstand. Your human-relations skills will help you to build good relationships with employees and thus minimize the possibility of negative reactions. You may never have someone under your supervision who becomes so disenchanted that she (or he) sets out to get you. But the possibility exists. Despite your own abilities, the role itself makes you more vulnerable. Knowing that a supervisor or manager is more vulnerable to negative human-relations problems is in no way intended to keep you from wanting to become a supervisor; it simply means that there are disadvantages you should consider in advance.

MANAGERIAL AND LEADERSHIP ESSENTIALS

Other Leadership/Management Considerations. While it is impossible to cover all the elements of management/leadership in a single book, anyone pursuing a position as a supervisor or manager should at least understand the basics of management[1] and leadership.[2] For example, you should have a solid foundation in the four management functions of planning, organizing, leading, and controlling. Also, you should understand the multifaceted leadership essentials that

[1] Also available from this publisher is Robbins/DeCenzo, "Supervision Today!" 5th ed., 2007, Prentice Hall, Upper Saddle River, New Jersey 07458.
[2] Also available from this publisher is Chapman/O'Neil, "Leadership: Essential Steps Every Manager Needs to Know," 3rd ed., 2000, Prentice Hall, Upper Saddle River, New Jersey 07458.

include empowering followers, creating a vision, practicing the mutual-reward theory, communicating effectively, making decisions, being a positive force, and influencing others. And, you should understand motivation.[3]

Successful managers and leaders also know how critical it is to understand leadership and communication basics, including your own leadership and communication styles. A good place to start in learning more about yourself is to take seriously your emotional intelligence (EQ) (see discussion of EQ in other chapters of this book). Having a healthy EQ that is firmly grounded by a positive attitude can be your greatest asset to help you remain calm when assessing and making decisions under stressful conditions and in potentially volatile situations. As you work at both understanding and managing your emotions, you will become better at understanding and managing your relationships with others. In a managerial/leadership position, your EQ becomes critical to achieving success in your role—every single day.

Consider how the many elements of management fit your style

Incremental Steps to Management/Leadership. Management and leadership competencies are not learned overnight. Neither is a person, under most circumstances, thrown into a managerial or leadership position for which he (or she) is totally unprepared. Preparation is the key to success, and taking progressive steps to achieve a goal makes good sense.

What you have learned about human relations will help you build your skills at a higher level. As you take additional steps toward building your career—especially steps that include education, training, and work experience—you will give yourself a competitive edge when positions of more responsibility become available to you. Evaluate your progress at every opportunity you get so you can benefit and learn from your mistakes, successes, and overall experiences.

To give you a better picture of whether management/leadership is on your horizon, complete the following activity to see how you rate as a supervisor.

[3]Also available from this publisher is O'Neil, "Motivation: An ATM Card for Success," 2003, Prentice Hall, Upper Saddle River, New Jersey 07458.

ACTIVITY

Supervisor Analysis Scale

If you have not had the opportunity to think about whether or not you would like to become a part of management, the following scale should help. Read both statements carefully for each of the ten items, then circle the number that indicates your views about a management position. A "10" indicates you have or appreciate the qualities needed for management. A "1" indicates you are not interested, at this time, to take on management/leadership responsibilities.

1. I can develop the confidence to become an outstanding supervisor.

   10 9 8 7 6 5 4 3 2 1

   I could never be close to being an average supervisor.

2. I have the capacity to build and maintain productive relationships with workers under my supervision.

   10 9 8 7 6 5 4 3 2 1

   I'm a loner. I do not want the responsibility of building and maintaining relationships with others.

3. It does not bother me that supervisors are move vulnerable and subject to criticism.

   10 9 8 7 6 5 4 3 2 1

   I could not handle the criticism that most supervisors receive.

4. I can develop the skill of motivating others.

   10 9 8 7 6 5 4 3 2 1

   I could never develop the skill of motivating others.

5. I can be patient, fair, consistent, and understanding with others.

   10 9 8 7 6 5 4 3 2 1

   I have no patience and understandingfor others and could not develop it.

6. I could learn to be good at disciplining those under me—even to the point of terminating a worker after repeated violations.

   10 9 8 7 6 5 4 3 2 1

   It would tear me up to discipline a worker under my supervision. I'mmuch too kind and sensitive.

7. I can make tough decisions of all kinds.

   10 9 8 7 6 5 4 3 2 1

   I do not want decision-making responsibilities.

8. It would not bother me to isolate myself from those I would supervise.

   10 9 8 7 6 5 4 3 2 1

   I have a great need to be liked; I want to be one of the gang, and I enjoy working with others.

9. I would make an outstanding member of a management team.

   10 9 8 7 6 5 4 3 2 1

   I hate staff meetings and would be a weak or hostile member of a management team.

10. My human-relations training will make me a superior supervisor—better than anyone for whom I have worked.

    10 9 8 7 6 5 4 3 2 1

    Despite my human-relations training, my potential as a supervisor is so low it is not worth developing.

Total Score _____

Now, total your scores for the ten items. If you scored 80 or higher, it would appear that you have the potential to become an excellent supervisor. If you scored between 50 and 80, you may need to gain more confidence, but you seem to have the potential to become a highly successful leader. If you rated yourself under 50, you probably are not ready for a supervisory role at this stage of your life.

GROWING IN YOUR POSITION

Once you have made the decision to move into management, you will have an entirely new set of responsibilities that will demand your attention. Many of the new responsibilities will require you to learn as much as you can—about the job itself and how to become a better leader/manager. One of the best ways to increase your leadership and managerial skills is to pursue further education and training—keeping a positive attitude as you do. Consider the brief discussion of the elements that will help you grow in your position.

- *Accept the edge you already possess, but admit you have much to learn.* Many capable supervisors study human relations after they get their jobs. Many also admit they started out with a handicap because they did not have a strong enough human-relations background. Keep in mind that human relations is not the only thing a supervisor must know. There are many special supervisory skills that must be learned. Learning how to delegate, to conduct formal appraisals, to set priorities, to make decisions, and to manage one's time are critical supervisory skills.[4] If you wish to succeed in a management role, it will be necessary for you to become competent in these areas. You may wish to study these skills in anticipation of your first supervisory role.

- *Management training is increasingly demanding.* Even if you prepare for and become an excellent supervisor, it is only a start. The more you aspire to upper-management roles, the more training you should receive. A worthy training goal, as well as an on-the-job focus, for any manager/leader is to work at turning weaknesses into strengths (and helping others do the same). The manager who learns how to turn problems into challenges will be an inspiration to followers. Practice, training, and experience will help the successful manager/leader grow into a style of her (or his) own—a style that is effective because it capitalizes on building good human relationships and on projecting a positive attitude.

  Life-long learning is a worthy endeavor

  Truly successful managers and leaders hone their managerial/leadership skills over a lifetime. They learn from other successful managers and leaders; and they pursue education and training. The Master of Business Administration (MBA) graduate degree has become the standard goal of many. Earning a MBA means taking demanding courses in statistics, computer science, information systems, management theory, finance, and other areas. If you decide to take this route to the top, keep in mind that in most cases you can earn a MBA while working full time.

[4]Also available from this publisher is Goodwin/Chapman, "Supervisor's Survival Kit," 10th edition, 2006, Prentice Hall, Upper Saddle River, New Jersey 07458.

■ *Your personal attitude is more important in a management role—not less!* As a supervisor, manager, or anyone else in a leadership position, maintaining your own positive attitude—staying out of attitudinal ruts—is critical. A negative attitude in front of employees is a luxury a person in management cannot afford.

There is little doubt that the significance of an "applied" human-relations meaning of Einstein's equation, $E = mc^2$ (a topic presented in other chapters in this book), is all the more important in a management/leadership role. That is, as a leader, YOU must be the example of energy and enthusiasm (E). YOU must demonstrate motivation (m), not only to build strong relationships but also to ensure high levels of productivity from your unit. And, YOU must be committed (c) to the success of your unit or deparment. Because the "c" in the formula is "c^2," "commitment" is very critical. YOU as a committed leader/manager need to show your commitment as well as encourage others to be committed; then, together, continuously strive for quality and self-improvement.

Mobilize Your Positive Force. All in all, successful supervisors and leaders at all levels have the ability to create a positive force that pulls employees into a circle of involvement and activity. Once this force gets started, it seems to generate confidence among all team members and leads to constructive action and higher productivity.

How do you create a positive force?

Like a pebble dropped into a quiet pool, the power of your positive attitude gets things started. Thus, as a leader, your positive attitude is the source of your power. A positive attitude of a supervisor/manager/leader builds positive expectations in the minds of workers, whereas a negative attitude destroys them.

Positive attitudes build positive expectations and outcomes

Your positive attitude communicates to those being led that they are headed in a direction that will eventually provide benefits. There are exciting goals within reach. Something better lies over the horizon.

Summary

This chapter has pointed out how dual competency (technical and human-relations skills) are important to build your self-confidence for greater personal and career success. You have also learned that your sensitivity in human relations is a valuable asset in moving up to leadership/management. While there are many considerations you need to ponder before you make the decision that a leadership/management role is for you, you are wise to take your time to analyze your own abilities and skills. Personal evaluations will be useful to guide you in learning about and developing a career path. Because there are so many essentials of management and leadership that are critical to success in a managerial/leadership position, you will still have much to learn.

The management/leadership challenge is, for many, exciting and rewarding. Those who have taken a leadership career path claim that the challenge has forced them to recognize that a positive attitude is, indeed, a priceless possession.

Now that you have achieved new insights into human behavior and the importance of your own attitude, you are in a better position to decide whether formal management or leadership roles are for you. Whatever you decide, your personal success is what really counts. Thus, you should always use your skills—including your management and leadership ability—to contribute your best in whatever position you occupy.

Good luck! And always keep in mind that *Your Attitude Is Showing!*

Test Your Understanding

Respond to the following items to test your understanding of the chapter.

Part A: Circle the correct answer (T = True; F = False) for each of the following statements.

T F   1. An individual who has both technical and human-relations skills is said to have a double competency.

T F   2. Employees who practice self-confidence and good human relations take just as long to become supervisors as those who don't.

T F   3. Ambitious people who like more responsibility, enjoy decision making, and are sensitive to the needs of others should seriously consider becoming supervisors.

T F   4. Excellent employees make excellent supervisors because they are successful at correcting the bad behavior of those who work for them.

T F   5. Becoming a supervisor will force you to live closer to your potential.

Part B: Circle the letter of the correct answer for each of the following items.

6. Improving one's human-relations skills also makes one (a) less susceptible to criticism and rumor, (b) more technically capable, (c) more self-confident, (d) less sensitive as a supervisor.

7. Supervisors who create a positive force usually are not successful at (a) identifying an exciting path ahead, (b) building positive expectations of workers, (c) using the power of their positive attitudes to build momentum, (d) building reward systems because they lack drive and creativity.

Part C: Write a short response to demonstrate your understanding related to the following item.

8. Discuss several factors that should be analyzed when an employee considers a leadership/management role.

Turn to the back of the book to check your answers.

> If you could assume
> the attitude of your choice,
> is Yours the one you would select?

Think and Respond

Respond to the following items with two or three complete sentences.

1. Explain what is meant by having "dual competency"?

2. Discuss two things related to human relations that can boost your self-confidence.

3. Suggest two factors you should consider before making the decision to move into management.

4. Discuss two of the essential elements for management and leadership roles.

5. Explain the stance one should take in regards to education and training as well as the significance one should place on one's personal attitude in a management/leadership position.

My Personal Business Plan for Leadership/Management

In the space provided below, outline a path you consider appropriate for you to move into a leadership/management role. You may wish to refer back to other chapters as you develop your outline. Suggest questions/answers, statements, or factors that will help you weigh the advantages and disadvantages of taking on a leadership/management role.

Finally, add a statement or two about how you can be more positive in the future because you know that, at all times, *Your Attitude Is Showing!*

My Personal Business Plan for Leadership/Management

_____

_____

_____

_____

_____

_____

_____

_____

_____

Because I know that, at all times, MY *Attitude Is Showing*, I will be more positive by

_____

_____

_____

CASE 24

Sensitivity

"I'm chained to my present role."

Angelina is, without question, the most popular and respected employee in her division. She has the rare talent of being able to build meaningful relationships quickly, but she is even better at maintaining them. Her sensitivity to the needs of others is amazing. Coworkers come to her for help on both work-oriented and personal problems, and she seems to have sufficient patience to handle them all.

One fellow employee, however, puts it this way: "Angelina is a pleasure to know and to work with. I sometimes wish she was our supervisor, but I'm afraid the job would chew her up. She is just too nice. It would be difficult, perhaps impossible, for her to get tough and set a firm discipline line. And problem employees would worry her to death."

Recently, management invited Angelina to become a supervisor of one of the departments in the division. Management believes she is so well liked by coworkers that she obviously has leadership potential.

A. Discuss: Assume that you are a close friend. Would you recommend that Angelina accept the invitation?

B. Expand Your Understanding: Conduct some extensive research about careers in management and leadership. Once you have consulted a number of articles, books, and other Internet sources, make a list of essential characteristics, skills, and competencies one should possess for achieving success in a management/leadership position. Draw some conclusions about leadership/management relating to (a) desireable leadership and managerial factors and elements, (b) the role of human-relations conpetencies, and (c) the importance of a positive attitude. From your conclusions, make some suggestions for Angelina, as well as for yourself, to consider in deciding whether or not moving into a management/leadership position is a feasible move. Finally, add a summary statement about why a person in any type of position should exercise whatever management and leadership skills he (or she) has developed.

Answers to End-of-Chapter Assessments

TEST YOUR UNDERSTANDING

Chapter 1: 1 = T, 2 = F, 3 = F, 4 = T, 5 = T, 6 = c, 7 = b, 8 = see text page 11

Chapter 2: 1 = T, 2 = T, 3 = F, 4 = F, 5 = T, 6 = a, 7 = d, 8 = see text page 22

Chapter 3: 1 = T, 2 = T, 3 = F, 4 = F, 5 = T, 6 = a, 7 = b, 8 = see text page 36

Chapter 4: 1 = T, 2 = T, 3 = T, 4 = F, 5 = T, 6 = a, 7 = d, 8 = see text page 47

Chapter 5: 1 − T, 2 = F, 3 − F, 4 = T, 5 = T, 6 = c, 7 = d, 8 = see text page 63

Chapter 6: 1 = T, 2 = F, 3 = T, 4 = F, 5 = T, 6 = b, 7 = d, 8 = see text page 76

Chapter 7: 1 = F, 2 = T, 3 = F, 4 = T, 5 = T, 6 = b, 7 = d, 8 = see text page 90

Chapter 8: 1 = T, 2 = T, 3 = T, 4 = F, 5 = T, 6 = c, 7 = a, 8 = see text page 104

Chapter 9: 1 = T, 2 = F, 3 = T, 4 = F, 5 = T, 6 = a, 7 = d, 8 = see text page 122

Chapter 10: 1 = T, 2 = T, 3 = T, 4 = T, 5 = T, 6 = c, 7 = a, 8 = see text page 141

Chapter 11: 1 = T, 2 = T, 3 = F, 4 = T, 5 = T, 6 = d, 7 = c, 8 = see text page 156

Chapter 12: 1 = T, 2 = F, 3 = T, 4 = F, 5 = F, 6 = b, 7 = b, 8 = see text page 170

Chapter 13: 1 = T, 2 = F, 3 = T, 4 = T, 5 = F, 6 = a, 7 = d, 8 = see text page 182

Chapter 14: 1 = F, 2 = T, 3 = T, 4 = T, 5 = T, 6 = d, 7 = d, 8 = see text page 196

Chapter 15: 1 = T, 2 = F, 3 = F, 4 = F, 5 = T, 6 = a, 7 = c, 8 = see text page 209

Chapter 16: 1 = F, 2 = T, 3 = F, 4 = F, 5 = F, 6 = b, 7 = a, 8 = see text page 225

Chapter 17: 1 = F, 2 = F, 3 = F, 4 = T, 5 = T, 6 = b, 7 = b, 8 = see text page 241

Chapter 18: 1 = T, 2 = F, 3 = F, 4 = T, 5 = T, 6 = a, 7 = d, 8 = see text page 255

Chapter 19: 1 = T, 2 = T, 3 = T, 4 = T, 5 = T, 6 = c, 7 = c, 8 = see text page 271

Chapter 20: 1 = T, 2 = T, 3 = F, 4 = F, 5 = T, 6 = b, 7 = a, 8 = see text page 287

Chapter 21: 1 = F, 2 = T, 3 = T, 4 = T, 5 = F, 6 = d, 7 = a, 8 = see text page 300

Chapter 22: 1 = T, 2 = F, 3 = T, 4 = T, 5 = T, 6 = d, 7 = d, 8 = see text page 314

Chapter 23: 1 = F, 2 = T, 3 = T, 4 = F, 5 = T, 6 = a, 7 = a, 8 = see text page 329

Chapter 24: 1 = T, 2 = F, 3 = T, 4 = F, 5 = T, 6 = c, 7 = d, 8 = see text page 342

Suggested Responses to End-of-Chapter Activities

CASES

The human-relations cases presented at the end of each chapter in this book are designed to be springboards for individual thinking and discussion purposes. There are no exact answers to any of the cases.

In the first place, only the most essential facts of each case are outlined. It is therefore impossible to give definite or complete answers to any case. Without all the facts, anything approaching a definite or complete answer would be dangerous indeed. Also, different points of view are always possible (even encouraged) in discussions of human-relations cases.

The following so-called suggested answers, then, are nothing more than an account of how to approach the case with the available facts. They should serve only as a guide to the independent thinking of the reader and the discussion leader.

CASE 1: REALITY

It is easy to understand why Rod was disturbed when the other two received promotions ahead of him. His pride was hurt because he had worked hard and efficiently at his job. But there is some evidence that Rod was not taking his full human-relations responsibility. He did not seem to make enough effort to cooperate and build good relationships with his coworkers. While he concentrated on his personal productivity, he did not appear to consider how his poor human-relations skills were affecting his career progress.

Rod was not fully justified in saying, "It isn't what you know but who you know that counts." Rod was escaping from his human-relations responsibility by trying to rationalize his unwillingness to build better relationships. He was reminded twice by his supervisor to be more a part of the group. He did not take the advice.

Rod did not understand why he had a responsibility to work closely with others in his department in order to help their productivity. On the other hand, Rod's supervisor might have counseled him sooner, more often, and in a more sensitive manner. The supervisor might have pointed out both desirable and undesirable behaviors. Rod appears to need feedback about the specific negative behaviors he demonstrates, the impact they have on others, and some suggested alternatives. The supervisor must assume some of the responsibility for Rod's poor human-relations performance.

Rod's case shows that an ambitious employee who works hard and efficiently does not necessarily make career progress. Rod needs to develop a better balance between productivity and human-relations skills to reach his potential.

CASE 2: ADJUSTMENT

It would appear that George must learn to relax and give more of himself if he wants to find an environment in which he can be happy and productive. He will never make his maximum contribution to his job and his company if he stays deep inside his shell and expects others to come to him.

George would probably have to make some concessions before he finds another job in which he would be happy. He failed to understand that when he was aloof and distant, he made it uncomfortable for others. He failed to comprehend that his fellow workers might have needed to communicate with him on a friendly basis whether or not he needed to communicate with them.

In discussing the matter with George, his supervisor might try to increase George's confidence to reach out and communicate more with others. George does not yet fully sense why he should communicate more. Thus (using specific examples that George would appreciate), stress could be placed on why it is difficult to work next to a poor communicator. That is, people who act aloof or distant have a way of irritating others. It could also be pointed out that such behavior is often misinterpreted—a negative or avoidance response from a person with whom you try to become friendly can cause you to withdraw. The supervisor's success with George would depend, in part, upon the supervisor's skill in getting George to talk more while the supervisor talks less and listens more effectively.

CASE 3: CREDIT BLUES

Although some people can control their consumer-credit financing patterns, others seem to get in over their heads. They soon struggle to keep up with the interest charges on their statements in addition to making payments on principal amounts. When this occurs, a drastic cutback in living standards is often dictated. Only a few people seem to go through such an experience without its having a negative impact on their attitude. Their academic goals and careers are often permanently derailed.

Because it appears that Manuel is facing serious financial problems, some suggestions for him include the following:

1. Curtail consumer spending immediately. If necessary, Manuel should destroy his credit cards.

2. Seek less-expensive forms of recreation.

3. Accept financial guidance from an expert.

4. Prepare and follow a monthly budget.

5. Anticipate a slow recovery.

Once Manuel is able to see the light at the end of his financial tunnel, his boss and coworkers will probably notice an improvement in his attitude and his career will be back on track. Manuel might have learned that his positive attitude could be his most priceless possession.

CASE 4: BOUNCE BACK

Counseling a highly sensitive individual on any facet of attitude is a difficult challenge. That Frank is a male nurse shouldn't make it more difficult, but the fact that Frank is one of her supervisors and an authority figure might. Frank will need all of his counseling skills. Once Sue Ellen relaxes and senses that Frank really wants to help, progress is a possibility. Frank should try to reach these goals:

1. Convince Sue Ellen that there is probably nothing personal about people stepping on her attitude—it is simply a characteristic of the work environment. Patients can be unreasonable. Doctors, under pressure, also can be unreasonable. She should endeavor to not take such verbal abuse personally.

2. Illustrate that everyone gets their attitudes stepped on and everyone must learn how to cope with it in their own way. Sue Ellen needs to know that she is not being singled out.

3. Assure her that, with effort, her personal confidence will increase; and encourage her to make a goal out of whipping the problem.

Frank may want to make it a goal between the two of them so Frank can compliment her on the progress she shows. With the reinforcement Frank provides in this manner, Sue Ellen will become a stronger person and will have a brighter career future.

CASE 5: DECISION

It is a smart strategy for Bernie to concentrate on building good horizontal relationships—but not to the point at which he ignores any opportunity to build a relationship with Gloria, his aloof boss. Even though Gloria may appear to be unapproachable, Bernie should continue to wait and watch for opportunities to build a stronger relationship through hard work, friendliness, suggestions for improvements, and other means.

Just because others have failed to build a healthy relationship with the supervisor doesn't mean that Bernie should give up. He could easily make the mistake of putting all of his human-relations eggs in one horizontal basket.

CASE 6: MESSAGE

The decision to pass Jeff over for the supervisory position is a good one for the following reasons:

1. It would be natural for Jeff's coworkers to resent him as a supervisor. He failed to build good horizontal working relationships with them when he had the chance. Productivity, under his leadership, could drop substantially.

2. An individual who doesn't learn how to build good horizontal relationships as an employee will probably have trouble building good vertical relationships as a supervisor. By neglecting his horizontal working relationships when he first joined the department, Jeff made a classic human-relations mistake.

3. A supervisor achieves more departmental productivity by building good relationships than from the work he (or she) actually performs. Jeff would be a poor risk as a supervisor.

Jeff's supervisor should have counseled him more and pointed out other examples of how high producers were passed over at promotion time. He should have explained the relationship between human relations and productivity when he first recognized that Jeff had a problem—that might have enabled Jeff to understand the "big picture." Thus, Jeff would have had a fair chance to correct his human-relations problem and ready himself for the next supervisory position opportunity.

CASE 7: INSIGHT

Ted's impatience and exasperation are understandable. But the supervisor had a point and was right in counseling him to keep his cool and not further damage his horizontal relationships. Ted was well along the way to becoming a supervisor. If he had continued being critical of others, he might have forfeited his opportunity.

It should be pointed out, however, that Ted was in a tough spot. Due to jealousy and other conflict-causing human factors, it is a human-relations challenge to maintain a personal productivity level above that of your coworkers and still maintain good relations with them. However, if Ted really wanted to be the next supervisor, this was the price he might have to pay.

The supervisor was wrong in not giving Ted the "human-relations story" before he became frustrated and damaged his horizontal relationships. Ted must learn, however, that few supervisors are perfect and that he must protect his future by being human-relations sensitive even when his supervisor is not.

CASE 8: CHOICE

You have a difficult choice. The older, Theory X supervisor might give you the following advantages:

1. He has been with the company longer and has had more experience, so he may be able to teach you more.

2. Although he may demand more from you, in the long run you may be a stronger person and eventually a better supervisor yourself because of it.

If you choose the younger, Theory Y supervisor, you may enjoy the following advantages:

1. You would probably become more involved under her leadership and, as a result, more productive.

2. This supervisor would probably move up the management ladder sooner. If you work hard, you may be able to take her place and move even higher later on because of her influence from above.

In answering the problem, consider the following:

1. In which work environment would you be most motivated and productive?

2. How would your personality and your values work with each supervisor?

3. How ambitious are you to get into management?

If you fully understand the leadership styles of each of the two supervisors, you should be able to make the best decision. If you are adaptable, though, neither environment should hurt your personal progress.

CASE 9: CURRENCY

When money is the only currency one finds important, in the long run he (or she) is apt to be shortchanged. Ralph's approach may be a better way to build a case since those who select careers in harmony with their values often come out ahead financially, too, because they build stronger human ties and remain more positive. Those who stay true to their values often enhance their leadership qualities (they gain more respect from followers) and, as a result, qualify for higher-paying positions. There is no documented evidence that those who deal only in the currency of money wind up with more of it.

CASE 10: CONTROVERSY

It is easy to justify the comments of both Justine and Zeke. It may sound simplistic for Justine to say that "if we treated everyone as an individual," life would be better for everyone. Justine's advice, however, is a sound principle of good human relations. Zeke, of course, has a point in saying that people need to be rated on their performance in the work environment and on their value as human beings in society as a whole. Taking sides becomes a tricky and complicated part of the conversation. A combination of both views is probably the best response. Adding discussion about the four Cs of team membership would be an excellent way to expand on Justine's and Zeke's comments.

CASE 11: FRUSTRATION

A divorce can be a devastating event in one's life. Many other personal things also can affect one's overall behavior; however, Allen needs to get a grip on his frustration and aggressive behavior. He needs to consider how negative his attitude has become and how it is affecting him and everyone around him. He can't continue to blame everything on his personal life—and chastise others for it. He appears to be looking for ways to alienate people. His lashing out at work, at home, and even in public against people he doesn't even know suggests he has very deep-seated anger.

Suggestions for improving his attitude include doing some physical exercise in which he can get physically tired and find a release for his negative energy. He should consider directing his aggression to tennis or swimming, to yard work or house cleaning, or to similar activities as a diversion. He must find some positive ways to rebuild his life—to stop his self-pity. It's not going to be an easy road for Allen, and maybe some professional help is needed; but, unless he takes action to turn his behavior around, he faces considerably more risk—possibly losing his job, alienating his children, becoming a loner, and being nothing but miserable.

CASE 12: RESTORATION

The chances of a full restoration are slim, but the luncheon meeting stands a good chance of pushing the conflict underground so it will not be so obvious to other workers. In other words, both Noreen and Krystal may learn to have more respect for each other and work together on a higher human-relations level than in the past.

Also, if Mrs. Raji does not have a good possibility for a transfer option, she should not suggest such an option. Her transfer suggestion could make both supervisors resentful of her and the conflict then becomes a three-way conflict.

CASE 13: COMMUNICATION

Ariele may want to take the long view and find his best solution by communicating freely and openly with his family, especially his wife. There is the strong possibility that Ariele can slowly build a mutually rewarding relationship with Yoshio. For example, Yoshio could reward Ariele by giving him more responsibility and authority, while Ariele could reward Yoshio by helping him improve his communication skills. With this exchange, Ariele may eventually earn a promotion or an even better job in the same organization, all of this without removing his family from its present comfort zone.

The big danger for Ariele is that he might permit the new situation (Yoshio getting the job Ariele wanted) to turn him negative on a permanent basis. This often happens.

CASE 14: NONPROFESSIONAL

Helen is in a delicate position. The behavior of Tyrell in apparently plagiarizing Helen's ideas would be considered unprofessional, if not unethical, by most people. But, if she blows the whistle on Tyrell without written proof, her accusation could be interpreted by management as "sour grapes" and her own image could be damaged. Although Helen may be tempted to confront Tyrell with the matter in front of others, she should resist. Confronting Tyrell could irritate and embarrass him, causing him to go behind her back and perhaps hurt Helen even more at a later date. It could also make Helen look bad to coworkers. Helen could, however, confront Tyrell in private, so that he knows what he will be up against in the future. She could also protect her creative ideas in the future by refusing to discuss them informally in advance and by submitting them in writing after they have been fully developed.

Openness is a vital part of human relations. Devious coworkers often destroy the element of trust that is vital in any long-term relationship.

The reader is encouraged to isolate and learn from other examples of nonprofessional behavior.

CASE 15: CONFRONTATION

Jonas did the right thing under the circumstances. After two months, he had had sufficient time to discover that the cause of Ms. Robertson's critical attitude was deep-seated and that time alone would probably not solve the problem. Jonas took time to investigate and gather some facts. He discovered, among other things, that two former employees in his position resigned because of Ms. Robertson and her attitude. In other words, this was not surface teasing or testing.

Although Jonas took a serious human-relations risk by standing up to Ms. Robertson, he had at least a fair chance of resolving the problem and helping his future. If he was successful, everybody would come out ahead, including the company and Ms. Robertson.

The reader may not fully agree with the way Jonas approached Ms. Robertson or the way in which he expressed himself. To some, it may appear that he was too direct and forceful. To others, he may have appeared to be overly apologetic. Everyone must go about confrontations of this nature in her (or his) own individual manner. But the principle remains that the cards must often be laid on the table if a sound working relationship is to be created or restored.

As a supervisor in a similar situation, the supervisor should initiate a three-way discussion to air differences openly. The supervisor could then introduce the MRT concept and suggest that Ms. Robertson and Jonas try to find a few mutual rewards that might help them build a positive relationship. Lastly, the supervisor should follow through by complimenting both employees on any progress made, in the hope that such recognition would encourage them to continue to make a strong effort to build a sound relationship.

CASE 16: BALANCE

Lorraine's absenteeism is getting out of hand and could be called chronic. Her firm could make a reasonable effort to help her learn how to do a better job of balancing home and career. Learning the proper balance could be accomplished through a series of discussions or in a seminar focused on the importance of attendance. Lorraine needs to see the negative impact of her sporadic absenteeism upon company productivity and coworker relationships. Once this has been achieved, it would be advisable for Lorraine to identify what she can do to reduce her absenteeism.

When an employee "owns" the problem, he (or she) must do the problem solving. Accepting problem ownership will preserve self-esteem and maintain a healthy manager-employee relationship. With such an attitude, Lorraine and Mr. Hodges should have no trouble working out an action plan that everyone can live with as the problem is addressed. They also need to agree on a time period that will allow Lorraine to bring her absenteeism under control. To start with, she must begin by calling in to Mr. Hodges each and every time she needs to be absent. Being certain that she is truthful every time she gives a reason for her absence will also help Lorraine build both her credibility and her self-discipline, presuming that she values her job and wishes to remain employed there.

If such efforts do not bring positive results, the firm would be justified in starting termination procedures according to personnel policy and legal restrictions. One employee cannot be permitted to drag down the productivity over an extended period of time. Lorraine, of all people, should appreciate the need for following procedures—she works with policies and procedures whenever she is on the job!

CASE 17: MOTIVATION

Bjorn seems to be out of tune with the modern, high-tempo workplace. He seems to be operating on the ultrasimplistic premise that management has the sole responsibility to motivate employees. Perhaps this comes from Bjorn's past, in which he leaned too heavily on his parents, teachers, and mentors for motivation.

First, Bjorn must be willing to listen to his supervisor and other seasoned employees while learning not to underestimate them. They apparently have Bjorn's best interests at heart and want him to succeed. He will need also to consider the principle of openly admitting his mistake (that he "may not have been trying as hard as he could have") to his supervisor. Since he is a new employee, his supervisor will most likely give Bjorn another chance to perform at his competence level. On his own, Bjorn also needs to start associating with some ambitious coworkers who are scrambling for better roles and greater effectiveness in the workplace. He will soon discover the depth of their self-motivation and will decide whether he is interested in applying his exceptional skills and competencies to become competitive and demonstrate commitment to his job and the organization.

CASE 18: DILEMMA

Keejo made two mistakes. First, she accepted as fact a comment that was not authenticated and could easily have been a rumor. Her second mistake was more serious: She permitted the possible rumor to disturb her emotionally, to the point where it noticeably hurt her productivity.

The facts were not presented in the case, but it is quite possible that the real reason Mr. Young was made department head instead of Keejo was that Keejo's efficiency on the job had dropped to the point at which management decided to pass her over. If this was what happened, Keejo permitted a simple rumor to do the greatest possible damage to her future.

CASE 19: CONFLICT

Goal-oriented people usually want to get on with their lives and may run out of patience waiting for those who are still searching. A marriage seems to work best when both partners are goal-oriented and have some strong common goals they are trying to reach. It would appear that it is best for Deric and RayLyn to go their separate ways at this juncture. If, in a few years, they discover that their love for each other has been sufficiently strong to hold up during periods of separation, their relationship could be restored.

CASE 20: PREFERENCE

Angelo has an intriguing but difficult decision ahead of him. In making it, he should take a long look at himself and the direction he desires his career path to take. How important is immediate monetary success versus long-range security to him? What are his long-term goals? If Angelo becomes impatient and frustrated over slow but steady progress, he should think twice about joining a company that has modest growth potential and makes a practice of promoting from within. The zigzag route to the top may be best.

However, if Angelo is comfortable with slower but more secure growth, Company B may be his better choice. Company B may provide more and better training, will perhaps encourage him to get an advanced college degree in management at its expense, and will offer a more comprehensive benefit package. Of course, all of this depends upon the future stability of the company. Even firms with strong PFW policies must sometimes go through reorganizations, consolidations, and layoffs.

If Angelo is seeking more immediate upward mobility and is willing to take the higher risks involved, Company A may be his best choice. Company A may push more responsibility his way sooner. He should keep in mind that he may have to get more training, and there is always the possibility that he may need to scramble to another company.

CASE 21: CHANGE

Both Ingrid and Darla may be successful in adjusting to the dynamic changes of the future, but Darla appears to be more realistic. When change occurs in most organizations, it is not business as usual and most employees can benefit from a new approach.

Darla is to be applauded for her philosophy of trying to turn change into opportunity, but "looking out for number one" often has a devious connotation that implies a departure from normal ethical and sound human-relations principles to get ahead. If deviousness is Darla's strategy, her efforts could prove to be counterproductive because she could injure relationships that might provide support she could need at a later date.

Perhaps a combination of maintaining high productivity and sound human relations (Ingrid) with a creative approach to turning change into opportunity (Darla) is the best approach. It should also be added that education is the best possible preparation for adapting to change.

CASE 22: INTERVIEW

The following answers can be considered models:

1. "In doing my pre-interview investigation, I discovered that you have an ambitious expansion program and that you have an excellent reputation within the industry for treating people fairly. These features appeal to me."

2. "I will bring my present professional sales skills with me—I feel competent in organizing client data, in my ability to close sales, and about handling rejection—and I would develop other skills such as handling objections on your product line. My goal would be to reach a role in which my leadership would help build a stronger organization through teamwork and a balanced emphasis on productivity and sales."

3. "I have concentrated on developing my human-relations competencies. I can build good relationships with coworkers and superiors. When I make a mistake, I can repair a relationship. I have received compliments for my skills in problem solving. I am also sensitive to the needs of others. I am a good listener. I understand the positive associations between high productivity and good human relations—especially in situations in which clients are concerned."

4. "I have trouble maintaining my enthusiasm over a long period of time, and I tend to scatter my energy in too many directions. I'm working to make improvements in both areas."

Note: Giving more specifics on how you are turning your weaknesses into strengths will focus you and the interviewer on your positive versus negative attributes.

CASE 23: FOCUS

All of the adjustment techniques could help Cathy, Lupe, and Arnold, provided they first recognize that they are in an attitudinal rut and need a major renewal program. Cathy may benefit most from exchanging her shopping (which is not satisfying her) for a workout or physical training routine (Adjustment 5) as well as placing more emphasis on her winners (Adjustment 2). Lupe may benefit most from revitalizing her attitude by giving it away to others (Adjustment 3) and looking better to herself (Adjustment 4). Arnold might benefit most from the "flip-side" technique (Adjustment 1) and placing more emphasis on his winners (Adjustment 2).

It is, however, most difficult for an outsider to designate any specific adjustment for another individual. Cathy, Lupe, and Arnold could experiment with all the techniques and then concentrate on those that help the most.

CASE 24: SENSITIVITY

It is suggested that Angelina stay where she is until she completes a formal course in supervision and/or managerial leadership. Once she has training, she will be in a better position to consider the demands of such a job in light of her own personality, values, and goals. It is quite possible that Angelina would agonize so deeply over making hard "people" decisions that she would be ineffective as a supervisor.

Not everyone who is highly effective at human relations should become a supervisor. Many people who were exceptionally competent at working with people at the nonmanagement level have failed completely in a leadership role. In this respect, it would appear that management may have made a mistake in inviting Angelina to become a supervisor at this early stage. They may be trading their best producer for a supervisor who won't be happy and may leave the organization. This would be a loss to all concerned. However, with time and experience, people change, mature, and need new challenges. A successful management career is not out of the question for Angelina and may become a very rewarding and fulfilling career choice for her.

Index